BREAKING AWAY
from the TEXTBOOK

HOW TO ORDER THIS BOOK

BY PHONE: 800-233-9936 or 717-291-5609, 8AM–5PM Eastern Time

BY FAX: 717-295-4538

BY MAIL: Order Department
Technomic Publishing Company, Inc.
851 New Holland Avenue, Box 3535
Lancaster, PA 17604, U.S.A.

BY CREDIT CARD: American Express, VISA, MasterCard

Second Edition

BREAKING AWAY
from the **TEXTBOOK**

*A New Approach to
Teaching American History*

Shelly Kintisch
Wilma Cordero

Paul Harvey Library
Notre Dame College

TECHNOMIC
PUBLISHING CO., INC.
LANCASTER · BASEL

Breaking Away from the Textbook (Second Edition)
a TECHNOMIC®publication

Published in the Western Hemisphere by
Technomic Publishing Company, Inc.
851 New Holland Avenue
Box 3535
Lancaster, Pennsylvania 17604 U.S.A.

Distributed in the Rest of the World by
Technomic Publishing AG

Printed in the United States of America
10 9 8 7 6 5 4 3 2 1

Main entry under title:
 Breaking Away from the Textbook: A New Approach to Teaching American History
 (Second Edition)

A Technomic Publishing Company book
Bibliography: p.

Library of Congress Card No. 92-64059
ISBN No. 0-87762-933-1

To our families and friends who supported and encouraged this endeavor and to our students who inspired it. This second edition is especially dedicated to the memory of Jack Kintisch. We also want to express special thanks to Esteban Cordero for his constant support.

Table of Contents

FOREWORD xvii

INTRODUCTION TO THE SECOND EDITION xix

INTRODUCTION xxi

ONE/**Exploration of the New World** 1
   Introduction 1
   Project List 1
   Homework Assignments 2
     Venturing into the Unknown 2
     Selected Explorers 3
   Classroom Activity 1: Rate the Mate 4
   Classroom Activity 2: Does the End Justify the Means? 5
   Classroom Activity 3: What Made Them Tick? 6
   Classroom Activity 4: What Would You Think? 6
   Classroom Activity 5: Skippers' Yarns 7
   Classroom Activity 6: If Columbus Had Stayed Home 8

TWO/**The Colonists** 9
   Introduction 9
   Project List 9
   Homework Assignments 11
     Who Came and Why 11
     New England Colonies 12
     Middle Colonies 14
     Southern Colonies 14
     The Colonial Frontier 15
   Classroom Activity 1: Writing the Mayflower Compact 15
   Classroom Activity 2: Town Meeting in Plymouth 16
   Classroom Activity 3: Colonial Norms and Values 17
   Classroom Activity 4: Grain Buffet 18

Classroom Activity 5: Colonial Survival Stories 18
Classroom Activity 6: Interviewing the Colonists 19
Classroom Activity 7: Panel of Experts 19
Classroom Activity 8: Rewriting History 20

THREE/The American Revolution and the
Declaration of Independence **23**
Introduction 23
Project List 23
Homework Assignments 26
    Events Leading to the Declaration of Independence 26
    The Declaration of Independence 27
    The War 28
    Culminating Questions about the American Revolution 29
Classroom Activity 1: Choosing Independence 29
Classroom Activity 2: Choosing Independence: Part 2 30
Classroom Activity 3: Choosing Independence: Part 3 30
Classroom Activity 4: Choosing Independence: Part 4 31
Classroom Activity 5: Taking a Stand 32
Classroom Activity 6: How Angry Would You Get? 33
Classroom Activity 7: Read the Declaration of Independence 33

FOUR/The Constitution and the Bill of Rights **35**
Introduction 35
Project List 35
Homework Assignments 36
    Articles of Confederation 36
    Constitutional Convention and Ratification 37
    The Constitution 38
    The Bill of Rights 40
Classroom Activity 1: Ready for Change 41
Classroom Activity 2: A New Constitution 41
Classroom Activity 3: How Good Are You at Compromising? 42
Classroom Activity 4: Debates 43
Classroom Activity 5: Happy Birthday Constitution 43
Classroom Activity 6: Rights and Responsibilities 43

FIVE/Establishing the New Nation **47**
Introduction 47
Project List 47
Homework Assignments 49
    George Washington's Term of Office 49
    Events under the John Adams Administration 50

Thomas Jefferson's Administration 50
The War of 1812 51
The Monroe Doctrine 51
Classroom Activity 1: Selecting a Cabinet .52
Classroom Activity 2: Upon His Retirement 52
Classroom Activity 3: Improvisations 53
Classroom Activity 4: Debates 54
Classroom Activity 5: Political Party Campaign 55
Classroom Activity 6: What Would You Do? How Would You Feel?   55
Classroom Activity 7: Using Power 56

SIX/Expansion and the Frontier **59**
Introduction 59
Project List 59
Homework Assignments 61
Manifest Destiny and the Pioneer Spirit 61
The Acquisition of New Territories 62
Pioneer Life 63
Native Americans 64
Classroom Activity 1: What Can You Do? .65
Classroom Activity 2: Where Lies the Truth? 66
Classroom Activity 3: What Would They Say? 67
Classroom Activity 4: The Trail of Tears 67
Classroom Activity 5: Weighing What to Take 68
Classroom Activity 6: Choices 68
Classroom Activity 7: Starting Over 70
Classroom Activity 8: Survival Manual 70
Classroom Activity 9: Law Enforcers Versus Law Breakers 71
Classroom Activity 10: Vigilante Justice 71
Classroom Activity 11: Tall Tales 72

SEVEN/The Civil War **73**
Introduction 73
Project List 73
Homework Assignments 75
The Slave Experience 75
Differences That Grew between the North and the South 76
Events That Led to the Civil War 77
The Civil War 78
Classroom Activity 1: Spoon Fashion 79
Classroom Activity 2: Classroom Writing 80
Classroom Activity 3: Could You Be an Abolitionist? 80
Classroom Activity 4: How Important Is Freedom to You? 81

Classroom Activity 5: The Webster/Hayne Debate 82
Classroom Activity 6: Stagecoach Quartet 82
Classroom Activity 7: The Dred Scott Decision 83
Classroom Activity 8: Lincoln-Douglas Debate 84
Classroom Activity 9: Secession 84
Classroom Activity 10: Reading Aloud 85
Classroom Activity 11: Point of View Questionnaire 86
Classroom Activity 12: Writing about Slavery 86
Classroom Activity 13: Using Movies in Class 87

EIGHT/**Reconstruction** **89**
    Introduction 89
    Project List 89
    Homework Assignments 91
        Political Issues 91
        Social Issues 92
    Classroom Activity 1: Reflections on the War 93
    Classroom Activity 2: How to Treat the South 93
    Classroom Activity 3: Would Things Be Different If . . . ? 94
    Classroom Activity 4: Adjusting to Change 94
    Classroom Activity 5: On Fear 95
    Classroom Activity 6: Interviewing the People 95
    Classroom Activity 7: "O Captain! My Captain!" 96

NINE/**Life Across the United States: 1865–1900** **97**
    Introduction 97
    Project List 97
    Homework Assignments 99
        Innovations That Changed American Life – 1865–1900 99
        Rural Life – 1865–1900 100
        Life in the Cities – 1865–1900 101
    Classroom Activity 1: Time 101
    Classroom Activity 2: Necessity and Inventions 102
    Classroom Activity 3: What's Left to Invent? 102
    Classroom Activity 4: Progress or Problem? 103
    Classroom Activity 5: "Modern" Round Robin 103

TEN/**The Industrial Revolution** **105**
    Introduction 105
    Project List 105
    Homework Assignments 107
        Mass Production and the Factory System 107

The Growth of Corporations 108
Labor Unions 109
Classroom Activity 1: Working on an Assembly Line 110
Classroom Activity 2: Efficiency Experts......................111
Classroom Activity 3: How Strikes Affect People's Lives 111
Classroom Activity 4: What Will You Do? 112
Classroom Activity 5: Deciding on Demands 113
Classroom Activity 6: Business Ethics.......................114
Classroom Activity 7: Union Versus Management 115
Classroom Activity 8: Fair and Reasonable 116
Classroom Activity 9: Rating the Industrial Revolution..........116

ELEVEN/Immigration **119**
Introduction 119
Project List 119
Homework Assignments 121
  Why and How Immigrants Came to the United States 121
  The Immigrant Experience in the United States................121
  Laws Affecting Immigrants 122
Classroom Activity 1: Freestyle Writing 122
Classroom Activity 2: Role-Playing 123
Classroom Activity 3: Making Choices......................123
Classroom Activity 4: A New Start..........................124
Classroom Activity 5: Illegal Aliens 124
Classroom Activity 6: Problem Solving 125
Classroom Activity 7: Discussing Feelings 126
Classroom Activity 8: Multiple Choice Exercise—Problems of
  Immigrants 127
Classroom Activity 9: A Multicultural Class 129
Classroom Activity 10: Debates Dealing with Immigration Today 130
Classroom Activity 11: Images of Immigration 130
Classroom Activity 12: Culminating Activity—International Fair 130

TWELVE/The United States Becomes a World Power **133**
Introduction 133
Project List 133
Homework Assignments 135
  The Spanish-American War...............................135
  Panama Canal 136
  Steps into World Involvement 137
  World War I 137
Classroom Activity 1: Foreign Policy Hearings 139

Classroom Activity 2: What Is Your Foreign Policy? 139
Classroom Activity 3: Find the Facts........................140
Classroom Activity 4: Civilians at War......................141
Classroom Activity 5: If We Had Stayed Home 142

THIRTEEN/**The Twenties** **143**
Introduction 143
Project List 143
Homework Assignments 144
Why the Twenties Roared 144
The Other Side of the Twenties 145
Prohibition 146
The Stock Market Crash 146
Classroom Activity 1: History Repeats Itself 146
Classroom Activity 2: Sound Effects 147
Classroom Activity 3: Time Capsule 148
Classroom Activity 4: Seeing the Opposite Point of View 148
Classroom Activity 5: Roundtable Discussion about Prohibition   149
Classroom Activity 6: You Are the Jury.....................150
Classroom Activity 7: Investing in the Stock Market 150

FOURTEEN/**The Great Depression** **153**
Introduction 153
Project List 153
Homework Assignments 155
Effects on People......................................155
The New Deal 156
Classroom Activity 1: Continue the Story 156
Classroom Activity 2: How Would You Feel If . . . ? 157
Classroom Activity 3: Meeting with President Hoover 157
Classroom Activity 4: Experiencing the Depression............157
Classroom Activity 5: Viewing Pictures.....................158
Classroom Activity 6: Town Meeting.......................158
Classroom Activity 7: New Deal Hit Parade 159

FIFTEEN/**World War II** **161**
Introduction 161
Project List 161
Homework Assignments 163
Events That Got Us into the War 163
The Home Front 164
Overseas..165

Japanese Internment Camps 165
The End of the War 166
Classroom Activity 1: Group Decision Making 166
Classroom Activity 2: Reaction Register 167
Classroom Activity 3: Panel Discussion on Alternatives 169
Classroom Activity 4: Public Service Advertising Campaign 169
Classroom Activity 5: Dear Mr. President 170
Classroom Activity 6: Election Campaign of Roosevelt
Versus Dewey 170
Classroom Activity 7: *Hiroshima No Pika* 171

SIXTEEN/The Post-War Years: 1945–1959 .... **173**
Introduction 173
Project List 173
Homework Assignments 175
Return to Peacetime 175
Culture During the Fifties 176
Civil Rights During the Fifties 176
Fear of Communism 177
Foreign Affairs 178
Classroom Activity 1: Congressional Committees 178
Classroom Activity 2: NATO Debate 179
Classroom Activity 3: Mediation 179
Classroom Activity 4: Fallout Shelter Decisions 181
Classroom Activity 5: Conforming 181
Classroom Activity 6: Debates 183
Classroom Activity 7: The Fifties Juke Box 183
Classroom Activity 8: To Confess or Not to Confess 184
Classroom Activity 9: The Dinner Party
(A Culminating Activity) 185

SEVENTEEN/The Sixties **187**
Introduction 187
Project List 188
Homework Assignments 190
Moving into the Sixties 190
The Kennedy Years 191
The Johnson Years: Domestic Accomplishments 192
Civil Rights in the Sixties 193
Vietnam: A War at Home and Abroad 194
The Space Program 194
How Life Changed 195

Classroom Activity 1: Moving into the Sixties 195
Classroom Activity 2: Interviews 196
Classroom Activity 3: "Ask Not . . ." 196
Classroom Activity 4: A Great Society 200
Classroom Activity 5: Checklist for a Great Society 200
Classroom Activity 6: Stuck in an Elevator 201
Classroom Activity 7: How Far Would You Go? 202
Classroom Activity 8: "Sixties-In" 204

EIGHTEEN/**The Seventies** **205**
Introduction 205
Project List 206
Homework Assignments 208
  Vietnam Continued: A War at Home and Abroad 208
  Social Issues and Movements 209
  Nixon's Presidency and Watergate 210
  The Carter Presidency 211
Classroom Activity 1: Trial of Lt. William Calley 212
Classroom Activity 2: Sexual Stereotypes 212
Classroom Activity 3: Debates on Issues of the Seventies 214
Classroom Activity 4: Reverse Discrimination? 214
Classroom Activity 5: Identifying Feelings 215
Classroom Activity 6: Multicultural Multimedia Celebration 216

NINETEEN/**The Eighties—Moving into the Nineties** **217**
Introduction 217
Project List 217
Homework Assignments 220
  Health, Environment, and Technology 220
  Social Issues 221
  Ethics in Government and Business 223
  The Persian Gulf War 224
Classroom Activity 1: Interviewing the Experts 225
Classroom Activity 2: Interaction with Senior Citizens 226
Classroom Activity 3: Who Gets the Heart Transplant? 226
Classroom Activity 4: A Question of Ethics 227
Classroom Activity 5: Independent Decision Making 229
Classroom Activity 6: What's Wrong Here? 229
Classroom Activity 7: Advice for Future Generations 230
Classroom Activity 8: Where Should the Money Go? 231
Classroom Activity 9: Difficult to Resolve 231
Classroom Activity 10: Social Action Groups 232

Classroom Activity 11: Return of the Hostages 232
Classroom Activity 12: Wish List for the Twenty-First Century 233

TWENTY/Current Events—The Nineties and Beyond **235**
Introduction 235
Expressing Opinions.......................................235
Cooperative Learning 236
News Broadcast 236
Classroom Writing...236
Political Cartoons...237
Skill Honing...237
Debate..237
News as Research 237
Know Your Newspaper 238

TWENTY-ONE/Term Papers **239**
Introduction 239
Choosing an Appropriate Topic 239
Locating Information 240
Writing an Outline 240
Note-Taking..241
Revising the Outline 242
Writing a Rough Draft.....................................242
Rewriting the Final Draft...................................242

**TWENTY-TWO/A Special Classroom Library—
Beyond Reference** **243**
Introduction 243
Introducing a Unit..244
Enhancing Lessons..244
Using Children's Picture Books 245
Independent Silent Reading 246
Presentations 246
Historical Magazine 246
Lending System 247
Guidelines for Book Reports Based on Historical Fiction........247
Guidelines for Book Reports Based on Biographies.............248
Book List for U.S. History..................................248
  Early Colonial Life......................................248
  American Revolution 248
  Pioneers and Westward Expansion 248
  Slavery and the Civil War 249

Women in the 19th Century 249
Immigration 249
Industrial Revolution, Early Urban Life, and Labor 250
World War I 250
The Depression 250
World War II 250
Civil and Constitutional Rights 250
Vietnam 251

DEBATES 253

ABOUT THE AUTHORS 257

Foreword

Many students consider social studies their least favorite subject, often with good reason. They complain of tiresome classes in which teachers dispense meaningless information, of countless assignments to answer the unimaginative questions at the end of a lifeless textbook chapter, and of weekly quizzes and examinations for which they hastily memorize irrelevant and soon forgotten trivia.

This sort of tedious, uninspiring grind contradicts everything educational researchers have learned about effective instruction: students should be active not passive, creative and not merely receptive, and they should be put in a position to exercise their judgment and not simply be required to recall disconnected bits of information. In sum, students benefit most if they are involved in the process of creating knowledge, if they are expected to collect and evaluate information and given an opportunity to propose and question generalizations. This is particularly important in social studies which has a special responsibility for citizenship education.

Fortunately, the leaden routine too often associated with social studies classrooms is not universal. Many social studies teachers successfully engage students in active learning and thereby arouse the spirit of inquiry and the habit of thoughtful reflection that are the hallmarks of educational excellence and enlightened citizenship. Wilma Cordero and Shelly Kintisch, the co-authors of *Breaking Away from the Textbook*, are two such teachers. And the book they have written is a compilation of many of the assignments, projects, and activities they have used through the years to spark the imagination of their students and to involve them in the creative process of learning.

The title of the book is a bit misleading. It is not intended to suggest that students and teachers abandon the use of social studies textbooks. Rather, the principle underlying *Breaking Away from the Textbook* is that texts are best used as sources of information and not as manuals which define the content and organization of a social studies program. The way the authors envision social studies students using textbooks is analogous to the way Albert Bushnell Hart, the famous Harvard historian, once described history's ultimate intellectual challenge. History, said Hart, requires the historian to transform "the lifeless lead of the annals" into "the shining gold" of historical understanding. This is an apt metaphor for *Breaking Away from the Textbook*. Each of its many teaching strategies is based on the fundamental insight that facts do not speak for themselves, that students must breathe the breath of life into historical facts and thereby create vital and meaningful understandings.

For the students with whom I work in the Social Studies Program at Teachers College, Columbia University, *Breaking Away from the Textbook* has proven an invaluable resource. As prospective teachers, these bright, well-educated, and enthusiastic students, have one very obvious shortcoming—classroom experience. That is why they turn so often to *Breaking Away from the Textbook*, especially when student teaching. Its practical wisdom reveals the way two experienced teachers think about teaching and prepare for instruction, and its myriad examples explain the way the social studies curriculum may be transformed into an exciting and creative program of learning. In short, *Breaking Away from the Textbook* is a treasure chest of tested ideas that teachers, both novice and experienced, can use to challenge and inspire their social studies students.

MICHAEL WHELAN

Assistant Professor of History and Education
Coordinator of the Social Studies Program
Teachers College, Columbia University

Introduction to the Second Edition

Our second edition of *Breaking Away from the Textbook* contains three new chapters and many additional classroom activities, homework assignments, and projects. We have updated our work to include recent issues and events. We have also added material that better reflects the unique multicultural nature of this country.

Our format for the chapters on current events, research papers, and a classroom library is different from our previous chapters. We wanted to share our experience in developing and using these ongoing processes. The material included in these chapters may be integrated into any unit of study in the U.S. history curriculum.

One of the joys of having written this book is the response we have gotten from our colleagues. We welcome feedback on your experiences using this material. Too often we teach in isolation and this book has given us the opportunity to connect with you, the classroom teachers who share our profession.

Introduction

Do these words really mean anything to the students of today, or have they become empty, meaningless cliches tossed about by politicians and the media? Young people today are exposed to so much publicity that they sometimes appear to have only superficial understanding of these terms. In a world that often does the opposite of what it says, children are left confused, distrustful, and cynical.

Yet, our country's history is based on the above principals. We feel that, rather than preach or force-feed students, we, as teachers, should offer them the opportunity to explore and rediscover for themselves what freedom means, how individualism can lead to both rewards and problems, what responsibilities democracy entails, and so forth. The framework of American society and history itself is so complex that often, in our zeal to cover material and give our students the most information, we overlook the in-depth analysis that is essential to any understanding of the American way of life and the democratic standards on which this life has been built.

For example, freedom can have many meanings. Students should examine the opportunities it provides along with its corresponding limitations. Do students really understand all the aspects of freedom of speech? Does it really give us the right to say anything we want, at any time, in any place, about anyone or anything? Obviously not. Does this make our Bill of Rights a lie? Of course not. Yet the student who only learns the facts without developing the skills to analyze them is left with mere empty words.

Too often, facts and curricula get in the way of students' independent thinking. Learning the facts becomes an end in itself. The mind is blurred by names, dates, and events. We hope to present a means to take the students one step beyond the concrete so that they can explore an infinity of ideas, values, and alternatives. We also hope that the students will internalize the concept of citizenship and learn that participation is meaningful and necessary for a democracy.

Through long-term projects, homework assignments, and classroom activities, we hope to teach the following skills:

- independent thinking
- problem solving
- taking a position and justifying it

As the students become comfortable with these skills, they will be able to:

- move from the concrete to the abstract
- question critically
- take an historical fact and both personalize it and see it in more far-reaching terms
- analyze the consequences of events, actions, and ideas
- participate in open-ended discussions of controversial issues
- defend a point of view in an argument or a debate

These are not unreasonable demands. In more than twenty years of active classroom teaching we have been rewarded with the great joy of seeing students of all learning abilities and backgrounds achieve these goals.

HOW TO USE THIS BOOK

This is not a textbook. Our book is designed as a teaching supplement for any U.S. history course of study. It can be used in its entirety or can be used selectively to fill in gaps left by traditional textbooks and curricula. It can also be used for enrichment.

Each chapter in this book coincides with an era in U.S. history. The chapters are organized chronologically. Within each chapter are sections for projects and research work, homework assignments, and classroom activities. We have not divided the work into elementary or secondary school levels because often the same assignment can lead to wonderful, if different, responses. For example, a child of eight and a high school senior can both rewrite the national anthem. The assignment will be equally stimulating to each student, and yet, the results will reflect each one's level of maturity and ability.

We suggest that the projects and research assignments be given out at the beginning of each unit of study. They provide an exciting introduction, stimulate interest in the new unit, and allow the students enough time to gather data and budget their time adequately. For example, the Family Tree assignment in the Immigration Chapter requires time for the students to contact relatives in order to trace family history. Once the information is gathered, the student needs time to map it out in a clear and attractive format. In our experience this seemingly simple assignment has brought us hundreds of different approaches. Some have been presented in the form of trees. Other students have presented charts with flags, family photographs, and colorful drawings. In a project such as this, students are able to develop and utilize organizational, artistic, and creative skills. Although projects are individual efforts, teachers can help the students by providing reading lists, library visits, and information about local groups and institutions that might be helpful. Critical thinking cannot occur until the students have a basic set of facts. Choosing what goes into the report or project is the starting point for evaluation and independent thinking.

Teachers may want to set up their own standards and requirements for written reports (for example: bibliography, length of report, footnotes, and organization). These would vary according to the age and the ability levels. The same is true for constructions. We always make it very clear that all constructions and endeavors must be conceived and executed by the student. Store-bought models are not acceptable because they do not reflect any original effort.

It is always beneficial for the teacher to set aside time for the students to present their projects to the rest of the class. At this time, they can share not only the information they gathered, but also the methods they used. Our students always enjoy asking questions, and the presenter has the chance to be the teacher for the moment.

Our homework section is meant to offer thought-provoking assignments that can be used with or without textbooks. They are designed as follow-up assignments to content lessons and can be used by most teachers to reinforce and expand upon the material covered during class sections. These assignments will help the students sort and evaluate factual material they have learned and take them one step beyond those facts. We have found that in doing the "Dear Abby"-type of assignment, such as the one in Chapter 11, the students become so personally involved that they naturally recall the facts in the process of writing the creative assignment. Thus, learning becomes both pleasurable and meaningful.

Teachers using this book can find appropriate homework assignments in each chapter under topic headings. For example, the assignments in our Immigration Chapter have the following headings:

- Why and How Immigrants Came to the United States
- The Immigrant Experience in the United States
- Laws Affecting Immigration

The classroom activities section is used to supplement the teacher's regular content lessons. In each chapter we offer a variety of ideas from which a teacher may choose, according to the needs of his or her class. They are designed to stimulate interest throughout the unit and to promote meaningful classroom participation by as many students as possible. Many of our activities do not require prior knowledge. Therefore, you will find that even your most reticent students will feel comfortable participating. For example, our Immigration Chapter includes an International Fair as the final activity. Every student can take part in such an activity.

Our last section offers topics for debates. These are general topics that come up frequently during social studies discussions but that do not specifically fit into any particular unit. They are often an outgrowth of current events lessons. Debate topics that clearly fit into a specific unit will be found in the classroom activities section of that chapter.

These approaches offer student and teacher alike a stimulating and dynamic classroom atmosphere—one that nurtures the curiosity and love of learning that we hope to instill in our students.

CHAPTER ONE

Exploration of the New World

INTRODUCTION

The stories of the exploration of the New World are probably unequalled in history in terms of bravery and adventure.

This chapter first highlights the fears, uncertainties, and problems the explorers faced as they ventured into the unknown. Although these events occurred hundreds of years ago, young people today can certainly identify with the feelings experienced by these men.

This chapter is also designed to help students evaluate the actions and accomplishments of some of the explorers and the men who accompanied them in terms of the ethics of their behavior.

PROJECT LIST

1. Make a model of a Viking ship.
2. Make a map showing the routes taken by European explorers to the New World.
3. Make a map or globe showing the land in the New World that was claimed by the English, Spanish, French, and Portuguese.
4. Make a model of a ship sailed by a famous explorer of the fifteenth or sixteenth century.
5. Write a log of a famous explorer describing his journey to the New World.
6. Make a poster illustrating early inventions that made sailing somewhat safer for European sailors of the fifteenth and sixteenth centuries.
7. Make a poster or scrapbook illustrating some of the things that Europeans wanted to get from Asia.

8. Make a diorama, an illustrated book, or a play about the adventures of one explorer.

9. Make an instruction manual, with diagrams, showing how to build a sailing ship like the ones used by the explorers. Include the materials to be used.

10. Make a series of cartoons illustrating the problems and dangers that early explorers faced.

11. Do a research report on one of the English, French, Spanish, or Portuguese explorers. Include:
   (a) Why he went
   (b) What he hoped to find
   (c) What he actually found and its value
   (d) How he handled the native population (if applicable)
   (e) Your evaluation of the accomplishments and methods used by this explorer

12. Write a TV script on the activities of Sir Francis Drake.

13. Do a research report on the treatment of the Native Americans by explorers such as Cortés or Pizarro.

14. Research how the economic theory of mercantilism affected the exploration and colonization of the New World.

15. Make a chart of all the major explorers of the fifteenth and sixteenth centuries who sailed for Portugal, Spain, France, and England. Include names, dates, and their discoveries.

16. Do an illustrated report on the adventures and problems faced by Magellan and his men as they sailed around the world.

17. Make a detailed diagram of an explorer's ship, such as Columbus's *Santa Maria*. Label everything clearly.

18. Make a board game of an explorer's trip to the New World. Include dangers, real and imagined.

19. Using recent articles and books, write a case for or against Columbus's accomplishments.

20. After doing research write a series of speeches by Native Americans about the European explorers who came to their lands.

HOMEWORK ASSIGNMENTS

VENTURING INTO THE UNKNOWN

1. Pretend you are a European king. Write a farewell speech for a sea captain whose voyage you are financing. Remind him that he is sailing for "God, glory, and riches."

2. Make up a dialogue between a European king and his advisor about whether or not they should spend money to finance a ship seeking a short cut to the Indies.

3. If you were a businessman living in medieval Europe, which item from the Indies would you want most? Why?

4. Make a drawing of things feared by sailors in the Middle Ages.

5. If you were an early sailor, what would frighten you most about going out to sea?

6. Can you think of any ways to test a person's ability to endure hardships such as those faced by early seafarers? Explain.

7. Make a list of foods that could be stored without refrigeration or other modern preserving techniques on a ship traveling to the New World.

8. Write a poem or make a drawing which expresses the fears that early sailors had about sailing into unknown seas.

9. In what ways is space exploration today similar to the exploration of the earth by the early explorers?

10. Make a list of personal qualities and characteristics that you would want in your sailors if you were the captain of a ship that was on an exploring mission (to be used with Classroom Activity 1).

11. What would you take with you as a memento of home (other than a photo) if you were going out on an exploration mission? Why would you choose that?

12. Make up a riddle in rhyme to describe an explorer.

13. Of the following problems faced by the early sailors, which one would bother you the most and why?
    (a) Scurvy
    (b) Eating moldy food
    (c) Rats and roaches on the ship

14. Would you have wanted to sail with the explorers? Why? Why not?

15. Write a poem or rap song entitled, "Into the Unknown."

16. Make a list of the "unknowns" in modern life that can be frightening.

SELECTED EXPLORERS

1. Why were the Spanish explorers called "conquistadores," which means conquerors, rather than just explorers?

2. Pretend you are Columbus. Make up a speech to convince Queen Isabella to finance your trip.

3. Pretend you are Columbus. Make up a pep talk for your crew to keep them from panicking after sailing for a month without sighting land.

4. Why was Columbus's chief concern at sea the morale of his men?

5. Pretend you are a roving reporter. Ask ten people who they think actually discovered America. Be prepared to report back to the class.

6. Pretend you are Magellan. Make up a help wanted ad seeking sailors for your voyage.

7. When Magellan set sail, why did he keep his route a secret from his crew?

8. Ponce de León set out to find the Fountain of Youth. Instead, he found Florida. Was he a failure? Explain.

9. Imagine that you are Jacques Cartier. Write a letter to King Francis of France explaining your discovery of the St. Lawrence River. Tell him why you think it is the Northwest Passage to the Indies.

10. Pretend you are the king of France. Write a proclamation ordering Samuel de Champlain to establish a French colony in North America. Explain why.

11. How did the French desire for furs affect the way they explored the New World?

12. Sir Francis Drake sailed the seas for England, pirating Spanish ships for their gold. Would you have joined his crew? Why? Why not?

13. Make up a "Wanted – Dead or Alive" poster for Sir Francis Drake. Include his crimes and a reward offered by the king of Spain.

14. Choose three of the explorers studied in this unit. Make up three titles for adventure movies that deal with their exploits.

15. Of all the explorers studied by the class, which one do you think made the most important discovery or had the most difficult experience? Explain.

16. Describe the encounter between Columbus and Native Americans from both points of view.

CLASSROOM ACTIVITY 1

RATE THE MATE

Using the answers that your students provided in Homework 10 (Venturing into the Unknown), conduct a discussion on the ideal characteristics of a sailor on an exploring ship.

Using a scale of one to five, have the students rate the following characteristics with one denoting most desirable, and five denoting least desirable.

___ kind	___ loyal
___ considerate	___ neat
___ responsible	___ intelligent
___ sense of humor	___ strong
___ obedient	___ stubborn
___ family man	___ overweight
___ poor	___ underweight
___ rich	___ talkative
___ adventurous	___ nail biter
___ curious	___ drinker
___ orphan	___ liar
___ criminal record	___ nervous

As you go through the list, you can poll the class and follow up with the following questions:

1. Why is this important? Unimportant?
2. How can this be useful on a long voyage? Helpful? Harmful?

CLASSROOM ACTIVITY 2

DOES THE END JUSTIFY THE MEANS?

Unquestionably, the explorers were brave and daring men. In order to reach their goals, they often made unusual decisions. It will be stimulating for the class to discuss their accomplishments from a values approach and to answer the question, "Does the end justify the means?" The teacher may further direct class discussion with the following questions:

- In what way was this harmful?
- What was achieved?
- What was the motivation of the explorer?
- Would you have done the same?
- What else could have been done?

1. Columbus kept two logs and misrepresented the distance they had sailed to his crew.
2. When Cortés realized that the Aztecs thought that he and his men were gods, he encouraged this in order to conquer them.
3. Pizarro made a deal with his captive Atahualpa, the Inca king. In exchange for a roomful of gold, Atahualpa could have his freedom. Pizarro kept the gold, killed Atahualpa, and claimed Peru for Spain.

4. Magellan started out with five ships and 237 men. Three years later, one ship returned with eighteen men. During the trip, the men were reduced to eating sawdust, leather fittings from the ship, biscuits that had turned to powder and were filled with worms, and rats which came to be considered a delicacy. Magellan refused to turn back and is credited with proving that the world is round.

5. The French and Spanish felt that it was their duty to convert the Native Americans to Christianity in order to save them, even if it was against their will.

6. French explorers sold liquor and guns to Native Americans in exchange for furs.

CLASSROOM ACTIVITY 3

WHAT MADE THEM TICK?

Columbus is considered by many to be the greatest of all the explorers. We know a great deal about his voyages, but some mysteries remain. The teacher can engage the class in a discussion of the following:

1. Everything went so well on Columbus's voyage—enough food, good weather, no storms, calm seas, and no damage to the ship—that the men became anxiety ridden. Why?

2. When Columbus landed and met the Arawak Tainos of San Salvador and saw their tiny, gold nose ornaments, he concluded that they had reached the Indies. He was wrong. Why did such a bright man use such flimsy evidence for his conclusion?

3. Why did Columbus stubbornly insist, after four voyages across the Atlantic, that he had reached China, when all logic should have told this brilliant mariner that he had found a new continent?

CLASSROOM ACTIVITY 4

WHAT WOULD YOU THINK?

Putting themselves into the shoes of the explorers will help the students to understand their decisions, fears, and feelings. Use the following questions to start a class writing assignment or a class discussion. There are no right or wrong answers among the choices.

1. You are about to set sail. Your greatest fear is
   (a) Your ship will fall off the edge of the earth.
   (b) You will be killed by a sea monster.
   (c) You will never see your family again.

2. You have agreed to sail west in order to reach the east. You do so because
   (a) You will be paid a lot of money.
   (b) The adventure appeals to you.
   (c) You want to be famous.

3. Your son/brother/boyfriend is about to set sail. You
   (a) Decide he's a loser and won't wait for him.
   (b) Think he's a hero.
   (c) Think it's unfair that you can't go along with him.

4. You have been at sea for a month without sighting land. Rations are running out, and several sailors are organizing a mutiny.
   (a) You join them.
   (b) You tell the captain.
   (c) You try to convince them to wait.

5. You are on a ship that is nearing the shore. You see different-looking people on the land.
   (a) You make a plan to attack them.
   (b) You assume they will be friendly.
   (c) You are afraid of them.

CLASSROOM ACTIVITY 5

SKIPPERS' YARNS

Sailors are known for their exaggerations and for the colorful sagas they tell. Divide the class into two teams for the purpose of exchanging stories about rough sea voyages. The teacher can give an example of how this may be done.

Team One: "We saw a twenty-foot sea monster."

Team Two: "We saw a thirty-foot sea monster."

Team One: "Ours attacked the ship."

This activity makes use of the students' knowledge as well as their imaginations.

CLASSROOM ACTIVITY 6

IF COLUMBUS HAD STAYED HOME

This activity allows students to let their imaginations take charge as they brainstorm in small groups. The teacher will say, "What would the U.S. be like if Columbus had stayed home?" Each group may answer the question by first discussing and then writing or drawing a description of their own. If students need help the teacher might direct the activity by asking the following questions:

1. What would be different?
2. How do you think people would be living?
3. What would be the role of animals?
4. How do you think the land would be used? How would it look?

After the groups are finished they would share their work. The teacher might arrange to decorate a bulletin board with their descriptions.

CHAPTER TWO

The Colonists

INTRODUCTION

The colonists, by and large, were an independent group of people — resourceful, energetic, and capable of adapting to their environment and circumstances. We want the students to be able to envision themselves in the shoes of these colonists, and throughout, we want them to attempt to make decisions that were made by these resourceful people whose lives were often physically difficult.

The colonists were a heterogeneous group, and the assignments reflect this variety of backgrounds, jobs, religions, personalities, and accomplishments. These threads are basic to American society today.

PROJECT LIST

1. Do a piece of creative writing on the adventures of the first Pilgrims who went to America on the *Mayflower.*
2. Make a special edition of a gossip magazine or newspaper revealing the life of Anne Hutchinson.
3. Do an interview with a Puritan leader such as John Cotton, Cotton Mather, or Jonathan Edwards in which they tell about their lives and their philosophies.
4. Make a diorama or poster illustrating people at work in Massachusetts Bay.
5. Pretend you are Roger Williams. Write a journal describing your life and your ideas.
6. Trace the roots of democracy in America. You may want to include such things as:
   (a) Town meetings

9

(b) The Fundamental Orders of Connecticut

(c) The trial of Peter Zenger

7. Pretend you are the owner of an antiques store specializing in everyday colonial tools and furniture. Make a diorama of your store and all the things you would sell. Make up a name for the store and prepare an inventory.

8. Write an original play about the Salem witchcraft trial of 1692.

9. Write an original version of a Puritan textbook for school children.

10. Make a poster or series of cartoons that illustrate the reasons why people settled in the colonies.

11. Make up a *Book of Etiquette of Puritans* living in the Massachusetts Bay colony.

12. Make an illustrated map of the thirteen colonies. Using a legend, you can indicate all or some of the following:
    (a) Major occupations in each
    (b) Special features
    (c) Origin of early settlers

13. Make a chart of the thirteen original colonies including:
    (a) When each was started
    (b) How
    (c) By whom
    (d) Major occupations
    (e) Contributions to democratic traditions

14. Many American customs and holidays originated with the colonists. Make a collection of greeting cards or illustrations reflecting them.

15. Make a collage, poster, or museum display of all the things that were grown and/or produced by the colonists around 1700.

16. Pretend you are William Penn. Make a pamphlet or brochure which illustrates and describes the benefits that people will have if they choose to settle in Pennsylvania.

17. Make a *Book of Beliefs* that guided Quaker life.

18. Write an illustrated biography of the life of William Penn or Benjamin Franklin.

19. Make models of things made in colonial America by carpenters or other craftsmen.

20. Make an original magazine of *Social Life in the Colonies* illustrating how colonists used their leisure time.

21. Make a labelled drawing illustrating a southern plantation.

22. Make a diorama of a southern plantation.

23. Make a filmstrip or illustrated story of Nathaniel Bacon's rebellion in 1676.

24. Make up an "Awards Ceremony" for the most outstanding people who founded colonies. Make a certificate for each one.

25. Make up a script for a TV talk show in which the host interviews a variety of types of people who lived in the colonies (Puritans, Quakers, slaves, merchants, owners of small farms, plantation owners, fishermen).

26. Make a poster illustrating all the advantages that life in the colonies could offer a European who would settle there.

27. Make up a board game illustrating the problems faced by the colonists.

28. Make up a ballad about relations between the colonists and the Native Americans.

29. The colonists were very different from each other in many ways. Make a collage or mobile that illustrates this idea.

30. Write a paper tracing the beginnings of slavery in colonial America.

31. Make an illustrated travel brochure describing the history and lifestyle of one of the thirteen colonies.

32. Pretend you are a war correspondent. Do a series of news articles about the French and Indian War.

33. Make a map illustrating major battles fought in the French and Indian War.

34. Send away to any universities that were founded during colonial times and ask for a bulletin and information on their history and philosophy. Write a report on your findings.

35. Do a report on the lives and roles of women in the colonies.

36. Construct a pioneer cabin used on the colonial frontier. Include puncheons and furniture.

HOMEWORK ASSIGNMENTS

WHO CAME AND WHY?

1. If you and your family could move to a new place, where would you go? Why?

2. If a satellite colony were started in space or under the sea, would you be willing to go? Explain.

3. Pretend you are a poor English tenant farmer. Make up a speech telling your family why you want to move to the colonies. Write the family's response. This can also be done as a dialogue.

4. Make up an argument to convince an English teenage boy that it will be a good idea for him to go to the colonies as your indentured servant.

5. You are Lord Baltimore. Write a letter to your king requesting a parcel of land in the colonies.

6. You are the king of England. Write a proclamation granting proprietorship of Maryland to Lord Baltimore.

7. Pretend you are an English aristocrat, and you have been disinherited by your father. Write a farewell letter telling him how you will make your own fortune by going to South Carolina where the king has granted you land for a plantation.

8. Pretend you are an English debtor in prison. Write a letter to James Oglethorpe telling him why he should take a chance on you and send you to Georgia.

9. Write a poem expressing what freedom of religion means to you.

10. Pretend you are a stockholder in the Virginia Company of London. Make a poster advertising land and opportunity for anyone who will go to settle there.

11. Make a list of all the things that might change if people had to follow a religion that was dictated by our government.

12. Pretend you are the king of England. Write a proclamation announcing the formation of the Virginia Trading Company. Explain its purpose and how it will make England a greater power.

13. Pretend you are a German farmer. Write a letter to your cousin explaining why you want to move to the English colony of Pennsylvania. Try to convince him to join you.

14. Pretend you are about to run away from home to the colonies. Write a letter to your parents explaining why.

NEW ENGLAND COLONIES

1. Make a list of things that might have gone wrong if the Pilgrims had not signed the Mayflower Compact.

2. Pretend you are a Pilgrim living in Plymouth in 1620. Write a letter

to your cousin in England telling him why you choose to stay in Plymouth rather than return to England.

3. Make a menu of your last traditional Thanksgiving Day dinner. Star those foods that originated with the Pilgrims.

4. Make up a poem of thanks that the Pilgrims might have said before their first Thanksgiving Day meal.

5. Make a list of the first things you imagine the Pilgrims did when they got off the *Mayflower*.

6. Pretend you are a Pilgrim mother or child. Describe your fears about life in this strange new land.

7. Pretend you are a Pilgrim meeting your first Native American. What questions would you ask him or her?

8. Why weren't preachers in Massachusetts Bay allowed to hold political office?

9. In what respects was Anne Hutchinson a woman ahead of her time?

10. Pretend you are a district attorney. Write a summation for a court trial outlining the reasons why you feel Roger Williams should be banished from the Massachusetts Bay colony.

11. Make up a help wanted section for a Boston newspaper in 1635. Include as many types of jobs as you can.

12. Pretend you are a Jew who wants to move to Rhode Island. Write a letter to Roger Williams telling him of your plans and the reasons why you are choosing to settle there.

13. You are a Puritan attending the first meeting to form the New England Confederation. Write a speech explaining why you want to blackball Rhode Island.

14. Why do you think a replica of the "Sacred Cod" is displayed in the Massachusetts State House in Boston?

15. Make up a newspaper advertisement to sell passage on a ship going to New England in 1650.

16. What can you infer about New England colonial life from knowing that the most important building in any town doubled as a church and a meeting house?

17. List all the things that the colonists could have made from timber.

18. Write an oral history describing Native American reactions to the first European settlers.

19. List all the things you would take with you if you were a member of a Pilgrim farm family about to leave for the colonies.

MIDDLE COLONIES

1. Sometimes the Middle Colonies are referred to as a melting pot. Make a cartoon or a pop-art drawing which illustrates this idea.

2. Do you think the purchase of Manhattan Island by the Dutch from the Native Americans was a fair deal? Explain. Did anyone get cheated? If so, who? Why do you think so?

3. Make up some original sayings in the style of *Poor Richard's Almanac*.

4. Bring in something made from a grain to be shared with the class in a "Grain Buffet." Explain what it is and how it is made. (Refer to Classroom Activity 4.)

5. Write a diary entry of a Jewish person explaining why he or she thinks Pennsylvania is the best place to settle.

6. Write a poem or limerick describing how the life-style in the Middle Colonies is unique.

7. What would you like to stand up and say if you were attending a Quaker meeting?

8. Make a cartoon of Peter Stuyvesant ruling New York.

SOUTHERN COLONIES

(A more in-depth study of the issue of slavery is covered in Chapter 7.)

1. Write an original ending to the mystery of what happened to the people of the lost colony of Roanoke, Virginia.

2. If you were Captain John Smith of Jamestown, Virginia, what would you say to the men to convince them to stop looking for gold and to start farming?

3. In Virginia, in 1619, the first shipload of slaves arrived, and the House of Burgesses met for the first time. Why is this ironic?

4. Make up a list of "characters" that would be found on a southern plantation. Describe the role of each one.

5. Pretend you have just been hired as a tutor to a child on a plantation. Write a plan for a day's lessons.

6. Imagine returning to the old South in a time machine. With all you know, what advice or warnings would you give the tobacco and cotton planters?

7. Write a poem about tobacco called "The Evil Weed." In it, tell why it

is nicknamed the weed and how it encouraged the growth of plantations and slavery.

8. Write a dialogue between two aristocratic plantation owners in Virginia discussing their feelings about the poor independent farmers.

THE COLONIAL FRONTIER

1. If you were living during colonial times, would you have chosen to leave an established colony and go off to live in the wilderness? Why? Why not?

2. Pretend you are Nathaniel Bacon. Write a letter to the governor of Virginia telling him what you are angry about.

3. Write a song about Daniel Boone called "The Great Pathfinder."

4. Draw or diagram one way that pioneers traveled to reach the Ohio Valley.

5. How did the rivalry between France and England in Europe lead to war in the colonies?

6. Make a list of words that could describe the reaction of the colonists to the Proclamation of 1763.

7. Write a speech that Pontiac might have made to convince the Native Americans that the white men had to be stopped.

8. What was the difference between how England and France wanted to use the land around the Ohio River?

9. Do you think history would have been different if the Native Americans had refused to take sides during the French and Indian War? Explain.

10. What do you think would have happened if the French had won the Battle of Quebec?

CLASSROOM ACTIVITY 1

WRITING THE MAYFLOWER COMPACT

This activity will be most effective if the class does it before they actually study the Mayflower Compact. In this way the students will be in a better position to recreate the situation that the Pilgrims faced.

After a journey of sixty-five days, the *Mayflower* sighted the New England coast. Since there were no established laws or lawmakers to govern them, they had to establish some sort of order.

Tell the class to imagine that they are the Pilgrims on the *Mayflower* and are about to land, but before they do they must work out some rules to live by. Divide the class into groups of three to five students and have each group attempt to decide on a simple agreement, a Mayflower Compact, to live by.

When they are done, have each group report back to the class. The teacher will record the results on the chalkboard, checking off those rules that are repeated. After all the groups are done, the teacher can use the following questions for a wrap-up discussion:

1. Did your group have difficulty in reaching an agreement? Were you able to resolve your difficulty?
2. Looking at the chalkboard, which rules were repeated most? Why do you think so?

To culminate this activity, the teacher may read the actual Mayflower Compact or a summary of it and compare it with the work of the students.

CLASSROOM ACTIVITY 2

TOWN MEETING IN PLYMOUTH

Town meetings are often considered the purest form of democracy because they gave the colonists (at least, the qualified voters) an opportunity to meet, plan, and air their concerns at public meetings and then vote on them by majority rule.

Tell the class that you are going to try to recreate a town meeting. Write each of the following issues on a separate slip of paper:

1. We have to elect a sheriff.
2. We have to elect a tax collector.
3. We need to elect a collector of stray hogs for the town.
4. We have to hire a new schoolmaster. How shall we go about finding one?
5. There are some poor people in this town who need help. Shall we build an alms house where they can be taken care of?

The teacher will distribute the slips of paper at random, call the town meeting to order, and have the students bring up their concerns by reading aloud what is written on the slips of paper. After each one is read aloud, the teacher can stimulate discussion by asking one or more of the following questions where appropriate:

1. Does anyone care to voice an opinion about this or ask a question about it?
2. Does anyone have any suggestions to make?
3. Does anyone disagree? Agree? Why?
4. Shall we vote?

Once all of the issues have been handled, the teacher can wrap the activity up with a brief discussion of how local issues are resolved in their community.

CLASSROOM ACTIVITY 3

COLONIAL NORMS AND VALUES

Many of the customs that were an accepted part of the colonial way of life might be rejected or viewed as peculiar by today's standards. It is only when we investigate or explore the reasons behind the customs that we gain insight and understanding.

Read the following customs and discuss each one using these questions:

1. Why do you think this was a custom/value?
2. Is this true today? Would it be accepted today? Why? Why not?

CUSTOMS

1. Unmarried girls over twenty-one were considered old maids.
2. Widows remarried immediately. One widow served the left-over refreshments from her first husband's funeral at her second wedding.
3. Women had many children. One Massachusetts woman had twenty-seven children.
4. Bundling was the custom where heating was a problem. A couple would get together in bed, fully clothed, and cuddle to keep warm.
5. Bleeding was a common way to treat illnesses, and when the doctor was unavailable, a barber was called in.
6. Lawyers were looked down upon in colonial society. They were considered to be useless windbags and were sometimes classed with drunkards and procurers.
7. Workers (laborers) often ate at the same table with their employers' families.

8. Letter carriers delivering long-distance mail sometimes entertained themselves by reading the letters they carried.
9. Education was mostly for boys.
10. Most voting was limited to male property owners.
11. Hogs roamed the streets as garbage collectors.
12. Stage plays were forbidden by law in some places because they were considered to be immoral and a waste of time.
13. Funerals and weddings provided a good excuse for drinking liquor.
14. Colonial women smoked pipes in public.

CLASSROOM ACTIVITY 4

GRAIN BUFFET

Since grain was a most important crop in the Middle Colonies and continues to be a basic crop in this country today, it will be enlightening and informative for the students to participate in the preparation of the grain buffet. It will enable them to savor the versatility of grains as a basic food.

Two or three days in advance of this activity, the teacher must assign Homework 4 from the Middle Colonies homework section. The teacher may wish to divide the class into "grain groups" so as to get a broader sampling of foods from those grains that were harvested in the Middle Colonies: wheat, corn, rye, and barley. Each group can meet and decide what the members will prepare and bring in.

On the day the assignment is due, set up a large table and have the students display the foods they brought in. Each one may quickly present his or her food, explaining which grain it contains.

After all the presentations have been made, the class can eat the foods.

The teacher can wrap this activity up with the following discussion questions:

1. Which grain does your family use the most? What foods do they buy or make that contain that grain?
2. In what ways are grains basic to our diets? To our economy today?

CLASSROOM ACTIVITY 5

COLONIAL SURVIVAL STORIES

The colonists faced uncountable dangers and innumerable problems as they reached their destinations and settled down.

The teacher can motivate this activity by asking the class what problems they might face if they found themselves stranded on a desert island. Have the class brainstorm all the problems that newcomers to an unsettled land might face. As they suggest problems, the teacher can write them on the chalkboard. Undoubtedly, their suggestions will include all or some of the following: unfriendly Native Americans, hunger, cold, lack of shelter, lack of food or fresh water, illness.

Once the brainstorming is over, the teacher can divide the class into writing groups of two to four students with each group selecting or being assigned a different problem. Each group will meet and pool their ideas for a story which revolves around their assigned problem.

When they are done, they can share stories. It would be especially rewarding for volunteers to type and reproduce the stories as a magazine.

CLASSROOM ACTIVITY 6
INTERVIEWING THE COLONISTS

Interviewing is the formulation of appropriate questions. It is an excellent way to stimulate critical thinking among students.

Ask the students who they would like to interview if they could go back in time to colonial days. It is unnecessary for them to name a specific person. Encourage the students to think of types of colonists who intrigue them and who they would like to learn more about. The teacher can make suggestions if the class does not come up with enough ideas. For example: a Puritan minister, a student in a New England school, a slave on a southern plantation, a plantation owner, the child of a plantation owner, a Quaker living in Philadelphia, an indentured servant.

Divide the class into groups, or have the students work in pairs. Tell them to make a list of interview questions for the person of their choice. When they are done, call one group at a time to read their questions. It might be fun to draw a stick figure on the chalkboard and print the name of the character being interviewed. In this way the students will have a point of focus. As each group reads their interview questions, the teacher can encourage discussion of the more thought-provoking ones by asking the class: What do you think the person being interviewed might have answered? Why?

CLASSROOM ACTIVITY 7
PANEL OF EXPERTS

This activity is excellent to use toward the end of this unit—once the students have become familiar with the major characteristics that differentiate the colonial regions from each other.

Choose nine volunteers to work in groups of three. Each group will serve as a panel of experts or Chamber of Commerce representing the New England, Middle, and Southern Colonies. They will have to answer questions posed by the other members of the class about life in the colonies that they represent. Each group should be allowed time to review the information about their area (colonies) regarding geographical, social, economic, political, and educational characteristics. While they are doing this, the rest of the class can work independently or in pairs preparing questions to ask the panelists. The questions should be directed toward gaining information that would help them to decide which colony or area to settle in. Tell the students that their questions should reflect their own lives and likes and desires, as if they were contemplating an actual move to one of the areas but were undecided as to which one. The teacher might use himself or herself as an example with one or two of the following questions:

1. Are there jobs for teachers in your area?
2. What kind of clothing will I need?
3. My husband/father needs a job. What is available?

These questions may be addressed to all the groups or to just one or two groups.

Once the students are prepared for the activity, separate each set of panelists into a distinct group, so that the rest of the class can distinguish one from the other. A large sign card would be helpful.

After the activity is over, the teacher may ask the class by a show of hands:

1. How many of you would move to the New England Colonies? Why?
2. How many of you would move to the Middle Colonies? Why?
3. How many of you would move to the Southern Colonies? Why?

CLASSROOM ACTIVITY 8

REWRITING HISTORY

It is fun for students to imagine the "what ifs" of history. In this activity the students will be broken into groups to rewrite U.S. history based on the following "non-events."

1. The first shipload of Africans was never brought to Virginia.
2. The Native Americans decided not to help the Pilgrims in Plymouth.

3. The Mayflower sank.
4. William Penn was a bigot.
5. The French won the French and Indian War.
6. The Dutch won permanent control of New York.
7. Neither tobacco nor cotton would grow in the South.
8. All the colonists decided life was too hard and went back to Europe.

CHAPTER THREE

The American Revolution and the Declaration of Independence

INTRODUCTION

Choosing independence is a difficult decision and involves many new experiences. At the beginning of the conflict with Britain the colonists still considered themselves British and wanted the rights of British citizens with the protection and backup of their mother country's government. But as time went by, they became more independent, less willing to be treated as an immature colony, and more experienced in self-government and determination. They, in fact, followed the stages of child, adolescent, and young adult.

This chapter stresses these changes, and most of the classroom activities are geared toward helping the students understand and identify with the process of becoming independent. Our project list and homework assignments focus on the wealth of ideas and people involved in this period of our history and offer the students ample opportunity for research and creativity.

PROJECT LIST

1. Make a poster showing uniforms worn by British and American troops during the American Revolution.
2. Make a booklet of maps showing campaigns and battles of the American Revolution.
3. Write pages from a British history textbook with descriptions and interpretations of five of the following events and people. (The teacher may change the number depending on the ability of the students.)
   (a) Navigation Acts
   (b) Currency Act

(c) Sons of Liberty
(d) Boston Massacre
(e) Boston Tea Party
(f) Patrick Henry
(g) Lexington and Concord
(h) The Declaration of Independence
(i) France's role in the Revolution
(j) Capture of Cornwallis
The student or teacher may substitute other events and people. This project may then be compared to coverage of the same events and people in any U.S. history textbook.

4. Make a booklet or poster showing weapons used in the American Revolution.

5. Pretend you are a reporter for a newspaper. Describe any battle from the American Revolution in detail. Include interviews with soldiers as well as who won and the importance of the battle.

6. Write a song book with at least ten songs describing the feats of heroes from this period of U.S. history. Examples are Thomas Paine, George Washington, and Thomas Jefferson. You may use familiar melodies of today if you wish.

7. The American Revolution was as much a revolution of ideas as it was of battles. Write a paper using the above sentence as your thesis with specific quotes and examples to back up your opinions.

8. Make an illustrated time line. Include events leading to the American Revolution, the Declaration of Independence, and important battles and campaigns of the Revolution.

9. Read a biography of one of the following people. Using your information, write a proposal for or against admitting him or her into a U.S. history "Hall of Fame."
Abigail Adams
Thomas Paine
Paul Revere
Crispus Attucks
Haym Salomon
Betsy Ross
Alexander Hamilton
Daniel Boone
Benedict Arnold
Nathan Hale
Thomas Jefferson
Benjamin Franklin

George Washington
John Adams
Samuel Adams

10. Read primary sources of information from the time of the American Revolution. Write the following:
    (a) Short summary of what you read
    (b) The point of view of the writer with specific quotes to back up your opinion
    (c) Comparison of the primary material to textbook coverage of the same event or ideas

11. Write the script for a TV program showing the many ways colonists began to feel and show American nationalism during the years preceding the Declaration of Independence.

12. (For students living in one of the original colonies represented at the Second Continental Congress.) Research and write a report on the position and arguments of your state's representative regarding the Declaration of Independence.

13. Do research and write a series of letters that illustrate the difference of opinion between the British and colonists on:
    (a) Taxation
    (b) "Natural" rights of people

14. Do a documentary TV program on the blockade of Boston Harbor. Include the hardships faced by the people and the efforts of other colonies to come to their aid. Include interviews with people having various opinions and feelings about what is going on.

15. Write the script for an eyewitness minute-to-minute news broadcast on the battles of Lexington and Concord.

16. Write a report on Virginia's Bill of Rights and Constitution.

17. Do a study of July fourth traditions in your own town or city.

18. Write a short story on what might have happened if George Washington had accepted the offer to be king of America.

19. Research and write a report on slavery during the period of the American Revolution.

20. Make a diorama showing a scene from any important event during the American Revolution.

21. Read *April Morning* by Howard Fast. Write a book report telling how the Revolution affected the lives of the main characters of the book.

22. Do a booklet of illustrations of scenes from the story and a book jacket for *April Morning* by Howard Fast.

23. Make an encyclopedia of important names and events from the American Revolution.

24. Paint a picture of any important event during the American Revolution.

25. Research the role of any foreigner who fought in the American Revolution. Write a diary describing what he does, sees, and feels. This may also be done as a series of letters home.

26. Read *Johnny Tremain* by Esther Forbes. Write a book report describing how this book makes the American Revolution come alive to you. Would you have liked to live during this time? Why? Why not?

27. Make a cartoon strip describing the role of John Paul Jones and the American navy during the American Revolution.

28. Using original songs from the American Revolution, make a musical videotape such as those seen on MTV.

29. Write your own version of *Common Sense*.

HOMEWORK ASSIGNMENTS

EVENTS LEADING TO THE DECLARATION OF INDEPENDENCE

1. Pretend that you are a colonist in the 1760s. Write an appeal to Parliament explaining why they should repeal one of the following acts. Give specific reasons.
   (a) Navigation Acts
   (b) Writs of Assistance
   (c) Sugar Act
   (d) Currency Act
   (e) Stamp Act

2. Would you have joined the Sons of Liberty? Why? Why not?

3. Write an editorial either praising or condemning one of the following actions:
   (a) Sacking of the Lt. Governor's home in Boston
   (b) Boston Massacre
   (c) Boston Tea Party

4. Choose one of the people below and write a list of grievances against Britain from his point of view.
   (a) Shipbuilder or manufacturer
   (b) Southern tobacco or rice farmer
   (c) Someone wanting to settle in the West

5. Make a political cartoon showing the difference between the Loyalists and the Patriots. It can be from either's point of view.

6. Pretend you are a British soldier or government official stationed in America. Write a letter home describing your feelings about the colonists.

7. Explain the First Continental Congress and the Association from the point of view of a British soldier, American patriot, or American moderate.

8. Draw illustrations for Longfellow's "Midnight Ride of Paul Revere."

9. Write the order that you think the British commander gave to his troops before sending them to Lexington and Concord.

10. Write a dialogue between a British soldier and a colonial homeowner in which the soldier demands to be quartered.

11. Write the answer a colonial parent would give to a child who had asked, "Mommy (Daddy), what is taxation without representation?"

THE DECLARATION OF INDEPENDENCE

1. Pretend you are a delegate to the Second Continental Congress. Make a list of reasons for and against becoming independent from England.

2. Make a "paid political announcement" for television on why the colonies should or should not be independent.

3. Prepare for a debate on whether the colonies should declare their independence. (Debate may be held the next day.) Write your reasons for both sides of the debate.

4. Write a headline and accompanying article for a British or American newspaper for July 5, 1776.

5. Pretend that you are an American living in 1776 and have just learned about the Declaration of Independence. Write a diary entry, short poem, or letter describing your feelings.

6. If television or radio had existed in 1776, how do you think the Declaration of Independence would have been reported on the news? Prepare your version for presentation in class tomorrow.

7. How do you think the Declaration of Independence affected American soldiers who were already fighting the British?

8. Who was left out of the statement, "All men are created equal"?

9. Imagine that you are living in 1777. Plan a July 4th celebration for the first anniversary of Independence Day.

10. Describe your last Independence Day celebration.

11. Interview your family and neighbors and ask what July 4th means to them. Be prepared to report your findings to the class.

12. In what ways are you independent? In what ways and on whom are you dependent?

13. According to the Declaration of Independence, people have the right to overthrow a government that is harmful and unjust. Do you agree? Why? Why not? Under what circumstances could you imagine joining a revolution to declare independence from your government?

14. Write your own Declaration of Independence to your parents or teachers.

THE WAR

1. Imagine that you are a general in the American army. Write a letter to your wife describing the problems you are having raising and leading your troops.

2. Make a recruitment poster for the American army.

3. Write a list of qualifications and characteristics you think a leader of the American army needed. You may put this into a help wanted ad.

4. Why were the "home front" and the war so interrelated during the American Revolution? Explain how one influenced and affected the other. Give examples.

5. Pretend you are a soldier at any battle taught in class. Write a letter home describing the conditions under which you are living and your feelings about the battle and the war.

6. If you had been a soldier listening to Washington's farewell to his troops, how would you have felt about him and what he said?

7. Write a poem, rap song, or ballad describing Bunker Hill, Valley Forge, the Capture of Cornwallis, or any other important event of the war.

8. Write a song or jingle to raise the spirits of the American soldiers.

9. Write a thank you letter to France for its help during the war.

10. Use the following sentence to begin or end a short newspaper article about the death of Nathan Hale: "I only regret that I have but one life to lose for my country."

11. If you had been assigned by George Washington to go to the Continental Congress to plead for funds, what would you have said? Write a speech and be prepared to deliver it in class.

12. Use as many of the following terms as possible in a short story, poem, or other creative writing about the Revolutionary War:

    redcoat, Yankee, inflation, paper money or Continental currency, war profiteer, patriot, spy.

13. Make a flag for the continental American army representing the thirteen colonies.

14. Could you be a mercenary the way the Hessians were? Why? Why not?

15. During the Revolution many people tried not to take sides. Why might this have been a temptation?

16. If you had lived during the American Revolution, would you have taken a side? Why? Why not? Which one would you have taken if your answer is yes?

17. Write a letter from Valley Forge describing Baron von Steuben's drilling of the troops.

CULMINATING QUESTIONS ABOUT THE AMERICAN REVOLUTION

1. If you could be any of the people studied during this unit, who would you choose? Explain.

2. Make up a set of baseball-type cards for your choice of five heroes of the American Revolution.

3. Make up a list of titles for any five leaders from the American revolutionary period. Example: Washington the Winner.

4. Very little has been written about the contribution of women during the American Revolution. What do you infer from this? Does it mean that they did nothing at all? Explain.

5. Write a letter to a grandchild explaining why you fought in the American Revolution or signed the Declaration of Independence.

6. Make up an agenda listing the first five things that must be done by the new country now that it is independent and has won the war.

7. Why do we celebrate July 4th rather than the day we won the war?

CLASSROOM ACTIVITY 1

CHOOSING INDEPENDENCE

Although a family provides love as well as structure, it can be compared to a government. The following exercises will allow students to see the similarities between family and government and to clarify their own position in their families. It will also help them to understand the relationship between a mother country and a colony. Choosing independence also means new responsibilities, and students will see this more clearly as they participate in these activities.

Students will write the answers to the questions below at the beginning of the class. The teacher may then have them share in groups, or can lead a discussion based on their answers. The teacher may stress that he or she is not prying into family business and should not offer suggestions or reactions to what the class says. This first exercise will lay the groundwork for the ones to follow.

1. Who makes the rules in your home?
2. Who makes the decisions?
3. What decisions do you make?
4. Is there anything you would want to change about the rules or decision-making process in your family?

CLASSROOM ACTIVITY 2

CHOOSING INDEPENDENCE: PART 2

Using the structure of Classroom Activity 1, the teacher will ask the following questions:

1. Who provides the basic needs for your family?
2. Describe the breakdown of chores at home. What do you do?
3. Who decided how these chores would be divided?
4. Do you get an allowance or any payment for what you do?

CLASSROOM ACTIVITY 3

CHOOSING INDEPENDENCE: PART 3

The teacher will now let the class prepare for independent lives outside the home. The students should form committees of three or four and discuss how they would set up a home together.

The teacher should give as little help as possible on this. Given time, most students will cover all their possible needs and problems. However, a few questions might get them started.

1. Think of all the economic and household responsibilities that you would now assume.
2. Think of new problems that might arise from living in a group and how they might be solved.

After the committees meet and report back, the teacher may lead a discussion or ask the students to write their thoughts on the following questions:

1. What are the benefits of living at home? Living on one's own?
2. Were you surprised by how many responsibilities independence gave you? Explain.

CLASSROOM ACTIVITY 4

CHOOSING INDEPENDENCE: PART 4

The teacher will read and discuss the following situations.

1. You are asked to join a street gang or neighborhood club. It offers protection and/or social activities. The members pay dues, wear special jackets, and spend most of their time together. Would you join? Why? Why not? What would you gain? What would you lose?
2. You live in a dormitory at college. Meals and linen are provided, and someone cleans your room once a week. There is a curfew and house rules about noise, visitors, and drinking. You are invited to join three other girls/boys in sharing an apartment. Would you go? Why? Why not? What would you lose? What would you gain?
3. You have a choice between two classes. One has a teacher who is very strict, piles on the work, and is known to have a terrible temper. He or she has a reputation for getting everyone in the class to pass the city/state exams in that subject. The second teacher believes students should learn through trial and error and individual research. She or he does not prepare the students in a systematic way for standardized tests. Students are responsible for taking their own notes during class lessons and for keeping up with reading and other work. At the end of the term they must hand in a special project. Which class would you choose? Why? What would be the advantages and disadvantages of each?

CLASSROOM ACTIVITY 5

TAKING A STAND

It is not easy to take a stand. The heroes of the American Revolution often seem superhuman. Yet, there were many unsung heroes as well as people who simply supported but didn't lead. All of them took some personal risk in order to be part of the American Revolution.

The situations below deal with school. The teacher should write these on the chalkboard. It would be best if the teacher reproduced the list of possible actions and handed them out to the students. For each situation, the students will decide on which action they would be willing to take. This is a personal decision, and except for possible discussion of terms (if necessary), the activity should start without very much teacher input. However, the following questions should be considered by the students as they make their decisions:

1. What risks are you taking?
2. What do you expect to win?
3. Is it worth the risk?

A class discussion or group sharing would end this classroom activity. It would also be helpful for the students to go over what they wrote and heard by doing a homework assignment about how they felt and what they learned about themselves during this activity.

SITUATIONS

1. The food in the cafeteria is terrible.
2. The dress code in school is very strict.
3. The school board has decided to add another hour to the school day.
4. The school board has decided to add another month to the school year.
5. One teacher in school is very unfair and seems to show discrimination against a particular group of students.
6. Your school insists that students only use notebooks, pens, and pencils with the school's name inscribed on them. They are sold in the school store and cost more than similar items found in other stores.

POSSIBLE ACTIONS: HOW FAR WOULD YOU GO?

1. Write a letter of protest.

2. Write and circulate a petition.

3. Sign someone else's petition.

4. Speak to someone in charge.

5. Have your parent speak to someone in charge.

6. Form a small group to speak to someone in charge.

7. Organize a sit-in in front of the school or school board's office.

8. Organize a school strike with protest picket signs.

9. Join a school strike or sit-in.

10. Make picket signs for the others but not appear yourself.

11. Boycott.

12. Simply refuse to do what you are told.

CLASSROOM ACTIVITY 6

HOW ANGRY WOULD YOU GET?

Students will pretend that they are colonists living during the days preceding the American Revolution. They are to rate their reactions to the following events as very angry, mildly angry, not angry.

1. Navigation Acts restrict trade to Britain only.

2. The Writs of Assistance provide for a general search warrant that invades privacy.

3. Taxes are put on all items using stamps.

4. The Townshend Acts are repealed except for the tax on tea.

5. You read about the Boston Massacre.

6. Boston Harbor is blockaded.

7. The British march from Boston to Lexington and Concord to seize arms and gunpowder believed to be hidden there.

After this is completed, the teacher should go back over the list and ask students at which point they would have been ready to take an action and what action they would have taken.

CLASSROOM ACTIVITY 7

READ THE DECLARATION OF INDEPENDENCE

Many students have only the vaguest idea of the meaning of the Declaration of Independence. Many have never read it. Some only know it said something about men being created equal. Often, it isn't even connected to July 4th celebrations.

We feel that it is imperative for all junior and senior high school students to read the entire document. It needs to be discussed and analyzed sentence by sentence, thought by thought. Students also need to understand its effect at the time it was written, what it was meant to do, and who it was written for, as well as the change in meaning and interpretation through the years.

The teacher may approach this as a study of literature with attention paid to style and vocabulary as well as content. After an initial reading, the teacher may want to break up the Declaration of Independence into short sections and assign students to analyze, explain, and read their own section to the class. Some other approaches include:

1. A choral reading
2. A reenactment of the signing of the Declaration while reading it aloud
3. A modern version written in committee and read aloud

CHAPTER FOUR

The Constitution and the Bill of Rights

INTRODUCTION

The Constitution has allowed our country to grow and change, to survive crises and problems, and even to make and correct mistakes (for example, the amendments for Prohibition and its repeal). The writers of the law of our land handed down a document that could breathe, expand, absorb change. The same Constitution of 1787 still exists today—still works today.

We hope to instill some of the wonder and appreciation of the Constitution and Bill of Rights in the assignments in this chapter. Special attention has been given to details of the Constitution and amendments in our homework section. No one is expected to use all of the questions.

We feel that it is essential for students to have copies of the Constitution and Bill of Rights for their study of this unit. If not provided in a textbook, we hope that the teacher will order a set for the class.

PROJECT LIST

1. Write a report on the Northwest Ordinance. In addition to explaining its provisions and lasting effect, write why it is often considered the most important accomplishment of the Congress during the days of the Articles of Confederation.

2. Make a booklet or poster of political cartoons showing all the reasons why the Articles of Confederation failed.

3. Make a booklet entitled *Who's Who at the Constitutional Convention.* Include all the participants, their backgrounds, and what they contributed to the Constitution.

4. Read *The Federalist* pamphlets. Summarize the arguments for ratifying the Constitution. Write any questions you would have liked to ask the authors James Madison, Alexander Hamilton, and John Jay.

5. Make a jigsaw puzzle of the three branches of government and how they work.

6. Make a picture book for young children explaining our system of checks and balances.

7. Make a dictionary of terms from the Constitution.

8. Choose any amendment after the Bill of Rights and write a report on its history.

9. Make a booklet for a new immigrant that describes the Constitution and Bill of Rights. Use your own words and cartoons or illustrations.

10. Write a short story in which any article or amendment of the Constitution plays an important part.

11. Research the background of any important decision of the Supreme Court. Then write how the case was decided and summarize the arguments involved.

12. Write a research report on checks and balances by using specific instances in which one branch of the government counteracted the other.

13. Using newspapers and magazines, compile evidence for a current events booklet which shows that the first amendment is used today.

14. Pretend that you are a lawyer. Research court cases dealing with the first amendment and use them to write an argument on behalf of your client's right to either freedom of speech, press, religion, or assembly.

15. Prepare a video or audiotape about the Bill of Rights today.

16. Research the treatment of the colonies by Britain in order to write an illustrated booklet on how the Bill of Rights was an effort to prevent any government from doing that again.

HOMEWORK ASSIGNMENTS

ARTICLES OF CONFEDERATION

1. Ask your parents and neighbors if they would pay a voluntary tax to help pay off the national debt. From their answers, do you think we could get it paid off? Explain.

2. What, or who, is the "Central Government" for your school? Do you think you could function without one? Why? Why not?

3. Make up a political cartoon for a newspaper in the 1780s about life without a Supreme Court.

4. Pretend you live in one of the original thirteen states under the Articles of Confederation. Write a letter to your state government as a:

    (a) Merchant asking them to tax goods from other states

    (b) Farmer urging them to set up a trade treaty with a neighboring state in which you sell your produce

5. Draw a ladder showing the steps needed for Congress to receive money from one state during the Articles of Confederation.

6. Would you have joined Shay's Rebellion or felt threatened by it? Give reasons for your answer.

7. Choose one weakness of the Articles of Confederation that you feel was most harmful to the country. Write a petition to Congress stating:

    (a) Why this is harmful

    (b) How the government might benefit from having more power in this area

    (c) Your ideas on how to make the changes

    (This homework should be assigned before doing Classroom Activity 1.)

CONSTITUTIONAL CONVENTION AND RATIFICATION

1. It is June 1787, and you are a delegate to a special congress in Philadelphia to improve the Articles of Confederation. Write a plea to the other members on why the happenings at these meetings should be kept secret from the public and why the windows should be kept shut even though it's so hot.

2. Write an oath of secrecy for the members of the Constitutional Convention in June 1787.

3. Discarding the Articles of Confederation was basically a lawless act and could have been considered a form of treason. Pretend that you are a member of the Constitutional Convention. How would you have voted? Write your reasons for your decision.

4. Write a dialogue between two delegates to the Constitutional Convention. One is for the Virginia Plan, and the second wants the New Jersey Plan.

5. Make a list of all the comforts of today that were missing during the Constitutional Convention.

6. Write an argument to your fellow delegates to convince them why they must accept the Great Compromise.

7. How does the Three-Fifths Compromise insult slaves?

8. Pretend you are a delegate to the Constitutional Convention. Write a journal entry on any of the following:

    (a) Doubts about the ability of people to vote intelligently

     (b) Fears about giving Congress power over trade with foreign countries

     (c) Questions about how your state will react to what the Convention has done

9. It has been said that few of the delegates were completely satisfied with the new Constitution. Choose any delegate or state and write a list of the positive and negative sides of the Constitution as they would see it.

10. Make a handbill for or against ratifying the new Constitution.

11. Pretend you were the host of a talk show back in 1788. Prepare a set of questions to ask the following guests about their positions on ratifying the Constitution:
     (a) Thomas Jefferson
     (b) Patrick Henry
     (c) Alexander Hamilton
     (d) Ben Franklin

12. Write a newspaper editorial about Jefferson's request that a Bill of Rights be added to the Constitution.

13. Make a commercial for or against ratifying the Constitution.

14. Write a headline and short news article about the ratification of the Constitution by either New York or Virginia.

15. Write the lyrics for a song called "Founding Fathers."

16. Some people think that the writing and ratification of the Constitution was the true American Revolution. Do you agree? Why? Why not?

17. Imagine that you were a delegate to the Constitutional Convention and had been present at George Washington's inauguration. Write a letter to a friend describing how this makes you feel about your work.

THE CONSTITUTION

1. Read the preamble to the Constitution. Why did the words, "We the people . . ." have such an impact on the world?

2. Write a poem, song lyric, or rap song using the words, "We the people."

3. Draw a political cartoon showing the reaction of any European king to the American Constitution.

4. Make a list of school rules and classroom rules. Compare this to the division of power between state and federal governments.

5. Find out at what age you may drive, drink, marry, vote, go into the army, and receive social security. Which of these are determined by your state? Which are determined by the federal government? Why?

6. Any of the following questions may be used after the class studies Article I of the Constitution:
   (a) Make a help wanted ad describing the job of and requirements for a senator or representative.
   (b) Make a ladder showing the steps needed for a bill to become a law.
   (c) Read carefully the powers granted to Congress, denied to Congress, and denied to the states. Write one modern example for each category.

7. Questions pertaining to Article II:
   (a) Using the information in Article II, write out questions for a job interview with a candidate for president.
   (b) Read the article carefully and find and write down the section that applies to the following events in modern history:
      • Lyndon Baines Johnson became president immediately after the assassination of John Fitzgerald Kennedy.
      • Richard M. Nixon resigned after articles of impeachment were brought against him.

8. For use with Article III:
   (a) How are your rights protected in this Article?
   (b) Why do you think treason was so clearly defined in the Constitution?
   (c) Why do you think Supreme Court judges are appointed for life?
   (d) Make a list of the qualities you think an ideal Supreme Court judge must have.

9. Read Article IV:
   (a) Draw a cartoon showing what would happen to someone who committed a crime in New York and escaped to New Jersey.
   (b) Send a telegram to the federal government from a state government requesting protection due to domestic violence. Explain the violence.

10. Article V states the provisions for amending the Constitution:
    (a) Why does this article truly make the Constitution a living document?
    (b) Read the amendments to the Constitution (excluding the Bill of Rights) and choose the three that you feel are most important to your life. Explain why.

11. For use with Article VI:
    (a) Why is it important for state as well as federal officials to take an oath to support the Constitution?
    (b) How does this article guarantee freedom of religion to public officials?

12. Article VII: Why do you think only nine out of thirteen states were necessary to ratify the Constitution?

13. Write a conversation between the Founding Fathers as they hear that we have just celebrated the 200th anniversary of the Constitution. What do you think they would say to each other?

14. If you could talk to any of the writers of the Constitution, what would you tell them today?

15. Write a proposal for an anniversary celebration for the Constitution. This should be read to the class and may be used for Classroom Activity 5.

THE BILL OF RIGHTS

1. Write your own definition of the word freedom.

2. Make a list of ways in which your personal freedom may be limited. Include economic considerations, family rules, and peer pressure in your answer.

3. Make a list of things that are legal but that you still wouldn't do. Explain your answer.

4. Make a cartoon illustrating the point that "my freedom ends where your nose begins."

5. Use the following questions for the First Amendment:
   (a) Is there any freedom you would want added? Explain.
   (b) How exactly do you use freedom of speech and the press?
   (c) How do you limit your own freedom of speech?
   (d) Interview a parent or neighbor on how they personally use the First Amendment.
   (e) Make a poster or a petition urging action on behalf of some cause you believe in.

6. Write an answer to people who use the Second Amendment as their reason for feeling that they should be allowed to own guns.

7. Imagine you lived during the days of the American Revolution. Write a letter to Congress urging them to pass the Third Amendment.

8. For use with Amendment IV:
   (a) Write the script for a scene from a TV police show illustrating how the Fourth Amendment is used.
   (b) Pretend that you are a police officer. Write a request for a search warrant. Be sure to include all the necessary information as prescribed in Amendment IV.

9. Read Amendments V, VI, and VIII and write a manual for accused people explaining clearly their rights under the law.

10. Write a letter from an American of 1789 to Congress giving reasons for the importance of Amendments IX and X.

11. Which of the amendments in the Bill of Rights is most important to you personally? Explain your answer.

12. Make a list of all the rights in the Bill of Rights that were denied to the slaves.

13. Make up an original amendment to protect the rights of Native Americans.

14. How do you think our history would have been different if the rights of the Native Americans and the black people had been protected?

CLASSROOM ACTIVITY 1

READY FOR CHANGE

(Students will do Homework 7 from the Articles of Confederation section before doing this activity.)

Each student will announce which weakness he or she chose to deal with. The teacher will then form committees in which the students will read their petitions to each other. They will combine, add, eliminate, argue, and compromise until each committee has produced one petition, which they will all sign. The final petitions will be read to the entire class.

If the same few weaknesses are chosen by everyone, the teacher may form more than one committee on the issue. It would actually be interesting to see how different committees handle the same assignment.

CLASSROOM ACTIVITY 2

A NEW CONSTITUTION

The writing of a constitution is a complex and difficult task. In order for this activity to be most successful, the teacher must be comfortable turning the class over to the students. They will be told that they have an opportunity to write a whole new set of rules for the school or classroom. The teacher simply states that and tells them that they can structure themselves any way they wish in order to complete the task. She or he then sits down and allows them to take over.

If this is not possible, the teacher may suggest the following:

1. George Washington was voted chairman at the Constitutional Convention. Maybe the class would like to vote for a chairperson to help organize things.
2. If there are no rules for running the meeting, it might lead to chaos.
3. Someone should take notes.

We strongly suggest that the teacher not use these but allow the students to discover them for themselves. Given the time and freedom, students will create their own order.

When this activity is finished, the new constitution should be presented. Students and teacher should discuss what similarities there are to the old system and what new ideas were included. If possible, some of the new ideas might be absorbed into classroom routines, or a committee might present ideas for the school to the principal or student council. The goal, however, is for the students to go through the process rather than focus on the end product.

CLASSROOM ACTIVITY 3

HOW GOOD ARE YOU AT COMPROMISING?

This activity is designed to help students understand the process of compromise. Two or three students will be assigned each topic. They will discuss it in front of the class until an agreement is reached. Not all discussions will lead to arguments or to compromises. The teacher will talk about the outcome with the class after each group has had its turn. Students may be asked to look for other options and areas of compromise when appropriate.

TOPICS

1. Choose a film to see.
2. Choose a dessert to serve.
3. Choose music for a dance.
4. Choose a place for a class trip.
5. Choose new school colors.
6. Choose a theme for a school party.
7. Choose a cause to raise money for.
8. Choose a soft drink for the cafeteria.
9. Choose one team for the school to support.
10. Choose an animal to be the school mascot or symbol.

CLASSROOM ACTIVITY 4

DEBATES

The following debates may be used throughout the unit as the class learns the relevant material.

1. Which should be adopted—the Virginia Plan or the New Jersey Plan?
2. Should there be direct popular vote for elections or an electoral college?
3. Which is more important—a strong central government or strong individual states?
4. Should we ratify the new Constitution?
5. Should a group such as the Ku Klux Klan have access to television as part of freedom of speech?
6. Should a group such as the neo-Nazis be allowed to have a public parade?
7. Should pornography be protected as freedom of the press?
8. Should anyone have the right to censor what students may read?

CLASSROOM ACTIVITY 5

(Assign Homework 15 from the Constitution section before doing this activity.)

HAPPY BIRTHDAY CONSTITUTION

Students will read their proposals and form committees to plan for the class celebration on the birthday of the Constitution. This may be done as a class project or be extended into a school or community project.

The celebration may be held during school time or on a weekend depending on what type of activities are planned.

CLASSROOM ACTIVITY 6

RIGHTS AND RESPONSIBILITIES

The Constitution and the Bill of Rights offer Americans freedom and responsibility. Neither stands alone. This activity will help students understand the relationship between their rights and their responsibilities.

The teacher will make up cards with the following categories:

> Right to vote
> Freedom of speech
> Freedom of the press
> Freedom of petition and assembly
> Freedom of religion
> Right to trial by jury

Students will pick a card, and then, all the students with the same card will form a committee. The job of each committee is to answer specific questions about their topic.

QUESTIONS

Right to Vote

1. What must a citizen do before he or she can vote?
2. What should a citizen know before voting?
3. Should people be obligated to vote by law?
4. What are some excuses people give for not voting? How can you respond to them?
5. Think of ways to urge people to make use of their right to vote.

Freedom of Speech

1. In what ways does the law limit freedom of speech?
2. In what ways could freedom of speech bring danger or harm to someone else?
3. What could happen if people don't bother to use their freedom of speech?
4. Is there anyone who you feel should not have freedom of speech?

Freedom of the Press

1. List everything and everyone besides newspapers that are guaranteed freedom of the press.
2. In what ways, besides writing, do we have freedom of the press?
3. How can the average citizen ensure his or her freedom of the press?
4. What responsibility does an editor of a newspaper have?
5. Who, if anyone, should censor what you read?
6. Is there anyone who you feel should not have freedom of the press?

Freedom of Petition and Assembly

1. What exactly do petition and assembly mean?
2. What are the responsibilities of people who organize and participate in a demonstration?
3. Write a list of ways to ensure that demonstrations are peaceful.
4. Write a list of causes that you feel should be demonstrated for or against. Why is it so important to do so?

Freedom of Religion

1. How might one person's freedom of religion hurt another person?
2. What limits should there be on what one believes?
3. What limits should there be on what one does or how one practices religion?
4. Give examples of how we separate religion from our government.
5. Give examples of how freedom of religion may be abused or denied.

Right to Trial by Jury

1. What do you know about jury duty?
2. What is meant by jury of peers?
3. Why is it important for people to serve when called for jury duty?
4. How would you convince people to take their jury duty?

This activity takes time, and the teacher may choose to do it over a two-day period. The class reports by each committee should be followed by questions from and discussion by the entire class.

CHAPTER FIVE

Establishing the New Nation

INTRODUCTION

With the ratification of the Constitution and the election of George Washington as president, the stage was set for the United States to establish itself as a nation. While the groundwork had been brilliantly laid by the framers of the Constitution, it remained to be seen whether the plan was workable. The United States had to establish itself as a viable political entity to the citizens, to the states, and to all the other foreign powers in the world. The success and endurance of the new nation would depend on the decisions and policies established by the leaders during the formative years.

For the sake of clarity, we have divided the homework section into five parts. The first three cover the administrations of George Washington, John Adams, and Thomas Jefferson as leaders who made the precedent-setting decisions which enabled our survival. The last two sections focus on the War of 1812 and the Monroe Doctrine, both of which established our identity in the eyes of the European nations.

A great deal of creative and sensitive decision making occurred during this era. This chapter will attempt to involve the students in assessing and analyzing those decisions and events so as to give them a deeper appreciation of the complexity of establishing the nation.

PROJECT LIST

1. Make a special commemorative magazine highlighting the accomplishments of George Washington as president.
2. Make a series of political cartoons both in favor of and in opposition to the Alien and Sedition Acts.

3. Make an original anonymous pamphlet attacking the Alien and Sedition Acts.

4. Make a series of political cartoons which illustrate our effort to stay out of involvements with European countries.

5. Write a diary about the life and accomplishments of Alexander Hamilton.

6. (For a more advanced student) Write an analysis of the economic policies that Alexander Hamilton made for the United States when he was Secretary of the Treasury. Evaluate them in your conclusion.

7. Make a map of the United States, illustrating in detail the Louisiana Territory. Include all or some of the following: rivers, resources, and the routes explored by Lewis and Clark and Zebulon Pike.

8. Do a special newspaper exposé on the life of Aaron Burr.

9. Make up a ballad or an epic poem about how Americans felt about the Embargo of 1807 and what they did about it.

10. Write a chapter for a British history textbook telling the story of the War of 1812.

11. Make a diorama of the burning of Washington in the War of 1812.

12. Make a model of a frigate, such as the *Constitution*, which was used in the War of 1812.

13. Make a diorama of one battle in the War of 1812.

14. Write a script for a TV special on the life and accomplishments of John Marshall, the first chief justice of the Supreme Court.

15. Write your own version of the Supreme Court arguments in the cases of *Marbury* v. *Madison* and in *McCulloch* v. *Maryland*.

16. Make a time line of the major events and decisions under the administration of George Washington.

17. Make a time line of the major decisions and events in foreign policy from 1796 to 1823.

18. Write a history of the treatment of the Native Americans by the administrations of Washington, Adams, Jefferson, Madison, and Monroe.

19. Make a fashion magazine illustrating fashions between the years 1789 and 1823.

20. Make a diorama of *Mount Vernon* or *Monticello*.

21. Read a biography of one of the first five presidents. Write a series of funeral speeches and eulogies that discuss the person's character, family life, accomplishments, and service to his country.

HOMEWORK ASSIGNMENTS

GEORGE WASHINGTON'S TERM OF OFFICE

1. Write your own version of George Washington's acceptance speech upon his election as president.
2. If you had been elected first president of the United States, list the things you might have tried to accomplish.
3. If you were the king of France or England, what do you think you would have said privately to your wife about the new nation, the United States.
4. What personal qualities do you imagine George Washington must have had to lead the new nation?
5. What do you think makes a good leader? Why?
6. If you had to run this school, how would you get everyone to obey the rules?
7. Pretend you are Alexander Hamilton. Write a speech for Congress to convince them to pay off the debts of the individual states.
8. Write an advertisement to convince citizens to invest in a national bank at $400 a share.
9. Make a list of all the people who might have opposed the tariff on manufactured goods. Who would have favored it? Why?
10. Pretend you are a manufacturer in 1790. Write a letter to Alexander Hamilton telling him why you appreciate the tariff on manufactured goods.
11. The United States owed $75 million to foreign nations, state governments, and individuals when George Washington took office. List all the ways that you think the government could raise money.
12. Make a poster urging people to support the Whiskey Rebellion.
13. Write an announcement urging people to join the militia to crush the Whiskey Rebellion.
14. Prepare for a discussion on the advantages of a government run by the wealthy, educated people as represented by the Federalist party or a government run by the masses.
15. Make up a slogan and a mascot to represent the Federalist party and the Jeffersonian-Republicans.
16. Make up a rap song to support Washington's Proclamation of Neutrality.
17. Is it more important to protect yourself or to help your friends? Why?

18. Make up a newspaper editorial either for or against Washington's foreign policy of isolationism.

19. Write a letter to the French government demanding the withdrawal of Citizen Genet.

20. President George Washington risked his reputation when he defended and supported the treaty that John Jay had negotiated with England. In what ways did he risk his reputation? Would you have done that? Explain.

21. What do you think would be an appropriate retirement present for George Washington? Why do you think so?

22. George Washington is remembered as the "Father of Our Country." Write a title that you would like to be remembered by.

23. Write your own version of Washington's Farewell Address.

EVENTS UNDER THE JOHN ADAMS ADMINISTRATION

1. Write a newspaper article and headline describing the XYZ affair.

2. Write a letter to President John Adams telling him why you object to the Alien and Sedition Acts.

3. Write a speech for John Adams conceding his defeat to Thomas Jefferson in the election of 1800.

4. Write an epitaph for the tombstone of John Adams.

THOMAS JEFFERSON'S ADMINISTRATION

1. Jefferson believed that farmers were the most important people in society. Do you agree? Explain.

2. Make a list of things that might have caused France to decide against selling us the Louisiana Territory.

3. Pretend you are Robert Livingston, the United States minister to France in 1803. Write a letter to President Jefferson explaining why you bought the entire Louisiana Territory instead of just buying New Orleans, as planned.

4. Make up a bill of sale for the Louisiana Territory.

5. Write a page in Jefferson's diary expressing his feeling of guilt over the Louisiana Purchase, since the Constitution did not specifically give the president that right.

6. Write a formal letter from the government of the United States to the London Foreign Office denouncing the attack on the *Chesapeake* by a British warship in 1807.

7. Pretend you are President Jefferson. Write a letter of condolence to the mother of one of the sailors who was killed on the *Chesapeake*.

8. Using the letters in the word EMBARGO, make up a slogan that shows the anger Americans felt about the 1807 Embargo.

9. Make up a limerick or rhyme that explains at least one reason why the Embargo of 1807 was a failure.

THE WAR OF 1812

1. Make up a dialogue between a British and an American sea captain regarding the impressment of American sailors.

2. Write a speech, as a War Hawk, urging Congress to declare war on England.

3. Do you think James Madison did the right thing when he asked Congress to declare war on England in 1812? Explain.

4. Write a newspaper headline and an account of the American naval victory of *Old Ironsides* or of Captain Perry's victory on Lake Erie.

5. Illustrate or explain the words of "The Star-Spangled Banner."

6. What do you imagine was going through the mind of Francis Scott Key just before he wrote "The Star-Spangled Banner"?

7. Pretend you are a French citizen. What is your opinion of the United States after learning about the terms of the Treaty of Ghent, ending the War of 1812?

THE MONROE DOCTRINE

1. Write your own version of the Monroe Doctrine in today's slang.

2. Make up a top secret note between Secretary Adams and President James Monroe revealing the real reason the Monroe Doctrine should be announced.

3. Make up an original descriptive name for the Monroe Doctrine.

4. Draw a cartoon about the Monroe Doctrine that could have appeared in a European magazine of the time.

5. What do you think would have happened if a European power had challenged the Monroe Doctrine? Explain.

CLASSROOM ACTIVITY 1

SELECTING A CABINET

In order to get the new government rolling, George Washington had to select able advisors that he could rely on. This is important for every good leader.

The teacher will divide the class into groups of three to five students. Each group will then make a list of all the qualities they think a person should have in order to be chosen for one of the following Cabinet positions:

1. Secretary of the Treasury
2. Secretary of War
3. Secretary of State
4. Attorney General

Since there were only four Cabinet positions during the first administration, it may be necessary to have more than one group working on the qualifications for each post. When they are done, the teacher will go over and discuss their lists. The teacher can record them on the chalkboard and then get a consensus on the order of importance of each.

CLASSROOM ACTIVITY 2

UPON HIS RETIREMENT . . .

George Washington's retirement from the presidency after two consecutive terms was emotional and momentous. He had successfully put the new nation on relatively sound footing, both internally and in foreign affairs. Largely through his strong non-partisan leadership at home, his wise foreign policy decisions, and his ability to delegate authority and surround himself with brilliant advisors, he successfully led the United States through its infancy. Because he affected so many people and so much history, this activity will give the students a better appreciation of the impact he made.

Have the class write a farewell letter to George Washington upon his retirement. It must be written from the point of view of any of the following people. The teacher may substitute other personalities, depending upon the material that was stressed in class.

1. The king of England
2. John Adams
3. Thomas Jefferson
4. John Jay
5. Alexander Hamilton
6. Citizen Genet
7. A soldier who fought under Washington in the Revolution
8. A Redcoat who fought against Washington in the Revolution
9. Martha Washington
10. The average new American

The teacher may suggest that they include in their letters:

1. Their feelings about Washington's retirement and his accomplishments
2. Why they feel that way
3. Whether they feel his successor can fill his shoes
4. What his presidency has meant for them

When they are done writing, they can get together in groups of three to read their letters to each other to get reactions or suggestions for improvement. After making any corrections or changes, the students can write their final drafts, after which they may read them aloud to the rest of the class.

CLASSROOM ACTIVITY 3

IMPROVISATIONS

Improvisations or role-playing can be wonderful techniques to get students to better understand how events in history occurred. Use the following scenes to have your students improvise what they imagine was said. This can be a lot of fun, since the students will inadvertently use their own slang in developing the scenes. Do not discourage it. If at first the students are shy, it is sometimes helpful for the teacher to take on one of the roles. That role can be handed over to a student as the level of comfort with the activity grows.

1. A British sea captain boards an American ship and orders the impressment of American sailors. The American captain objects and argues.

2. Robert Livingston, the United States minister to France (who is a little hard of hearing), and James Monroe are negotiating with the French over the sale of the Louisiana Territory. The United States only wants New Orleans and is willing to pay $10 million, but France wants to unload the whole territory for $15 million.

3. Thomas Jefferson and Chief Justice John Marshall, who are cousins, meet. Marshall has just made his decision in the case of *Marbury* v. *Madison*, giving the Supreme Court the right to declare a law unconstitutional. Jefferson thinks it's an abuse of power.

4. George Washington doesn't want to run for a third term of office. His friends think he should.

5. It is 1794. Farmers in Pennsylvania have been chasing tax collectors away and refusing to pay the whiskey tax. Washington and his Cabinet have to figure out how to handle the situation.

6. Alexander Hamilton and Thomas Jefferson meet at dinner. Hamilton feels it would be best for the United States to be friendly with England. Thomas Jefferson thinks we owe more to France.

CLASSROOM ACTIVITY 4

DEBATES

A number of controversial issues had to be resolved as the new nation was established. Due to lack of prior experience and precedence, many issues were debated. In order to give the students a more in-depth understanding of the issues, the teacher may have individuals or groups prepare for debates on all or some of the topics below. Since some of these topics were handled in the homework section, George Washington's Term of Office, it would be more meaningful to do this activity after the students have completed those assignments.

1. A government run by the wealthy, educated people is much better than one run by the masses.

2. Farmers are more important to a country than manufacturers.

3. A country must never pay ransom to free hostages.

4. It is more important to keep peace and trade with England than to go to war because of principle or to save face.

5. It is more important to help our friends than to stay out of foreign wars.

CLASSROOM ACTIVITY 5

POLITICAL PARTY CAMPAIGN

This activity can be used after the students have learned the basic differences between the first political parties in the United States: the Federalist party and the Democratic-Republican party.

In order to better understand how political parties are a vehicle for channeling ideas, divide the class in half. One half of the class can represent the Federalist party and the other half can represent the Democratic-Republican party. Each group can be divided into sub-groups to work out:

1. Campaign slogans
2. Campaign buttons
3. Campaign songs
4. Campaign speeches
5. Mascot
6. Fund-raising activities

When they are done, each group can make a presentation to rally support. Afterwards, ask the students:

1. How did you feel about participating in your party program?
2. What problems arose? How did you resolve them?
3. Did you feel the end results were true to the principles of your party?

CLASSROOM ACTIVITY 6

WHAT WOULD YOU DO? HOW WOULD YOU FEEL?

The "Founding Fathers" and leaders of the emerging nation risked their reputations as they made decisions about a variety of issues. Since U.S history classes often neglect to deal with the feelings of leaders as they agonize over certain decisions, it will be a broadening experience for the students to explore this aspect of the decision-making process.

Have the students divide a sheet of paper into two columns. In the first column they will write what they would do, and in the second column they can write how they would feel when facing the following accusations:

1. Someone calls you chicken because you don't want to fight.
2. Someone calls you a bully because you threaten to fight.
3. Someone says you'll be sorry if you don't pay for protection.
4. Someone says you are stupid because you give in all the time.
5. Someone says you're too weak to win a fight or argument.
6. Someone says they don't like you because you won't lend them money.

When they are finished writing, the teacher will go over and discuss their answers.

CLASSROOM ACTIVITY 7

USING POWER

One of the most difficult aspects of leadership is knowing how to be strong without being a tyrant. Although the Constitution provides safeguards against the usurpation of power by one group or individual, it is still a credit to our early leaders that they did not abuse the power they were given.

The teacher will divide the class into two separate groups. One group will be "Observers" and their task will be to observe and take notes about everything the other group does. The other group will be called the "Leaders" and they will be told that they have fifteen minutes to decide on any changes they would like to make in the school. The teacher must give as little direction as possible about this task.

It would be best if the class could be set up with an inner circle for the "Leaders" and an outer circle for the "Observers." However, if this is not possible, the teacher can divide the room in any way that she or he feels is suitable. After the "Leaders" have met for fifteen minutes, the teacher can lead a discussion. The following questions may be directed to the "Observers":

1. What did you notice about the way the "Leaders" acted with each other?

2. Did you think they used their time wisely?
3. How did they behave?
4. Did the things they suggested seem to show more personal interest or more care about the school?
5. How did you feel about not being able to participate?

Now ask the "Leaders" the following questions:

1. How did you feel when you discovered you were a "Leader"?
2. How did you feel about working with your group?
3. How did you feel about being observed?
4. Who would have been affected by the changes you came up with? Do you care?
5. Do you feel you accomplished anything?

The following questions can be used to wrap up this activity:

1. Did you learn anything about yourself today?
2. Did you see any connection between what you did and what goes on in politics?
3. If we do this activity again, what would you like to do differently?

CHAPTER SIX

Expansion and the Frontier

INTRODUCTION

This chapter deals with the acquisition of territory by the United States and the settlement of that territory by the pioneers.

Our "manifest destiny" was achieved through a variety of methods: purchase, conquest, and compromise. The students will find many opportunities in this unit to both analyze and evaluate those methods and their results.

Because of the abundance of available land, the American frontier became a symbol of opportunity for everyone. People who were dissatisfied with what they had, or who dreamt of something new or different, could pioneer west and attempt to make their dreams come true. The frontier tested the strength and courage of those hardy souls who ventured west and settled the vast wilderness. This same strength, courage, and sense of purpose was used to drive the Native Americans from their ancestral lands and eventually force them into reservations.

This is a complex story. Again, the projects, homework assignments, and class activities are designed to involve the students in the multiple aspects of the westward movement in terms of analysis and evaluation.

PROJECT LIST

1. Make a map of the United States showing all the major land and water routes used by the pioneers traveling west.
2. Make a model of a flatboat carrying pioneers and their livestock into the wilderness.
3. Write a series of poems that illustrate the frontier and the pioneer spirit.

59

4. Construct a model of a Conestoga wagon or a prairie schooner.

5. Make a diorama of a wagon train.

6. Make a poster that illustrates all the means of transportation used by pioneers going west.

7. Make a collage that depicts frontiers.

8. Make a map illustrating the growth of the United States from the Louisiana Purchase in 1803 on.

9. Make a chart showing additions to United States territory from colonial times. Include when the land was acquired, how it was obtained, from whom, and what it represented in wealth to the United States.

10. Write the history of the Mexican War with the United States for a Mexican news magazine.

11. Write the history of the Lone Star Republic as seen through the eyes of the Mexicans.

12. Make an illustrated time line of the major events in the expansion of the United States.

13. Make an *Official Book of Documents* with peace treaties or bills of sale for all of the land acquisitions made by the United States. Include the Louisiana Territory, Florida, Texas, the Mexican Cession, the Oregon Territory, the Gadsden Purchase, Alaska, and Hawaii.

14. Pretend you are a pioneer traveling west on the Oregon Trail. Write a diary of your experiences.

15. Make up a *Tour of Pioneer Landmarks*. Include a map and a pamphlet explaining why you have designated each site as a landmark.

16. Make up a board game about the problems and obstacles faced by pioneers traveling west. You can include such things as snowstorms, attacks by Native Americans, illness, raging rivers, tall mountains, etc.

17. Write a script for a TV special on the treatment of the Native Americans by the pioneers, the settlers, and the government.

18. Make up a series of claims by Native Americans to be presented to Congress regarding their treatment throughout U.S. history as the pioneers took over their land. Include maps and diagrams where necessary.

19. Write a booklet about the first people to open up the West. Illustrate how hunters, trappers, miners, and cowboys helped pave the way for the settlers who followed.

20. Make a series of posters of the most wanted outlaws of the old West.

21. Make a mail order catalogue of cowboy equipment and clothing, in-

cluding everything a cowboy might need both on the range and on a cattle drive.

22. Make up a short story or a TV or movie script about life in the "Wild West."

23. Make a scrapbook illustrating the variety of Native American cultures in the territory of the United States.

24. Make your own western movie or video from the point of view of the Native Americans.

25. Write a script for a TV special called *Visit to a Native American Reservation*. Do an in-depth coverage of the life and problems of today's Native Americans.

26. Write a survival manual for pioneers going west. Include chapters for scouts, miners, trappers, cowboys, and farmers.

27. Write a report on black and Mexican cowboys in the West.

28. Make a Sunday magazine supplement on the history of the Mormons in Utah.

29. Make a pictorial overlay map that illustrates the growth of the United States from colonial days through the acquisition of Hawaii, showing the wealth that was added with each acquisition (example: oil in Alaska).

HOMEWORK ASSIGNMENTS

MANIFEST DESTINY AND THE PIONEER SPIRIT

1. Do you feel that you have a "manifest destiny"? What? If not, what would you choose your "manifest destiny" to be?

2. It is said that there will always be a frontier. Do you agree? Why? Why not?

3. If you could participate in the opening of a frontier, which one would it be? Why?

4. If you were going on a pioneer scouting mission to Mars, what small personal items would you pack?

5. If you could open a small store for last minute purchases for pioneers today who are heading into unknown parts, what items would you stock?

6. What would frighten and excite you most about being a pioneer in some unknown area? Why?

7. Make a list of all the qualities you think a frontier person must have. Put a check next to those qualities you think you have.

8. The frontier represented a chance for all who pioneered west to change their lives. In what way might this have meaning for you to-day?

9. What is your personal frontier now? Explain.

THE ACQUISITION OF NEW TERRITORIES

(Homework assignments relating to the Louisiana Purchase can be found in Chapter 5 in the third part of the homework section dealing with the administration of President Thomas Jefferson.)

1. Make a list of charges against Major-General Andrew Jackson for his actions in Florida in 1818.

2. What excuse do you think the Spanish government could have made to their people to save face about why they sold Florida to the United States?

3. Make up an announcement by Stephen Austin inviting Americans to settle in Texas.

4. Many pioneers who settled in Texas brought their slaves with them. How does this contradict the pioneer spirit?

5. In 1835, when fighting broke out between the Texans and Mexicans, who do you think had more right to the land? Explain.

6. Make up a poem entitled "Remember the Alamo."

7. Make up a ballad called "Broken Promises" that enumerates the lies that the Mexicans felt the Texans had told them in order to get permission to move onto their land.

8. Make up a national anthem for the Lone Star Republic.

9. Pretend you are a Mexican government official. Write a note to the American special envoy John Slidell indicating that Mexico is unwilling to listen to his insulting offer to buy California.

10. Write an argument between the pro-war and anti-war people in Congress who are trying to decide whether or not to declare war on Mexico in 1846.

11. Pretend you are a reporter at a press conference with President James Polk in 1846. Polk wants Congress to declare war on Mexico. Make up a series of questions for him.

12. Make a list of all the places in the Southwest that have Spanish names.

13. Why do you think the United States didn't demand all of Mexico when they signed the peace treaty ending the war?

14. Write a newspaper editorial justifying the actions of the United States in the Mexican War.

15. Write a letter from the British government to President Polk suggesting a compromise for settling the Oregon Territory dispute.

16. Make up a paid advertisement urging the United States not to give up any of the Oregon Territory to England ("54°40′ or fight").

17. Do you think the United States overpaid in the Gadsden Purchase? Explain.

18. Make a cartoon to illustrate the idea of "Seward's Folly."

19. Make a pennant which includes illustrations of Alaska's resources.

20. List the ways in which Hawaii is different from any other territory the United States acquired.

PIONEER LIFE

1. Make up a slogan for a bumper sticker for a covered wagon going west.

2. Write titles for a series of soap opera segments about a wagon train going west.

3. Make up interview questions for a family going west on a wagon train.

4. When Iowa became a state in 1846, Iowa City had seven general stores, twelve lawyers, two weekly newspapers, a college, and a female academy. Choose one and explain what that tells you about Iowa City in 1846.

5. Write a headline and newspaper account of the discovery of gold in California.

6. Write an imaginary story about a forty-niner who did not find gold in California.

7. If you were heading for California during the gold rush, which route would you take? Why?

8. Make up an advertisement for gold seekers who would buy tickets on a boat going from New York to San Francisco, around South America.

9. What is your opinion of the businesspeople in California who charged outrageous prices to the forty-niners in order to get rich quickly?

10. Make up an inscription for the tombstone of a pioneer who died on the trip west. Include the cause of death.

11. Make a poster offering free land to homesteaders.

12. Make a list of all the possible problems that could occur on a wagon train going west.

13. Why was the West sometimes referred to as the Wild West?

14. Why is vigilante justice often unjust?

15. Write a story about how a Western boomtown became a ghost town.

16. Make a diagram of a general store in the West with a list of items it would carry.

17. What do you think a cowboy in the old West would have said about the idea of gun control?

18. You are a pioneer missionary. Explain why you want to move west to convert the Native Americans to Christianity.

19. Write a sensational headline and story for a supermarket newspaper about the Donner Party.

20. Make a community bulletin board advertising community events and entertainment for a pioneer town.

21. Make up a speech that might be given by Annie Oakley, Belle Starr, or Calamity Jane at a Girl Scout meeting.

22. Pretend you are a pioneer woman. Write a "Dear Abby"-type letter to a newspaper describing your problems.

23. Write an advertisement for a mail-order bride from a pioneer in California.

24. Write a day's list of things to do for a pioneer woman.

25. Write a poem that describes the cowboys' feelings about barbed wire and railroads.

26. Write a help wanted ad for a trail boss, a wrangler, and a chuck wagon cook.

27. You have been hired as a trail boss for a 1,000-mile cattle drive. Make a list of all the things you will need for your cowhands on the trail.

28. Design a brand for the cattle you own.

29. Pretend you are a black cowboy working in Arizona in 1875. Write a letter to your cousin in South Carolina, who is working as a sharecropper, and tell him why he should join you as a cowboy.

NATIVE AMERICANS

1. Write a poem or song explaining how the Native Americans see the use of land and nature.

2. Pretend you are the Shawnee spokesman, Tecumseh. Write a speech to convince all the tribes to unite against the white man.

3. Write a speech to be given by a Native American chief to his tribe explaining the 1825 Removal Policy.

4. Write a ballad or folk song about the "Trail of Tears."

5. Why weren't the white man and the Native American able to understand each other?

6. Make a political cartoon showing the irony of the 1924 declaration making the Native Americans citizens.

7. Imagine you are a young Native American living on a reservation today. Write a dialogue between you and your parents in which you discuss your decision to leave.

8. Can we do anything to make up for all that has been done to the Native Americans? If so, what?

9. Pretend you are a defense attorney for the Native Americans. Write a list of accusations against the United States for their treatment of your clients.

10. What do you think would have happened if the Native Americans had defeated the U.S. armies?

11. On the Dakota reservations the Sioux had a religious ceremony, the Ghost Dance, that celebrated the times when the Native Americans ruled and roamed the plains. Make up your own version of this ceremony.

12. Make a list, or draw pictures, of things that they lost as the Native Americans were forced onto reservations.

13. Write a poem called "I am Proud" from the point of view of a Native American.

CLASSROOM ACTIVITY 1

WHAT CAN YOU DO?

On the frontier, there was always a need to get something done, to build or to make something. This led to a natural cooperation among the pioneers. It was not a question of "Who are you?" but rather one of "What can you do?" By pooling their talents, abilities, and strengths, they were able to survive and construct a more comfortable life. Everyone was equal. There were no classes or castes.

Have half the class write their names on slips of paper and put them in a brown bag. The other members of the class will then pull a name from the bag in order to pair up with someone, much in the same way that random people came together on the frontier. As soon as everyone has a name, let them get together and make a list of all the things they can do for each other in some small or large way. Once they have decided, each pair can report to the rest of the class. This can be wrapped up with a simple question: Was anyone surprised at the ways you found you could be of help to each other? How? Why?

CLASSROOM ACTIVITY 2

WHERE LIES THE TRUTH?

The story of the acquisition of the Florida Territory is not as simple as it seems at first glance. There were a number of people who played a role in the story. Each one represents a different interest and gives a different slant to the story. In order for the students to more clearly understand how history is open to many interpretations, the teacher will do this activity after the students have studied the acquisition of Florida by the United States.

The teacher will divide the class into groups. Each group will represent someone from the list below. They will be assigned to write an explanation of the treaty in which Spain ceded Florida to the United States. In each case, their reputation and the reputation of their country is at stake, so the explanation they give should reflect their feelings and should defend their actions.

1. President James Monroe
2. United States Major-General Andrew Jackson
3. The representative of the government of Spain
4. A citizen of the United States who claimed damages against Spain because Native Americans from Florida burned down his home
5. A Seminole from Florida

When they are done, a member of each group can read their explanation to the rest of the class. In a wrap-up discussion, the class might discuss such issues as:

1. Were there clearly any good guys or bad buys in these accounts? Explain.
2. Why were these accounts so different from each other?

CLASSROOM ACTIVITY 3

WHAT WOULD THEY SAY?

The teacher will reproduce the following list of people or write it on the chalkboard. The students will be instructed to work independently or in pairs to write a sentence expressing what each of the people on the list might have said or felt about the war between Mexico and the United States:

1. President James Polk, who called for war
2. The Mexicans who lived in the Southwest
3. Abe Lincoln, a Congressman who questioned the necessity of the war
4. A Native American who lived in the Southwest
5. A slave in Texas
6. A plantation owner in Texas
7. An American missionary living in California
8. Santa Anna, the Mexican general
9. Zachary Taylor, an American general
10. A sixteen-year-old Mexican cadet who was killed by American troops in Mexico City
11. One of the Mexican leaders who signed the peace treaty

When they are finished writing, the students can share what they wrote and discuss it. The teacher can conclude this activity by asking the students why so many different feelings were expressed about this war.

CLASSROOM ACTIVITY 4

THE TRAIL OF TEARS

After the students have discussed what the Trail of Tears was and how the Native Americans were forced, at gunpoint, to march hundreds of miles from their homes to resettle in lands that were unfamiliar to them, have the class brainstorm words that come to mind when they think of this tragic event.

Once they are done have them choose one word as a theme or title for a journal entry or poem and have them do a piece of writing using the words elicited during brainstorming to help them. When they are done they can be put into groups of three or four to share their writing.

CLASSROOM ACTIVITY 5

WEIGHING WHAT TO TAKE

This activity should be done in groups of about four students. The teacher will explain that each group represents a family traveling west in a covered wagon around 1820. The average covered wagon can carry a weight of about 2,000 pounds. These 2,000 pounds consist of:

1. Things they will need to start a new life on the frontier
2. Basic supplies that they feel are necessary for the trip west

Each "family" must compile two lists of things that they want to carry west in their covered wagon, according to the above criteria. They can estimate the weight of the items, and where there is a lot of disagreement, the teacher can resolve it. The object of the activity is not to assess the weights accurately, but rather to reach a general consensus on the items which would be necessary to take on the journey. The weights are used to give the students a framework of limitations. The most important aspect of this activity should be the discussion and final agreement about which items to take.

After the "families" have compiled their lists, they can share them with the rest of the class.

CLASSROOM ACTIVITY 6

CHOICES

The opening of the West (the frontier) represented vast opportunity and choices for those people who wanted them and were willing to take the risks. The following multiple choice questions will give the students the opportunity to explore these choices for themselves:

1. Where would you prefer to settle?
   (a) In the mountains
   (b) On open farmland
   (c) In a small frontier town

2. What would you prefer to be?
   (a) A farmer
   (b) A cowboy
   (c) A miner

3. What would be the most difficult thing for you to endure?
   (a) Loneliness
   (b) Danger
   (c) Hard physical work

4. What would frighten you most about traveling west?
   (a) Crossing a raging river
   (b) Crossing the desert
   (c) Crossing the mountains

5. Which job seems the most dangerous?
   (a) Pony Express rider
   (b) Stagecoach driver
   (c) Boom town sheriff

6. What would frighten you most about a trip west?
   (a) Hostile Native Americans
   (b) Sickness (cholera)
   (c) Getting lost

7. What would appeal to you the most?
   (a) Settling in a small town and opening a general store
   (b) Building a farm
   (c) Starting a cattle ranch

8. What would be the most disappointing for you?
   (a) Looking for gold and not finding it
   (b) Getting free farmland and finding it was not fertile
   (c) Discovering you were cheated when you bought your supplies for your trip west

9. What would you look forward to most as a pioneer?
   (a) Getting rich
   (b) The chance to start your life over
   (c) The opportunity to be on your own

10. Who would you like to travel west with?
    (a) Your family
    (b) Your best friend
    (c) Your next-door neighbor

11. Who would be most valuable on a wagon train?
    (a) Doctor
    (b) Sharpshooter
    (c) Business person

12. Who would be the biggest handicap on a wagon train?
    (a) Elderly woman
    (b) Baby
    (c) Ex-convict
13. Would you rather settle
    (a) Near a river
    (b) Near a lake
    (c) Near an ocean
14. Do you think the trip west would be harder for a
    (a) Man
    (b) Woman
    (c) Child
15. What would excite you most to find on your land?
    (a) Gold
    (b) Oil
    (c) A river
16. What would inspire you the most?
    (a) A beautiful sunset
    (b) Watching the birth of a calf
    (c) Sleeping under the stars at night

CLASSROOM ACTIVITY 7

STARTING OVER

Aside from offering adventure, the frontier represented an opportunity for people to start their lives over and to become successful in new ways.

Tell the students to list ten things they would do, or do differently, if they could go to a new place and start all over (they cannot include buying things). When they are done, have them look over their lists and put a check next to those items that will require physical work and a plus sign next to those items which will require mental work. They can then put a star next to those items that they think they could actually change now.

When they are done with this, call on volunteers to share their lists with the class. The teacher can stress that starting over can take many forms.

CLASSROOM ACTIVITY 8

SURVIVAL MANUAL

Divide the class into groups that will work on different chapters of a *Survival Manual* for pioneers going west. Students should include advice for both physical and mental survival. Diagrams, cartoons, and drawings can be used to make the advice clearer. Include the following chapters:

1. Scouts
2. Trappers
3. Miners
4. Cowboys
5. Farmers
6. Women
7. Children

The completed manual can be reproduced and distributed to all the students in the class. It can also be displayed on the bulletin board as a class effort.

CLASSROOM ACTIVITY 9

LAW ENFORCERS VERSUS LAW BREAKERS

Many books claim that the law enforcers of the old West shared many of the same qualities as the criminals they chased.

Without any discussion, divide the class in half. Have one half make a list of all the qualities they think most law enforcers have. The other half of the class can list the qualities they feel most outlaws have.

When they are done, the students can read their lists aloud, and the teacher can record them on separate sections of the chalkboard. As the lists grow, the class will discover for itself how many of the qualities are shared by both groups. The teacher will then ask:

1. Can you think of situations where a law enforcer could become an outlaw?
2. What makes the difference?

CLASSROOM ACTIVITY 10

VIGILANTE JUSTICE

Vigilante justice was an important element of the "Wild West." It was not always just.

Students may understand this concept better if they discuss it in terms of today. Not all of the situations below have simple conclusions, and that is precisely the point of this activity. The teacher should encourage discussion but warn the students that not every situation below will have a neat conclusion. Students should be asked if they agree with the way the situation was handled, how else the situation could have been handled, and what they personally might have done.

1. A group of kids steals money that was collected for senior dues. The seniors form a group to beat up the gang and get the money back.

2. Mr. Hammer's house is in an isolated area. He is offered an illegal gun to protect himself. He says no.

3. Mr. Hammer's house has been robbed three times. He is offered the same illegal gun. He still says no.

4. Mrs. White has just been robbed of her social security check. She enrolls in a target practice class.

5. The city subways are considered dangerous at night, so twenty-one-year-old Alyssa carries a switchblade for protection.

6. Adam and Marchel see a man pushing a wire hanger through the opening of a car window. They run over, grab him, and begin to hit him as they yell at him for trying to steal the car.

7. Kristina's expensive bike was stolen. Her sister Alexandra sees a neighbor riding the same bike. She calls the police.

8. Mr. Smith's daughter was killed. The jury did not find enough evidence to convict the accused. Mr. Smith buys a gun and goes after the accused himself.

CLASSROOM ACTIVITY 11

TALL TALES

Cowboys often sat around the fire and told exaggerated stories of adventure, excitement, and danger to pass the time more pleasantly. The teacher will seat the students in a circle and lower the lights as if it were nighttime on the trail.

Let a volunteer begin and then go around the circle with each student adding another episode. If they are shy, the teacher can begin with the story of how she or he single-handedly stopped a stampeding herd of 1,000 longhorns.

CHAPTER SEVEN

The Civil War

INTRODUCTION

The Civil War was the most crucial test faced by this country. Secession and the formation of the Confederate States of America were a grave threat to the continued existence of the United States. At the same time, the country faced the moral ugliness of slavery—one of the most shameful aspects of our history.

The activities and assignments of this chapter are designed to help the students understand the moral, social, political, and economic aspects of this war and to examine their own beliefs about personal freedom and responsibility toward others.

PROJECT LIST

1. Write a TV script, stage, or radio play about the Compromise of 1850. Include roles for Daniel Webster, Henry Clay, John C. Calhoun, Stephen Douglas, William Seward, Jefferson Davis, and Alexander Stephens. Include their beliefs and arguments and the eventual provisions of the Compromise.

2. Construct a detailed slave ship.

3. Make a poster illustrating differences between life in the South and the North. Include a short summary in writing of the differences in outlook and lifestyle.

4. Make a tape of spirituals and give your own introduction to each.

5. Make an illustrated edition of *Uncle Tom's Cabin* by Harriet Beecher Stowe. Include a book jacket.

6. Write a report describing the effect of the Kansas-Nebraska Act. Be very specific.

7. Read the decision of the Supreme Court on Dred Scott. Summarize and analyze the reasons the judges gave for their decision. Write your own opinion.

8. Read a biography of Abraham Lincoln and do one of the following:
   (a) An illustrated time line of the important events and decisions of his life
   (b) The script and program for a memorial service honoring his life and accomplishments

9. After doing research, write a case for or against the following two men. Were they heroes or traitors?
   (a) Jefferson Davis
   (b) Robert E. Lee

10. Make a booklet of battle plans for either the Confederacy or the Union.

11. Read *Gone with the Wind* by Margaret Mitchell. Describe how the war directly affects the lives of the major characters.

12. Read poetry and songs about the Civil War. Describe the major themes found in this work.

13. Make a poster showing weapons and uniforms of the Civil War.

14. Make a diorama of any major battle and write a short account of it.

15. Draw a map showing General Sherman's march to the sea.

16. Write a report with diagrams of the strategy of either side by land and by sea.

17. Write an eyewitness account for a newspaper of the time of any battle or campaign of the Civil War.

18. Write a training manual for either the Northern or Southern soldiers.

19. Write a play, TV script, or short story describing in accurate detail how civilians were affected by the war.

20. Write a story about two brothers who join opposite sides in the war.

21. Make a three-dimensional illustrated time line showing what you consider to have been the most important events leading to the Civil War and battles fought during the war.

22. Make a series of ten to fifteen front pages for any newspaper using what you consider to be the most important events from 1850–1865.

23. Make a model of either the *Merrimac* or the *Monitor* or a diorama showing their battle.

24. Create a series of flash cards on all the important generals of the war. Write data about each.

25. Make a board game about the battles and campaigns of the Civil War.

26. Make a booklet of art or poetry describing the devastation of the South because of the war.

27. Do research on the slave experience by using primary sources of information. Write a script in which slave traders and slave owners are on trial for committing crimes against humanity. Include witnesses and detailed testimony as well as the defense of the slave traders and owners.

28. Write the program for an awards ceremony for slaves and abolitionists who helped people reach freedom. Include awards and acceptance speeches for Harriet Tubman, Sojourner Truth, William Lloyd Garrison, and Frederick Douglass, as well as for others you find in your research.

29. Do creative writing about any of the following:
    (a) Slave ship experience
    (b) Auction block
    (c) Work as a field hand
    (d) Work in the "great house"

30. Read *To Be a Slave* by Julius Lester. Write a book report, play, or series of poems using his material as your foundation. You may also draw a series of pictures to illustrate the major issues and events in his book.

HOMEWORK ASSIGNMENTS

THE SLAVE EXPERIENCE

1. Write a list of the many ways people can be slaves. (For example, addicts are slaves to their drugs.)

2. Write a response to a slave owner who says he treats his slaves very well.

3. Would you rather be a well cared for slave or take your chances on freedom? Explain.

4. Pretend you had been a slave and are now free and surrounded by your children. Tell them how it felt to be a slave.

5. Write your own song with code words to plot an escape from the plantation.

6. Write a list of accusations against the ship captains and traders who brought slaves to America.

7. Write a secret handbook that teaches slaves to resist their owners in many subtle ways.

8. What might a slave of the 1860s have thought about the role of black people today? Write negative and positive answers.

9. Would you have been willing to risk arrest to be part of the Underground Railroad? Explain.

10. Pretend you could be at a press conference for Frederick Douglass. What questions would you ask him?

11. Write a minute-by-minute account of the day of a plantation slave.

12. Write an answer to a TV editorial that stated that slaves were often better off than poor free people.

13. Write how one of the following contributed to the continuation of slavery: cotton economy, preachers who taught slaves to be obedient, or laws against slaves learning to read and write.

14. Prepare a speech for an abolitionist meeting in which you describe slavery as you witnessed it on a visit to the South.

15. Write a conversation between two cousins—one from the South and one from the North—in which they discuss slavery.

16. Write a poem describing the feelings of a child who was separated from his or her mother at an auction.

17. Pretend you are a parent who has been separated from your child at a slave auction. Write a letter to another member of your family describing your feelings about this.

18. Do you think all slave owners were evil? Explain.

19. Write a secret message to fellow slaves explaining ways to fight back.

20. Can slavery ever be justified? Give reasons for your answer.

21. What would be the worst aspect of slavery to you personally? Explain.

22. It has been said that, in order to treat people very cruelly, you must convince yourself that they are not quite human. Do you agree or disagree? Explain by using examples from the slavery experience.

23. Write an indictment against the United States for allowing slavery to exist for so long.

DIFFERENCES THAT GREW BETWEEN THE NORTH AND THE SOUTH

1. Pretend that you are a European expert on the United States and are lecturing a group of future immigrants. Write what you would tell them about the North and the South, including differences in type of work, environment, and culture.

2. Write two headlines and short news articles about the Missouri Compromise – one for a Southern state and one for a Northern state.

3. Pretend you are a fortune teller. Look into your crystal ball and explain why the Missouri Compromise doesn't lead to a lasting solution to the argument over slavery in the territories.

4. Make up a public service commercial for or against states' rights.

5. Write a letter to the editor from a Southerner explaining why a high tariff is unfair.

6. Read and summarize the provisions of the Compromise of 1850. Place checks next to those parts that would make the South happy and stars next to those parts that would satisfy the North.

7. Make a political cartoon or write a satire showing the Northern opinion on Southern feelings that their way of life is socially superior.

8. Write a description of life in the North from any point of view below:
   (a) A Southern plantation owner
   (b) A slave
   (c) A poor white Southerner who doesn't own slaves
   (d) A small shop owner from a Southern town

9. Write a description of life in the South from any point of view below:
   (a) A social worker
   (b) A factory worker
   (c) A wealthy merchant
   (d) An abolitionist

10. Make a chart reviewing differences between the North and the South. Include economic, social, and political differences.

EVENTS THAT LED TO THE CIVIL WAR

1. Write an advertisement for *Uncle Tom's Cabin* for a newspaper.

2. Pretend that you are a child in the 1850s and have just read *Uncle Tom's Cabin*. Write a letter to Harriet Beecher Stowe with questions and feelings about her book. You may choose to be a Southern or Northern child.

3. Write Harriet Beecher Stowe's answer in which she tells why she wrote the book.

4. Would you have been willing to break the Fugitive Slave Law and help runaway slaves? Why? Why not?

5. Make a page from a dictionary illustrating and explaining the following words:

    (a) Underground Railroad

    (b) Conductor

    (c) Station

6. If you had lived in 1854, would you have supported or opposed the Kansas-Nebraska Act? Give reasons for your answer.

7. Describe John Brown from the point of view of an abolitionist, slave owner, and pacifist.

8. Imagine that you are a lawyer. Prepare a case on Dred Scott's behalf or prepare an argument against his claim for freedom.

9. What advice would you have given Dred Scott if he had asked whether to fight for his freedom through the courts?

10. Make a poster urging people to join the Republican party.

11. Make a political cartoon about the Lincoln-Douglas debates.

12. Write a TV commentary of the Lincoln-Douglas debates.

13. Prepare for your own Lincoln-Douglas debate by researching one of the positions and writing it in your own words (for use in Classroom Activity 8).

14. Make a paid political announcement for or against popular sovereignty.

15. Can you think of any reason why you would urge your state to secede from the United States? Explain your answer.

16. Make a poster of original campaign buttons for the candidates in the election of 1860.

17. If you had been alive in 1860, would you have voted for Lincoln? Explain.

18. Why did the election of Lincoln lead to secession and the formation of the Confederate States of America?

19. Make a map showing the Confederate States of America and the United States of America in 1861.

20. Pretend you are Jefferson Davis. Write an entry in your journal on the morning you become president of the Confederate States of America.

21. Pretend you are a Southern child, and make up a list of questions you would ask your parents about secession.

22. Can you think of any way to have prevented the Civil War?

THE CIVIL WAR

1. Pretend that you are alive twenty years after Fort Sumter. Describe your memories of the day Confederate soldiers fired on it. You may choose to be a soldier on either side or a civilian.

2. Write a diary entry of a young man who is from a border state and is struggling to decide which side to fight for.

3. Describe the term *a house divided* by writing a poem or a song, or by doing creative art work.

4. Imagine that you are in charge of planning strategy for either the Confederacy or the Union. Write a speech to give to your men explaining the strengths and weaknesses of the other side.

5. Write a letter of resignation for Robert E. Lee to the U.S. Army explaining why he must join the Confederacy.

6. Write a news flash for any battle studied in class.

7. Write a folk song about the *Monitor* and the *Merrimac*.

8. Write the dialogue for a group of veterans after the war discussing their memories of any battle studied in class.

9. Pretend you were present at President Lincoln's Gettysburg Address. Write how you felt and how the people around you reacted.

10. Read the Gettysburg Address. Find and write down all the ideals that Lincoln said we were fighting for.

11. Write a letter of encouragement from one woman to another as they deal with the problems of civilians in the South during the war.

12. Make a sign recruiting women for the war effort. What would they do?

13. Who was freed by the Emancipation Proclamation? Who wasn't? What do you think Lincoln was trying to accomplish?

14. Write an editorial about the riots in New York City in 1863 against the draft.

15. Write a poem, short play, or eyewitness account of Lee's surrender to Grant at Appomattox.

16. Why do you think General Grant told his men not to fire guns to celebrate their victory after the surrender at Appomattox?

CLASSROOM ACTIVITY 1

SPOON FASHION

This activity only takes a few minutes but will leave an indelible impression on the students. When the teacher explains the slaves' experiences on the ships coming to America, he or she will describe the piling of people spoon fashion (head to feet) to save space. Instead of asking the students to imagine this, the teacher will show them how to lay down side by side on the floor. Desks or chairs can be used to pen in the space. Silence will be demanded. Students will be told that they would have been shackled to each other and would not have been allowed to move or change position. Depending on the age group, the teacher may keep them in that cramped position and space for as long as he or she feels is appropriate. When the activity is through, the students will write their feelings about the experience. Afterwards, the students may read their pieces or simply discuss how they felt.

CLASSROOM ACTIVITY 2

CLASSROOM WRITING

In order to obtain a deeper understanding of the meaning of slavery, the students will answer the questions below.

In what ways can the following be considered slaves?

1. A pet
2. Someone who can't give up smoking, playing video games, drinking, eating, or gambling
3. A baseball player in the days before they could be free agents

After writing, the students can read their papers to the class. Comparisons may be made to actual conditions of slavery in the South.

CLASSROOM ACTIVITY 3

COULD YOU BE AN ABOLITIONIST?

There were many ways in which people fought against slavery. Below is a list of some abolitionist tactics. Students will read the list and decide which of these tactics they would feel most comfortable doing. They will number each from one to ten—one is most comfortable and ten represents least comfortable.

1. Make speeches
2. Talk directly to slave owners
3. Become active in the Underground Railroad
4. Write pamphlets
5. Organize committees
6. Run for political office

7. Work on the campaign of someone running for political office
8. Kill slave owners
9. Organize a slave rebellion
10. Teach slaves secretly to read and write

After doing this, the students will sit in groups and discuss their decisions. They will also talk about what they learned about themselves. If the teacher feels that the class would be comfortable discussing this as a large group, he or she may begin by simply asking for a show of hands on how many students learned something new about themselves by doing this exercise.

CLASSROOM ACTIVITY 4

HOW IMPORTANT IS FREEDOM TO YOU?

Many slaves risked and lost their lives in order to obtain freedom. Today it is a concept that is often taken for granted. In order to gain insight into the meaning of freedom, the students may answer and discuss the following questions.

1. Which would you be least willing to give up?
   (a) TV set
   (b) The right to choose your friends
   (c) Your bed
2. Which of the following would you be most willing to fight for?
   (a) A member of your family
   (b) Your country
   (c) Your right to choose what you read
3. What matters most to you?
   (a) Your education
   (b) Your privacy
   (c) Your clothes
4. What makes you proudest?
   (a) Your accomplishments at school
   (b) Your popularity with your friends
   (c) Your ability to defend what you believe in
5. What would you be willing to do to keep personal freedom?
   (a) Fight with a parent
   (b) Bring charges against a teacher
   (c) Enlist in the army

CLASSROOM ACTIVITY 5

THE WEBSTER/HAYNE DEBATE

This activity will help students see both sides of the states' rights issue. The teacher must get copies of the speeches by Robert Hayne for states' rights and by Daniel Webster for a strong union. These primary sources may be edited by the teacher or used in their entirety, depending on the level of the students.

Two students will play Webster and Hayne. They will be given their material with ample time to study it and prepare for the debate. The rest of the class will take on the following assignments:

1. Reporters who will interview the two senators
2. Demonstrators who will prepare signs and arguments for each side
3. Other senators from the North and the South who will make up original short speeches of encouragement for their side
4. Artists who will sketch the proceedings
5. Button and banner sellers who will have a stand with items for each side

The teacher will orchestrate the proceedings, either having many things happening at once or one event at a time, ending with the debate.

This can be a lively activity, and the teacher should expect some noise.

CLASSROOM ACTIVITY 6

STAGECOACH QUARTET

What would happen if any four of the following people found themselves together on a stagecoach heading west? The teacher will set the scene and assign parts.

- Southern plantation owner
- slave
- Southern child who has been educated by a tutor
- Northern abolitionist
- Northern factory worker
- poor white Southerner hoping to start over in the West
- Northern factory owner
- black laborer from New York City who hopes to start over in the West
- female factory worker

- Southern female who has grown up on a plantation
- Northerner who believes in live and let live
- Southern secret abolitionist

Each quartet will discuss the following topics:

- slavery
- Nat Turner's slave revolt
- Fugitive Slave Law
- states' rights
- tariffs
- best way to live
- nationalism

Each quartet will act out their ride west and engage in conversation. The teacher may add any other characters or topics to this activity.

CLASSROOM ACTIVITY 7

THE DRED SCOTT DECISION

This activity should follow any lesson or reading on the Dred Scott case. Once the students have some familiarity with the subject, they may enrich their understanding with this activity.

The teacher will explain that while the case itself dealt with legal and constitutional issues, the students will now expand their outlook to moral, economic, and political issues. The class will be divided into four groups. The teacher will hand out a sheet with the major arguments of the decision, or the students will use their class notes. The four groups are:

1. Moral
2. Economic
3. Legal and constitutional
4. Political

Each group will discuss the Supreme Court decision from their assigned point of view. They may argue for or against the decision or analyze it. A committee secretary for each group will take notes. These will be read aloud at the conclusion of the class.

Students may do a follow-up assignment in which they explore the differences between the above points of view concerning modern issues such as abortion, surrogate motherhood, experimentation on animals, and so forth.

CLASSROOM ACTIVITY 8

(To be used after doing Homework 13 from the section on Events That Led to the Civil War)

LINCOLN-DOUGLAS DEBATE

STRATEGY 1

Students will break into two groups and pool their arguments on behalf of Lincoln and Douglas. A volunteer or elected member of each group will then carry out the debate.

STRATEGY 2

Analyzing political effect is an important part of studying history. Students will study the appearance, demeanor, and appeal of Lincoln and Douglas (many accounts exist). The teacher may simply read the descriptions to the class or prepare them ahead of time. A discussion will then follow. Some key questions are:

1. How would these men have done if the debates were held today and were televised?
2. What advantages and disadvantages would Douglas have had?
3. What advantages and disadvantages would Lincoln have had?
4. How would each man appeal to the public?
5. What seems to be important besides a politician's stand on the issues?
6. Should people care about anything except the issues?

CLASSROOM ACTIVITY 9

SECESSION

Secession was a difficult decision for many Southerners. The following exercise will help students examine how they might have felt and behaved. In all cases below, the students must try to put themselves in a Southerner's shoes, but they must also answer for themselves and not how they think someone else would. After each question is answered, students should explain their choices.

1. Which would anger you most?
   (a) Reading *Uncle Tom's Cabin*

(b) Hearing about John Brown's raid

(c) Losing money because of the high tariff

2. You think you treat your slaves well. You read some of the abolitionist literature and think:

(a) You are wrong and should free your slaves.

(b) The abolitionists don't understand the Southern way of life.

(c) Let the North clean up their own problems of slums and dangerous factories before they criticize you.

3. Slavery in the new territories is important to you because

(a) It upholds what you believe in.

(b) The more new states that have slavery, the stronger your position in Congress.

(c) You can't give in to the North.

4. People who help runaway slaves are

(a) Criminals and thieves

(b) Kindhearted but not too bright

(c) People who don't understand why slavery is necessary

5. Slavery is necessary because

(a) Slaves need their masters in order to survive.

(b) It's economically impossible to survive without it.

(c) It's the only right way for the races to exist together.

6. Although you are a patriot, you begin to feel the Union is not representing you because

(a) There are more Northern states than Southern.

(b) The North will never understand a cotton-growing economy.

(c) The Fugitive Slave Laws are not enforced enough.

7. Lincoln is elected. You know he is for a strong Union and against slavery.

(a) You feel you are no longer part of the country that elected him.

(b) You feel that you are no longer part of the country that elected him and have the right to secede and form a new country.

(c) You feel that you are no longer part of the country that elected him but must wait out the next four years. How can you secede from your own country?

CLASSROOM ACTIVITY 10

READING ALOUD

Any of the following can be read aloud and reenacted by the class for more immediacy.

- Gettysburg Address
- Scenes from *In White America*
- Songs from the Civil War
- Lincoln's second inaugural address
- Excerpts from *To Be a Slave* by Julius Lester

CLASSROOM ACTIVITY 11

POINT OF VIEW QUESTIONNAIRE

Students will choose to belong to one of the four groups below:

1. White Southerner
2. Black Southern slave
3. White Northerner
4. Black Northern free person

The teacher will then hand out the questionnaire. Students will answer the questions using their adopted point of view. When finished, the students may read their answers aloud or form groups to discuss their opinions.

1. How do you feel about black and white children
   - playing together?
   - dancing together?
   - learning together?
   - marrying each other?
2. How do you feel about freeing the slaves?
3. What is your opinion about high taxes on imported clothing?
4. Which do you consider yourself first—an American, a Northerner, or a Southerner?
5. Do you think runaway slaves should be returned to their owners?
6. How do you feel about Nat Turner?
7. How do you feel about Harriet Tubman?
8. Describe your ideas about the best way for people to live a good life.

CLASSROOM ACTIVITY 12

WRITING ABOUT SLAVERY

Classroom writing is a method of increasing skill as well as a jumping off point for classroom discussion. The following questions may be reproduced and handed out to the students. They would do their writing individually while in class.

1. Write an essay, poem, rap song, or monologue finishing the statement, "To be a slave means . . ."
2. Pretend you are a white child living in the South. You have grown up playing with black children on your plantation. Now your parents tell you that your friends are slaves and can no longer be playmates. Write:
   (a) All the questions you would have
   (b) How you would feel when you had to say goodbye
3. Pretend you are the slaves in question 2. Write:
   (a) What your parents might tell you about why you have to stop playing with your friend
   (b) What questions you would have
   (c) How you would feel

At the end of this writing activity students can share their work in groups. They may be grouped according to the question they answered or in mixed groups. A class discussion can follow. Students may even want to role play the responses to questions 2 and 3.

CLASSROOM ACTIVITY 13

USING MOVIES IN CLASS

GLORY

The teacher will show the movie *Glory* to the class. Afterwards the students may write a review of the film including their feelings about the characters, events, and music. Reviews may be read aloud or reproduced and made into a booklet. Students may then respond to reviews they agree or disagree with.

For a class discussion the teacher should ask the class why the film was called *Glory*.

THE RED BADGE OF COURAGE

The teacher will show the movie *The Red Badge of Courage* to the class. Students will then do a classroom writing assignment discussing the word "courage" and all it signifies in this story. Students may also want to write their own definition of the word "courage."

CHAPTER EIGHT

Reconstruction

INTRODUCTION

This chapter covers the years from 1865, when the Civil War ended, until 1877, when the last occupation troops were withdrawn from the southern states. Although this chapter spans only twelve years, those years marked a turning point in the development of the United States. As the nation was reunified, many of our political, social, and economic patterns changed. Although the nominal status of black people was redefined, unfortunately, little was done to provide for long-term advances. Thus, the stage was set for problems which still plague us today.

The students will have an opportunity to explore all of this and, hopefully, to sensitize themselves to the issues.

PROJECT LIST

1. Make up a memorial ceremony honoring Abraham Lincoln after his assassination. Include speeches reflecting the points of view of the new president Andrew Johnson, a northern member of Congress, a southern white person, and a black American.

2. Make up a play or epic poem about Lincoln's assassination.

3. Make an illustrated time line of the Reconstruction era from 1865 to 1877.

4. Pretend you are a freed slave. Write a diary describing both your feelings and all your hardships.

5. Write a play about the impeachment trial of Andrew Johnson.

6. Make an illustrated dictionary of words and terms from the Reconstruction era.

7. Pretend you are a psychiatrist. Write a report analyzing the problems of Andrew Johnson during Reconstruction.

8. Do a magazine exposé of the Ku Klux Klan during Reconstruction.

9. Write a chapter for a children's textbook that explains the meanings of the 13th, 14th, and 15th Amendments.

10. Make up a program for a "Half-Way House for Freed Slaves." Include a descriptive list of all the courses that would be offered.

11. Do a piece of creative writing called "Shattered Dreams" which describes all the different ways in which the ex-slaves were prevented from making progress.

12. Write an *Instructional Manual for a Better Reconstruction*, as if you had the power to recreate history.

13. Write the history of Reconstruction as seen through the eyes of a bankrupt southern plantation owner.

14. Write a report that describes how each of the following robbed black people of their rights and their dignity:
    (a) Poll tax
    (b) Literacy tests
    (c) Jim Crow Laws
    (d) Ku Klux Klan
    (e) Lynchings

15. Prepare a *Who's Who of the Reconstruction Era*. Include brief descriptions of their ideas and their lives.

16. Make an illustrated scrapbook of the contributions of black leaders during and after Reconstruction.

17. Do a research report on what the Jim Crow Laws were, how they came to exist, and the damage they did to black people and to American society as a whole.

18. Write a series of newspaper headlines and articles exposing all the corruption that existed during Reconstruction.

19. The election of 1876 was possibly the strangest one in the history of the United States. Make a series of cartoons that describe the:
    (a) Campaign
    (b) Election
    (c) Dispute
    (d) Compromise

20. Write a script for a TV news special about how the Democrats regained control in the South.

21. Analyze the 14th and 15th Amendments and then write a report on

how the southern states got around them by following the letter of the law but not the spirit of the law.

HOMEWORK ASSIGNMENTS

POLITICAL ISSUES

1. Why do you think the period after the Civil War was called Reconstruction? Make a list of all the things that had to be reconstructed. Put a star next to those items that are not physical.

2. Write a funeral eulogy for Abraham Lincoln.

3. Write a speech for or against the impeachment of Andrew Johnson.

4. How would you have felt if you were Andrew Johnson on trial for impeachment? What would you have done?

5. What do you think might have happened if Andrew Johnson had been found guilty at his impeachment trial?

6. Make a cartoon illustrating how Andrew Johnson alienated both northerners and southerners.

7. Pretend you are a southerner. Write a letter to a carpetbagger telling him how you feel about him and why he should go home.

8. Draw a caricature of a carpetbagger.

9. Pretend you are a northern Republican congressman. Make a speech to Congress explaining your feelings about the Black Codes and what you think Congress should do.

10. Write an explanation that Andrew Johnson might have given for his veto of the Civil Rights Act of 1866 and the bill extending the Freedmen's Bureau.

11. Write your reactions to the Radical plan for Reconstruction from the point of view of a southern plantation owner.

12. Make a list of adjectives that each of the following would use to describe a scalawag:
    (a) Ex-slave
    (b) White southern Democrat

13. Make a picket sign for or against the Radical-Republican plan for Reconstruction.

14. Write a list of things a southern state would have to spend money on during Reconstruction.

15. Write an explanation a southerner would have given to justify the legality of the poll tax and the literacy tests.

16. Make up a speech as a southern Democrat running for office. Tell the people of your state what you hope to do if elected.

17. Imagine that you are a voter. Write a letter to your senator expressing your feelings about the Compromise of 1877.

18. Make up a toast to the reunited nation.

19. Make up some New Year's resolutions for the reunited union.

20. Make up a list of laws to protect the newly freed slaves.

SOCIAL ISSUES

1. If you had been a slave, what is the first thing you would have done after hearing you were free?

2. Make a list of ways the ex-slaves could have earned a living. Why were they limited?

3. Pretend you are a Rebel soldier returning home to your destroyed plantation. Write a page in your diary describing your feelings.

4. Write a newspaper editorial against the Black Codes.

5. Write a dialogue between a tenant farmer and a landowner in which they work out their agreement on the use of the land.

6. Write a poem or a folk song called "Forty Acres and a Mule."

7. Write a sign on behalf of the Freedmen's Bureau offering services.

8. Make up a list of things that you think the Freedmen's Bureau should teach the ex-slaves. Explain why.

9. Pretend you are an ex-slave who has become a sharecropper. Write a letter to a newspaper in the North describing your situation and asking for advice.

10. Do you think the word *reconstruction* or the word *restoration* better describes the era after the Civil War? Explain.

11. Why can't "separate but equal" facilities ever be equal?

12. Write a will for Thaddeus Stevens in which he explains why he wants to be buried in a black cemetery.

13. What is the meaning of the word *radical*? How might a radical of today try to deal with the problem of race relations?

14. If you had been a plantation owner after the Civil War, what would you have done to help your former slaves?

15. Make a public service advertisement to re-educate the former southern rebels. This can be done in the form of a poster or newspaper advertisement.

CLASSROOM ACTIVITY 1

REFLECTIONS ON THE WAR

The end of the Civil War left deep feelings and scars in most members of American society, both about the war and about the future. Have the students do a piece of writing which would reflect the feelings of one of the following people:

1. A recently freed slave
2. Plantation owner
3. Rebel soldier
4. Northern soldier
5. Poor white southern farmer

Their writing can be done in the form of a poem, short story, ballad, letter, song, or diary.

When they are done, they can meet in small groups to share their work. Then they can write their final drafts and hand them in. The results can be posted as a bulletin board display.

CLASSROOM ACTIVITY 2

HOW TO TREAT THE SOUTH

The teacher can motivate this activity by asking the students how their parents deal with them when they do something wrong and what they think is the best way to teach someone a lesson.

In order to help the students to better understand the issue of how to treat the defeated southern states, they can pretend they are members of the Congress of 1866. Divide the class in half. One half must argue for the Johnson plan of leniency. The other half must represent the hard line Radical-Republicans. It will be helpful if the teacher lists the major points of each plan on the chalkboard. It is preferable to elicit this from the students, based on their own reading or a prior class lesson. The students can then argue why they feel one plan is better than the other. Use the following questions as a guide:

1. What do we hope to accomplish?
2. Is it important to punish the South? Why? Why not?
3. If we are hard on the South, won't we teach them a lesson? Why? Why not?

When they are done, let the class vote as to which plan they feel is better. The teacher can then inform them that the Radical-Republican plan won.

CLASSROOM ACTIVITY 3

WOULD THINGS BE DIFFERENT IF . . . ?

Often, in our lives, we imagine how different things would be if we had just done one thing in another way. It will be enlightening for the students to toy with some of the "what ifs" that historians sometimes engage in.

Divide the class into committees and let each one wrestle with one of the following. Would things be different today if:

1. Each ex-slave had been given forty acres and a mule, as promised
2. Each ex-slave had been given a better education
3. The South had been punished more severely
4. The South had been punished less severely
5. Jim Crow Laws, the poll tax, and literacy tests had been outlawed
6. Southerners had been policed and severely punished for participating in Ku Klux Klan activities and lynchings
7. The carpetbag governments had been more honest and efficient

When they are done, let each committee report back to the class.

CLASSROOM ACTIVITY 4

ADJUSTING TO CHANGE

Reconstruction was a time when everyone in the South was forced to adjust to radical changes. It was not easy. In order to help the students understand this concept better, it must be brought down to a more personal level. The teacher can open up the discussion by asking the students what the biggest change was that they have faced in their lives so far, and whether or not they adjusted to it easily. As each student responds, the teacher will list the elicited "change" on the chalkboard. The class can then discuss the problems as a whole, or they can break up into groups to analyze:

1. Why each change is hard to adjust to
2. What things they could do to make the adjustment easier

CLASSROOM ACTIVITY 5

ON FEAR

Because the southerners had lost so much as a result of the Civil War, they were terrified of losing what little they had left. When people are afraid, they often react in many unexpected and even aggressive ways.

Since people, especially children, may be reticent about revealing their own fears, it will be less threatening if the students observe and discuss the behavior of others. Give the students two days to observe how people express fear, either in actual situations or on television. Each student must be prepared to describe the situation. They must tell:

1. What they saw
2. What the person was afraid of
3. How the person acted

The teacher can culminate this activity by having the students discuss why they think the people behaved the way they did when they were afraid.

CLASSROOM ACTIVITY 6

INTERVIEWING THE PEOPLE

Students often gain great insight into an era and the minds of the people who lived in that era by formulating questions that they might ask individuals who lived in that time. We find that this type of activity works well with smaller groups.

Divide the class into groups of two or three students and tell them to imagine that they are teams of newspaper reporters preparing interview questions for one of the following people:

1. A rebel soldier who has returned to his destroyed plantation
2. A freed slave who has remained on his or her former master's plantation
3. A freed slave heading north
4. A freed slave leaving his or her plantation
5. A member of the Ku Klux Klan
6. A poor white southern farmer
7. A white Union soldier returning home
8. A black Union soldier heading home

9. A carpetbagger

10. A black senator during Reconstruction

11. A white northern teacher going south to work

12. A scalawag

As each group presents its interview questions the rest of the class may be asked how they think the individuals being interviewed would have responded.

CLASSROOM ACTIVITY 7

"O CAPTAIN! MY CAPTAIN!"

Have the students read Walt Whitman's "O Captain! My Captain!" Discuss: Who is the Captain? What is the ship, and what journey has it survived?

Wrap it up by having the students write one more stanza for this poem.

CHAPTER NINE

Life Across the United States: 1865–1900

INTRODUCTION

The late nineteenth century was a time of change. New inventions changed rural life and influenced the growth of cities. Labor-saving devices affected both the way people lived and the roles they played in their families and at work.

Our chapter provides homework and project assignments that deal specifically with the years between 1865 and 1900. Our classroom activities will help the students explore change and its benefits and problems on both universal and personal levels by expanding the time period to the present.

PROJECT LIST

1. Trace the population growth of any city in the United States from 1865 to 1900. Chart the results on a large graph.

2. Make a diorama of any scene from city life during the late nineteenth century. Be sure to include name of city, neighborhood, and source of information.

3. Do a series of pieces of original artwork on city scenes during the late nineteenth century.

4. Prepare a special issue of a woman's magazine for 1899 devoted to labor-saving devices and gadgets of importance. Include ads, articles, letters to the editor, and an editorial page.

5. Make a diorama of a modern home of 1899.

6. Read a biography of any of the following people and write a report describing their contributions to society:
   - Jane Addams
   - Julia Lathrop
   - Jacob Riis

7. Write and produce a performance of a vaudeville or burlesque show of the 1890s. Include posters advertising the show, costumes, and music. This is a project for more than one person.

8. Draw a detailed diagram of a trolley park (amusement park) such as Steeplechase in Coney Island, New York.

9. Make a model of a trolley park.

10. Make the covers for sheet music of ten top songs of the 1890s.

11. Write a series of political pamphlets describing the causes supported by the populist movement of the 1890s.

12. Prepare a library catalogue for 1899 with short descriptions of the most popular reading of the time.

13. Write a letter to Vassar or any other woman's college of the years 1865 to 1900. Ask for material on the history, philosophy, rules of behavior, and early courses taught at the college. Then write your own bulletin.

14. Read the philosophy of any of the people below. Write a paper describing it and its effect on the country.
    • Charles Darwin
    • John Dewey
    • Edward Bellamy
    • Henry George

15. Read poems by Walt Whitman or one of the novels by Mark Twain or Henry James. Write in your own words about the America they describe.

16. Write an epic poem describing the race to complete the transcontinental railroad.

17. Write an itinerary for a trip on the transcontinental railroad. Include places to stop for sightseeing visits and a map.

18. Write an illustrated biography of Clara Barton and her founding of the American Red Cross.

19. Make a catalogue of office machines and innovations for 1899.

20. Make an illustrated poster on advances in communication and transportation from 1865 to 1900.

21. Visit a hardware store and do a descriptive inventory of the gadgets it sells to make life more convenient today.

22. Write a history of the Grange movement and its importance to the lives of farmers.

23. Make a poster of "before and after" scenes for any labor-saving device of the nineteenth century.

24. Make a model of the perfect city or write a paper describing it.

25. Follow the growth of any industry or invention from its conception to its use and its effect on life today.

26. Write a tour guide for any large city. Include history, places to visit, important people and events.

27. Make a mail-order catalogue that would be of interest to a farmer of the late nineteenth century.

HOMEWORK ASSIGNMENTS

INNOVATIONS THAT CHANGED AMERICAN LIFE—1865–1900

1. Write a speech that could have been made as the golden spike was nailed joining the Union Pacific and Central Pacific railroads to form the first transcontinental railroad in 1869.

2. Write a message to be sent by cable across the ocean to Europe in 1866.

3. Make up a song or poem called "Thank You, Mr. Edison" in which you list all the important things in your life that use electricity.

4. Write a dialogue (you may make it funny) in which two housewives try to outbrag each other about the new gadgets and conveniences in their homes in the late nineteenth century.

5. Write a letter to the editor for or against the "progress" of modern life.

6. Draw or describe a time capsule in which you put the most important inventions of the late nineteenth century. Explain how they changed people's lives.

7. Draw and label all the parts of a modern kitchen in 1899.

8. Pretend you are a salesperson. Write a pitch to be given to the office manager of a company for one of the items below:
   • typewriter
   • adding machine
   • telephone

9. Make a list of modern inventions that can be traced back to either the typewriter, adding machine, or cash register.

10. Public libraries became more popular in the nineteenth century. If you could buy ten books for a new public library, which would you choose? Either choose your own favorites or books you feel are necessary for a library today. Explain your choices.

11. Design a costume for a woman to make it easier for her to go bicycling in the 1890s.

12. Make a classified ad for all the women's jobs in an office due to new inventions in the late nineteenth century.

13. Keep a diary of how often and for what reasons you use the telephone in a week.

14. (To be used with Classroom Activity 1) Do one of the activities below and check the time it takes.
    (a) Wash dishes completely by hand; prepare dishes for the dishwasher.
    (b) Sharpen a pencil manually; sharpen it with an electric pencil sharpener.
    (c) Sweep the floor; use an electric broom or vacuum cleaner.
    (d) Hang out wet clothes to dry; put wet clothes in a clothes dryer.
    (e) Write by hand; type or use a word processor.

15. (To be used with Classroom Activity 1) Keep a diary of leisure-time activities during any day of a weekend.

RURAL LIFE—1865-1900

1. Pretend you are a farmer during the close of the nineteenth century. What advice would you give a young person who asks whether he should become a farmer? Include the positive and negative aspects of farming.

2. Write a speech for a presidential or senatorial candidate in the late nineteenth century to be given at a meeting of farmers in which the following problems are already on an agenda for discussion:
   • drought
   • locusts
   • debt to banks
   • low prices
   • high-priced farm machinery
   • high rates on railroads

3. Write a slogan for a rally by farmers against the high interest rates.

4. Write a dialogue between a father and son in which the son tells the father that he wants to leave the farm to try life in the city.

5. Write the "doings" for a weekend's social activity in a small town newspaper.

6. Write the agenda for a Grange meeting.

7. Make a list of events and booths for a country fair.

8. Write your own story for a *McGuffey Reader*. Be sure it includes a lesson in values.

9. Read Edwin Markham's "The Man with a Hoe." What is the poet's message? What is his warning?

10. Make a banner for a populist rally.

11. Read William Jennings Bryan's "Cross of Gold" speech. Explain his position in your own words.

LIFE IN THE CITIES—1865–1900

1. Draw a picture or cartoon showing the difference between rich and poor sections of any big city in the late nineteenth century.

2. Describe or make a tape of sounds on an urban street of the nineteenth century. Include traffic noises, people, and animals.

3. Write a column for the fashion or gossip page of a New York newspaper describing the people in the Golden Horseshoe of the new Metropolitan Opera House.

4. Make up a headline for the famous prizefight between John L. Sullivan and Gentleman Jim Corbett in 1892.

5. Explain why spectator sports were so popular in the cities as a form of recreation.

6. Make up a theater playbill for a vaudeville or burlesque show.

7. Make up a cast of characters and a short synopsis of a melodrama for the 1890s.

8. Write a diary entry for a child's first visit to a trolley park.

9. Write a newspaper editorial on poverty in the big cities.

10. Pretend you are riding in an elevator for the first time in the 1870s. Describe how you might feel.

11. How did the elevator change architecture and life in the cities?

12. Compare the problems in the cities of the late nineteenth century to problems in modern cities.

CLASSROOM ACTIVITY 1

TIME

This activity should be done after Homework 14 from the Innovations homework section. Students will report their times on using labor-saving devices. The actual time saved will be charted on the chalkboard or on a large piece of paper. The teacher will then ask, "So what?" Students may write their answers individually or work in committees to form answers. Answers will be read aloud.

LEISURE

Since time is what's saved, students might benefit from examining how they spend their time. After doing Homework 15 from the Innovations homework section, they should report back to class on how they spend a day of leisure. The teacher may lead a discussion using the questions below.

1. Why do we have so much leisure time?
2. After looking at your diaries, were you satisfied with how you spent your time?
3. What changes (if any) might you make?
4. What restrictions do you have on your time?
5. If you had unlimited free time, what would you do?

CLASSROOM ACTIVITY 2

NECESSITY AND INVENTIONS

Which comes first—need or a new invention that creates need? Students might enjoy discussing this question.

Students will make a list of five items they feel are necessary in their lives. As they share their lists, the teacher will write the items on the chalkboard placing checks next to items mentioned frequently. Once this is completed, the most popular items will be circled, and the discussion will begin.

Students often choose hair dryers, stereos, telephones, and televisions. Using what the students of the class have chosen, the teacher will ask the following questions:

1. What need does this serve?
2. What did you do before you had it?
3. What could you do if you didn't have it now?
4. Do you think your life is easier/better/worse because of this item?
5. Is the world better because of it?

CLASSROOM ACTIVITY 3

WHAT'S LEFT TO INVENT?

Students will break into committees and brainstorm to answer the above question. The teacher might choose to leave the question open-ended or to specify certain categories, for example, transportation, entertainment, medicine, labor-saving devices, space exploration, anti-pollution devices.

After the committees meet, they will report back to the class. This activity might lead to further committee work on class projects in which the inventions are developed in more detail.

CLASSROOM ACTIVITY 4

PROGRESS OR PROBLEM?

Students may examine both sides of change by role-playing the following situations.

1. A farmer and his family discuss the pros and cons of taking out a loan to buy new machinery and expand their production.
2. A parent and child have an argument because the child has stopped reading books and only watches television.
3. The board of directors of an automobile company argues over the expense of including safety devices.
4. An older family member remembers life without air conditioners.
5. A city social worker in the late nineteenth century walks a newcomer to the city through an apartment and explains what everything is. The newcomer asks lots of questions.
6. A group of people discuss the problems that exist today because of early inventions and lack of foresight about the environment.
7. A city planner tries to convince a mayor and his or her budget committee to include parks in a new housing development.
8. The public relations department of an electric company prepares a TV commercial on how to conserve energy during a very hot summer (or on what to keep at home in case of a blackout).

CLASSROOM ACTIVITY 5

"MODERN" ROUND ROBIN

Since the period from 1865 to 1900 was so full of change and innovations, the teacher might want to reinforce all the material learned in class or expand it to the present. This is a short activity in the form of a game. The teacher will write some or all of the following words on the chalkboard:

- transportation

- attitudes
- slang
- medicine
- nutrition
- music
- machines
- entertainment
- fads

Students will copy the headings and write one example of something modern that belongs in that category; for example heart transplant might go under medicine. The teacher will choose the first student to read his or her answers and write them on the chalkboard under each category. Then students will read their answers in turn. Every time students duplicate another classmate's word they cross it off. The student with the most original words wins the game.

This game can also be played without writing. The teacher lines the students up as if for a spelling bee. She or he then says, "I'm thinking of a modern form of transportation (or any other category)" and the students take turns giving examples. When a student can't think of a word he or she sits down and the teacher starts another category. Students continue taking turns until there's only one "winner" left.

This game works best with younger students.

CHAPTER TEN

The Industrial Revolution

INTRODUCTION

The Industrial Revolution created vast political, social, and economic changes in this country. It led to the development of mass production, corporate expansion, and the need for labor unions.

Our assignments will expose the students to various experiences relating to the business world both from the perspective of labor and of management. They will also be involved in many decision-making activities and assignments dealing with issues and problems that many of them will face as adults.

PROJECT LIST

1. Make a map of the United States with a legend highlighting the major industrial centers.
2. Make a map of the United States which shows the locations of natural resources.
3. Construct a home-made model of the Model T Ford.
4. Make a poster illustrating some of the first automobiles made in the United States.
5. Make a manual called *How to Use and Care for Your Model T Ford*.
6. Make a model of a factory assembly line with a conveyor belt.
7. Write the life of Henry Ford in the form of a memoir.
8. Write a newspaper account of a famous strike such as the Pullman strike or the Homestead strike.
9. Make up a series of episodes for a soap opera dealing with the abuses of factory workers in early factories. Include child labor, low wages, long hours, and unsafe conditions.

10. Write a research report on the Triangle Shirtwaist Factory fire. Include eyewitness accounts.

11. Make an illustrated encyclopedia of the labor movement in the United States.

12. Research and write the biography of one famous labor organizer such as Samuel Gompers or Cesar Chavez.

13. Make a film or video describing the benefits of union membership to attract potential members.

14. Make a song booklet or a tape of original union folk songs.

15. Write to the AFL-CIO and to local labor unions. Make a scrapbook about them based on information received.

16. Do a piece of creative writing or a magazine exposé entitled "My Life in a Company Town."

17. Make up a special Labor Day program celebrating the labor movement in the United States. Include awards honoring important labor leaders of the past and present.

18. Make a poster diagramming or illustrating Andrew Carnegie's steel empire.

19. Do an illustrated report or poster on John D. Rockefeller's oil monopoly.

20. Make a poster illustrating how a corporation works.

21. Make a scrapbook illustrating the contributions of some of the early corporate giants such as John D. Rockefeller, Andrew Carnegie, and J. P. Morgan.

22. Make a chart or poster illustrating how a monopoly, trust, or holding company works.

23. Write a government bulletin informing business people of anti-trust legislation.

24. Make a chart illustrating the goals and accomplishments of progressive reformers of the early twentieth century.

25. Write a script for an in-depth TV *Muckraker News Special* exposing the evils of industry and society around 1900.

26. Write an information bulletin for workers describing the laws that protect them on the job.

27. Make a poster or chart showing the accomplishments of Theodore Roosevelt in terms of:
    (a) Square Deal for labor
    (b) Trust-busting
    (c) Land conservation

28. Make a descriptive catalogue of progressive literature that exposed the injustices of society around the turn of the century. Include fiction and nonfiction works by writers such as Jacob Riis, Lincoln Steffens, Upton Sinclair, and Theodore Dreiser.
29. Work out a union strike plan including:
    (a) Picket signs with slogans
    (b) Buttons
    (c) Chants
    (d) Mascot
    (e) Speech to gain public sympathy
    (f) Speech to gain total active support from the membership
30. Write and illustrate a business plan for a factory. Explain:
    (a) What you will produce
    (b) The things you will need
    (c) Where you will get the capital
    (d) Anticipated expenses
    (e) Organization of the assembly line
    (f) Who your potential customers are

HOMEWORK ASSIGNMENTS

MASS PRODUCTION AND THE FACTORY SYSTEM

1. Why is the Industrial Revolution called a revolution? Give specific examples of the drastic changes it created.
2. Make a list of the sounds and sights that would have surprised someone who was about to start working in a factory for the first time.
3. What do you think was the biggest change for a worker who stopped working at home and went to work in a factory?
4. Show how the Industrial Revolution could not have happened if one of the following had been missing:
    (a) Natural resources and sources of power
    (b) Inventors
    (c) Available workers
5. Name any manufactured item in your house and list all the natural resources that it is made from.
6. Name all the places where you see conveyor belts used.
7. Make a list of all the other industries that were stimulated as a result of automobile production.

8. Make up a magazine advertisement for the Model T Ford.

9. Write a dialogue between a salesman at a Model T Ford showroom and a doubtful shopper who owns a horse and buggy.

10. Name something you own or have seen that was handmade. How does it compare with a similar mass-produced product?

11. Write a poem describing work on an assembly line.

12. Interview an older person and ask him or her to name a product that was not available when he or she was young. In what ways does the product change the quality of his or her life?

13. If you had to give up one modern appliance, which one would be hardest for you to live without? Why?

14. If you had the money to open a factory today, what would you produce? Why?

15. How did the Industrial Revolution lead to the growth of cities?

16. In what ways is the Industrial Revolution still going on today? Give it a new name.

17. The Industrial Revolution led to waste and pollution. List all of the ways that you and your family could practice conservation and recycling.

THE GROWTH OF CORPORATIONS

1. Make up a motto that would describe the business philosophy of one of the robber barons.

2. What advice do you think the robber barons would have for the young people of today?

3. If you owned a business, list the things you could do to eliminate your competitors. Put a star next to those things that you would feel comfortable doing.

4. Write a dialogue between the owners of a small business who are discussing how a large monopoly is driving them out of business.

5. Make a cartoon illustrating the idea of the business world being a jungle.

6. Do you think corporations have a responsibility to their employees? Explain.

7. What do you think should be the golden rule for:
   (a) A business person
   (b) An employee

8. If you owned a business and made an unexpected large profit one year, what would you do with it? Why?

9. Write a letter to your congressional representative for or against a tariff on foreign cars.

10. Write an editorial for or against granting all the cable TV rights to one company.

11. Pretend you are a fund raiser for a charity. Write a letter to J. P. Morgan or Andrew Carnegie requesting a large donation.

12. Make a cartoon illustrating the idea of trust-busting.

13. Write an editorial suggesting ways in which you think the government should protect the public against dishonest or unethical business practices.

LABOR UNIONS

1. Pretend you are a child laborer in 1900. Write a letter to "Dear Abby" about your problems.

2. Write a day's entry in the diary of a sweatshop worker of 1900.

3. You own a sweatshop in 1900. What is your opinion of the workers?

4. Make up a "Yellow dog contract" for newly hired workers.

5. What would you do if getting hired for a job depended on your signing an oath promising not to join a labor union?

6. You have just been fired from your job and blacklisted because of union activity. Write a poem or rap song describing your feelings and your plans.

7. Imagine that you are a factory owner around 1900. You suspect that some people are trying to unionize your workers. Write a bulletin telling them what will happen if they join.

8. Describe a disagreement in which you compromised with another person.

9. Make a picket sign or a union button in support of a strike.

10. Interview someone who belongs to a labor union. Find out what the union does for him or her.

11. Pretend you are a judge. Write a court injunction ordering striking milk deliverers back to work. Explain why they must return.

12. Make up an agenda of items to be discussed at a collective bargaining meeting between union and management representatives to avoid a transit strike.

13. If you, as students, had a union, what things would you request in a collective bargaining session with teachers and administrators?

14. You want to be president of your union. Make up a speech to convince the members to vote for you.

15. Make up a handout announcing a union membership drive.
16. Find out what child labor laws protect you today.
17. If you found out that you could get fired for going out on strike, what would you do?
18. Make a list of money-saving measures your family could take if your parents went on strike.

CLASSROOM ACTIVITY 1

WORKING ON AN ASSEMBLY LINE

In order to illustrate and contrast the differences between assembly line work and craftsmanship, the class can be set up to mass produce an item. We have found that students especially enjoy making paper airplanes since that is generally regarded as a no-no in the classroom, but any paper folding, drawing, or building task can be substituted. The teacher will have to decide in advance how many tasks to include in the assembly line. In all probability, several assembly lines will be working at the same time, and this is advantageous because then they can compete with each other for speed of production. The teacher will number the tasks and then assign different students to learn each task.

Two students may be given the job of assembly line foreperson. They will walk around encouraging the students to work quickly and carefully. Sloppily made products will be discarded as rejects. Two other students may be seated separately with paper, scissors, markers, and other art supplies and allowed to work creatively and artistically at their own speed.

Once the class is set up with the supplies and they understand their tasks, the teacher can allow them to work for ten to twenty minutes without stopping. When they are done, they can discuss and compare their experiences through the following questions:

1. How many planes were made by each assembly line? By the artisan? Allow them to display their work.
2. Why did the assembly lines produce so many more?
3. In what ways are the assembly line products different from those made by the artisans?
4. Did you enjoy your work? Why? Why not?
5. Is there anything that would have made it more enjoyable?
6. Would you like to do this kind of work for the rest of your life? Why? Why not? If not, what would you prefer?

CLASSROOM ACTIVITY 2

EFFICIENCY EXPERTS

One of the basic ideas behind assembly line production is to break a task down to its smallest component, so as to eliminate wasted motion by the workers.

Divide the class into groups of efficiency experts who will work out the tasks for the assembly line production of one of the products listed below. The teacher may add or substitute products, so as to better motivate the particular students who are participating in this activity.

1. Pencil
2. Candy bar
3. Basketball
4. Looseleaf binder
5. Pair of blue jeans
6. Bicycle

When they are done, the groups can report back to the class. After each group reports, the teacher can ask the rest of the class if they can think of any way to break the tasks down even more.

CLASSROOM ACTIVITY 3

HOW STRIKES AFFECT PEOPLE'S LIVES

When service workers go on strike, the public is affected in many ways. Divide the class into committees to discuss the problems they personally would have and how they would solve or cope with those problems if one of the following unions went on strike. Each committee will deal with a different strike:

1. Transit workers
2. Teachers
3. Postal workers
4. Police
5. Sanitation workers
6. Firefighters
7. Electric company
8. Telephone company

After the committees have met and reported back to the class, the teacher may ask:

1. Have any of you ever experienced a strike? What happened?
2. Do you think certain workers should be prohibited from striking?
3. Do you think it is a violation of our freedom to prohibit someone from striking? Why? Why not?

CLASSROOM ACTIVITY 4

WHAT WILL YOU DO?

The teacher will tell the class that they are all members of the Ambulance Drivers' Union. Collective bargaining has failed. There will be no raise in salary and no improvements in conditions or benefits for the next year due to lack of funds. As union members, they now have to decide what to do about a series of problems and situations. As the scenarios change, they will have to put themselves in the position of the ambulance drivers. For each of the following questions, they must decide what they would do and why.

1. Will you support a strike?
2. Will you actively support it by speaking out and picketing?
3. You don't want to strike, but the majority does. Will you join the strike or cross your co-workers on the picket line?
4. Volunteers are driving the ambulances. A call comes in. There is a medical emergency at the neighborhood elementary school your children attend. What will you do?
5. A court injunction orders you back to work.
6. You are in violation of a court order and will be fined $100.00 a day.
7. Your spouse thinks you should return to work even though you don't want to. Your disagreement causes constant fights.
8. They will not raise your salary, but they will give one extra coffee break and increase the health and vacation benefits.
9. They will give you a 5 percent raise in salary but will not improve health benefits or working conditions.
10. The strike is nowhere near settlement, and you do not have the money to pay next month's rent.
11. The police have been called, and there may be violence because scabs have been hired to take your jobs.

As a wrap-up, the teacher may ask the students to discuss which problems seemed the most difficult to resolve and why.

CLASSROOM ACTIVITY 5

DECIDING ON DEMANDS

The teacher will reproduce the following list of union demands for the students. Leave a blank space next to each one, so the students can number them. Tell the students that, as members of the Telephone Worker's Union, they are a diverse group. It is time for them to decide on their next set of contract demands and to put them in order of importance. Distribute the list.

_____ Raise in salary
_____ Better health and dental insurance benefits
_____ Longer lunch time and shorter work day
_____ New lounge for employees
_____ College scholarship fund for children of employees
_____ Larger expense account
_____ Employees' cafeteria
_____ Larger life insurance policy
_____ More job security
_____ Day-care center for children of employees

The following groups of workers must meet to decide on the order of importance of their demands. The first three items on their lists must have clear explanations to go with them. The order on which they decide should be based on the needs of the group they represent.

1. Single men and women around twenty-one years of age
2. Single parents with children between the ages of three months and five years
3. Managers and supervisors
4. Men and women over fifty years old
5. Employees with large families, mortgages, and car payments

After they have met, each group will present its demands to the rest of the union members. The teacher will encourage the other students to raise questions and arguments during the course of the presentations. The entire class will then have to vote on the order of importance of their demands, based on the arguments they heard.

CLASSROOM ACTIVITY 6

BUSINESS ETHICS

The growth of the factory system and big business created opportunity, jobs, and fortunes for many Americans. At the same time, the industrial giants sometimes did cruel, unethical, and immoral acts as they built their corporate empires. It is important for the students to explore these issues in order to clarify their own ideas and feelings.

The teacher will ask the class, by a show of hands, to indicate whether they agree, disagree, or are unsure about the following statements. Where there appears to be interest or controversy, the students can discuss why they feel the way they do.

1. The object of business is to make as much money as possible.
2. Anything that is legal in business is okay.
3. Poor people are poor because of their own shortcomings.
4. The fruits of the labor of millions have been stolen to build the huge fortunes of millionaires.
5. It's alright to pay workers less than they deserve if they are foolish enough to accept it.
6. If a business person is smart enough to drive his or her competitors out of business, then they deserve what they get.
7. It's alright for a business person to give a discount to regular customers who spend a lot of money.
8. When profits go down, companies have to lay off employees.
9. Companies have no obligation to their employees after they've been laid off.
10. Sometimes it's necessary to undersell competitors in order to drive them out of business.
11. It is the job of the government to always watch what business people are doing.
12. It's alright for an employee to take home paper clips and other items without paying for them.
13. Workers should not do more than they are paid to do.
14. It's perfectly understandable that workers slow down when the boss is out.
15. It's alright to hire your friend as a manager even though there are other qualified people who have been working for you.

16. In order to make more money an employer has to hire younger people who accept lower wages and fire older, higher salaried people.

17. It's alright for a company to manufacture its products in countries where labor is cheap in order to get bigger profits.

CLASSROOM ACTIVITY 7

UNION VERSUS MANAGEMENT

Divide the class into groups of four. Within each group, two students will represent the interests of management, and the other two will represent the interests of the union members. Each group of four will try to resolve a different problem from among those below. The teacher can list the conflicts on the chalkboard or write each one on a separate sheet of paper for distribution to each group.

1. Profits have been going down in the factory. Management is planning to lay off 20 percent of the assembly line workers and cut back on production.

2. Group health insurance costs are rising; therefore, management wants the workers to pay for their family health insurance benefits. These were previously paid for by the company.

3. Truck drivers want new trucks for long hauls because the present trucks are breaking down, often causing delays on long trips. This leads to accidents because the drivers become overtired and fall asleep at the wheel.

4. The assembly line work in the soda bottling plant is boring. Workers want to rotate jobs. This requires more training and, therefore, will cost the company more money.

5. Workers want more fringe benefits: a cafeteria, an employees' lounge, a day-care center for their children, and a shorter work day on Fridays during the summer months.

When the groups have finished thrashing out their problems, each one in turn may present their problem and resolution, or lack of it, to the rest of the class. After the last presentation, the teacher may ask:

1. Did you learn anything new about union-management disputes? What?

2. What was the biggest problem your group had?

3. Why is it often very difficult for unions and management to resolve their differences?

CLASSROOM ACTIVITY 8

FAIR AND REASONABLE

Students will be divided into groups of four or five to work on a Bill of Rights and Responsibilities for workers, or a Bill of Rights and Responsibilities for employers. Their laws must be fair and reasonable.

After they have met they will present the results of their work to the rest of the class for a vote. As each item is discussed the teacher will record it on a large sheet of paper so the class can see it. The completed chart can be left as a bulletin board display.

CLASSROOM ACTIVITY 9

RATING THE INDUSTRIAL REVOLUTION

This activity might serve as a culminating activity on the Industrial Revolution. The teacher will write the following question on the chalkboard: "Are our lives better or worse because of the Industrial Revolution?" If necessary the teacher might lead a brief preliminary discussion about the benefits and problems of living in an industrialized society. Then students would be placed in small groups. Each group would respond to one of the questions below. Their answers may be written on the chalkboard as part of the lesson or the teacher may ask one member of each group to report back to the whole class. At the end of the session students would vote on whether their lives are better or worse because of the Industrial Revolution. They should also discuss the direction modern inventions and industry should now take.

QUESTIONS

1. What problems exist in our environment today because of our industrialized society?
2. What appliances and inventions make your life easier?
3. What inventions make your life safer?
4. What inventions make your life more fun?
5. What moral decisions and dilemmas do people face today that people 100 years ago didn't have?
6. What are some things that worry you about our society? Can an invention solve them? Explain.

7. What problems have not been solved by industrialization?
8. What problems can't be solved by a new invention?
9. What new inventions do you think we need?
10. What new inventions do you want just for fun?
11. List all the benefits of the Industrial Revolution.
12. List all the problems caused by the Industrial Revolution.

CHAPTER ELEVEN

Immigration

INTRODUCTION

The United States is a country of immigrants. The richness of our culture reflects the great variety of people who have come here to settle.

In many areas, such as New York City, immigration is an ongoing process. However, some parts of the country no longer have much movement or change in population. We hope that our assignments will help evoke the immigrant experience for students throughout this country.

PROJECT LIST

1. Make a family tree showing where your ancestors came from. Wherever possible include: why they came, when they came, any interesting stories about their trip over, and their experiences here.
2. Pretend you are an immigrant coming to this country around 1900. Write a diary describing your trip. This can also be done as poetry or in the form of a play.
3. Make a model of a 1910 steamboat that carried immigrants to the United States.
4. Make a poster of flags showing the different countries immigrants came from.
5. Make a scrapbook, collage, or mobile showing your interpretation of the immigrant experience in this country.
6. Make a model or map of Ellis Island.
7. Write a play about a family that wants to emigrate to the United States. Name the country they are leaving and be sure to include the reasons why they are leaving. You may choose any country from which a large number of immigrants came (example: Ireland).
8. Write a booklet of poems or a narrative poem expressing the feelings of immigrants.

9. Write a report or story contrasting what the immigrants imagined the United States would be like and what they actually found.

10. Do a photographic essay of any ghetto or immigrant area of your neighborhood, town, or city.

11. Make a filmstrip, film, or video telling the story of one immigrant's experience.

12. Do an illustrated cookbook of foods introduced by immigrants.

13. List all the streets and buildings in your city that are named after immigrants who settled here. Include their countries of origin.

14. Make a map of your state showing all the places that have foreign names.

15. Write a biography of an immigrant who you feel did something special in this country. Be sure to give your reasons why.

16. Write a report on a town or neighborhood settled by one particular group of immigrants.

17. Write a manual of instructions on how to become an American citizen.

18. Make a newspaper geared to immigrants in the early 1900s. Include articles and an advertising section for jobs and apartments.

19. Write a report about the contribution of immigrants to the labor movement.

20. Write a report on any group of immigrants or refugees who have been labeled "Boat People."

21. Write a report about how and why illegal aliens come into this country.

22. Make a list of agencies and services in your town, city, or state that provide help for newly arrived immigrants today. Explain what each one does.

23. Write a report about some of the laws that discriminated against immigrants in the past.

24. Make an illustrated glossary of words that were introduced to the American language by immigrant groups (example: rodeo, kindergarten).

25. Read a play or novel that deals with immigrant people. Write:
    (a) Short plot summary
    (b) Problems they faced
    (c) Solutions
    (d) Changes in life because of coming to the United States
    (e) Your feelings about the book and experiences it describes

26. Write a report about any famous defector (example: Mikhail Baryshnikov).
27. Using current periodicals, write a report on any new group of immigrants such as Haitians, Russian Jews, or Koreans.
28. Make a scrapbook illustrating some outstanding contributions made by immigrants to this country.
29. Using a tape recorder or camcorder do an oral history of an immigrant. Prepare your questions first. The tape and questions should be handed in together.
30. Write a fantasy short story or play describing what would be missing in the life of your town or city if one ethnic group had not emigrated.

HOMEWORK ASSIGNMENTS

WHY AND HOW IMMIGRANTS CAME TO THE UNITED STATES

1. What would have to happen in the United States to make you consider leaving it for another country? Why?
2. If you were an immigrant and could only take what you could carry with you, what things would you pack? Why?
3. Immigrants spent two weeks crossing the ocean by ship in the early 1900s. How do you think you would spend your time? Include how you would feel.
4. If you lived in another country, what would attract you most to the United States? Why?
5. Make a poster, newspaper, or magazine advertisement for passage to the United States.
6. Create a rap song telling why a group of immigrants wants to come to this country.
7. Read and analyze the Emma Lazarus poem, "The New Colossus."
8. Read the international section of your newspaper. Write about actual problems described in countries of today that you think would make people want to leave and come to the United States.

THE IMMIGRANT EXPERIENCE IN THE UNITED STATES

1. Write a letter to your cousins in the old country. Tell them why they should or shouldn't come to the United States.
2. Write a letter to your best friend in the old country describing how life is different in the United States.

3. What do you think the expression "streets are paved with gold" meant to the immigrants?

4. Write a letter to a "Dear Abby" column describing your problems as an immigrant and ask for advice. The next day, have the students exchange their completed assignments and write their advice about the problems. Then discuss or read them in class.

5. Is the United States a melting pot or a tossed salad? Explain your answer. Which would you prefer and why?

6. What do you think is the main reason why immigrants have endured so much to come and live here? Could/would you have done it?

7. Compare your first day at school with an immigrant's first day in the United States.

8. Make up a new national anthem with an immigrant theme.

9. Tour your neighborhood or any specified street and collect proof of the variety that exists because of immigrants' contributions. For example, a menu from a restaurant serving ethnic food, bills or flyers from stores run by immigrants, and so forth.

LAWS AFFECTING IMMIGRANTS

1. Do you think a quota system is fair? Why or why not?

2. Who, if anyone, do you think should not be allowed into the United States? Why?

3. Why do you think immigrants are required to live here for five years before becoming citizens?

4. Make up an original oath of allegiance for new citizens.

5. What was ungentlemanly about the "Gentleman's Agreement" with Japan regarding immigration?

6. Should boat people, who come here without permission, be sent home or be allowed to stay? Why?

7. Write your own opinions and feelings about the Amnesty Law for illegal aliens.

8. (To be used after teaching the Oath of Allegiance taken by new citizens) Would you take this oath? Why? Why not?

CLASSROOM ACTIVITY 1

FREESTYLE WRITING

By answering the following questions, the students will better relate to the immigrant experience.

Students will answer the following questions with the first thoughts that come into their minds. The teacher may then have them read their answers aloud or put students in small groups for sharing.

1. Name a way in which you would like to improve your life.
2. Can you think of something besides money that would make your life better?
3. If you could move somewhere else, where would you move?
4. Would you prefer the city or the country?
5. Would you want to live in an apartment or a house?
6. If you were given more freedom, what would you do with it?

CLASSROOM ACTIVITY 2

ROLE-PLAYING

By taking on the role of the family, the students will learn the decision-making process on a personal level. This can be expanded to leaving the country today. This activity can be used after teaching the problems in Europe that led to immigration. In discussing this afterward, stress can be given to the choice that exists between the security of a familiar situation and the risk, possible fear, and adventure of the unknown.

Role-play a discussion between parents, grandparents, and two children (age of the class). Half of them want to go to the United States and half don't. The students may choose their roles.

CLASSROOM ACTIVITY 3

MAKING CHOICES

Making choices is always a difficult process. It can be frustrating, sad, painful. Afterwards, one is sometimes left with a gnawing doubt as to whether or not the choice was correct. There is no formal procedure for making choices, but certainly we can train young people to analyze all the options, so that once they have reached a decision, they will feel comfortable with it. In the following activity the students will be forced to make uncomfortable choices. The teacher will stress that there are no right or wrong answers and read the following:

> Your family wants to leave their country of origin and emigrate to the United States where they can be free and have a chance to build a better life and future and educate their children, but they can only afford four tickets (on the boat/plane). Who stays behind and who goes?

1. You
2. Father, a 32-year-old laborer
3. Mother, 29 years old, a nurse
4. Grandmother, 72 years old, almost blind and totally dependent on the family
5. Father's brother, 28 years old, medical student, wanted by the police for anti-government activity
6. His wife, the only one who speaks English, a seamstress, six months pregnant
7. Two-year-old son who has a liver disease that can be treated in America

The teacher should feel free to substitute other relatives in terms of age, occupation, disability, or specific circumstances.

CLASSROOM ACTIVITY 4

A NEW START

The students will answer the questions below either verbally or in writing. The teacher will say:

You have the chance to be a modern day immigrant to a new country where you can start a new life.

1. What qualities do you personally have that will help you get along?
2. What change would you most look forward to?
3. Would it be more important to make money or to get a good education?
4. What problems, if any, do you think you might face?
5. What would be the hardest to leave behind?

CLASSROOM ACTIVITY 5

ILLEGAL ALIENS

The teacher will read or tell the following information to the class. When he or she is done, the teacher will divide the class into groups to discuss the statements relating to the information given.

Illegal aliens sneak into the country in many ways. They hide in trains and boats. They enter as tourists and then remain here. They swim across the Rio Grande and sometimes pay people to help them sneak in. They do it because they cannot get in legally and they want a chance to earn more money than they can make in their own countries, or they seek freedom from an oppressive government. Pretend you are a member of a Congressional Committee and have to argue for or against one of the following "solutions" to the problem of illegal aliens.

1. We can solve the problem of illegal aliens by letting everyone into the country.
2. We can solve the problem of illegal aliens by putting more guards along the borders.
3. We can solve the problem by harshly punishing all illegals who get caught.
4. We can solve the problem by creating towns and jobs for them in underpopulated areas.

CLASSROOM ACTIVITY 6

PROBLEM SOLVING

Children of immigrants often face tremendous conflicts in adapting to their new country and new environment. Old ways come into conflict with the new ways.

The teacher will read the questions below to the class and discuss all the possible solutions to the problems. This may also be done as committee work or as a role-playing activity.

1. Your parents speak Spanish at home, but they forbid you to speak Spanish.
2. Your parents speak Spanish at home, but it embarrasses you, and you refuse to speak it.
3. Your parents don't want you to be friends with a boy/girl of another background.
4. There is a new kid in school, and your friends tell you that he looks weird and you shouldn't be friends with him.
5. You want to finish high school and get a job. Your father says, "No. You must go to college."
6. You live in a shabby, run-down apartment and are ashamed to bring your friends home.

7. Your parents want to arrange a marriage for you.

8. Your parents don't understand what's in style and won't let you dress like the other kids.

9. Your parents are "old-fashioned" and won't let you
   (a) Date
   (b) Stay out as late as your friends
   (c) Go to parties

10. Your parents refuse to come to open school night because they don't speak English *or* you don't tell your parents about open school night because you're ashamed of how they dress and speak.

CLASSROOM ACTIVITY 7

DISCUSSING FEELINGS

Money was a major problem faced by the immigrants. They had to make many sacrifices in order to make money and meet expenses. How would the students feel about each of the following? The teacher will discuss anger, jealousy, unhappiness, resentment, and so forth. The teacher might go on to discuss alternative actions as a follow-up, once the students get into the activity. The class could also break up into groups and write lists of alternative solutions to issues that they specifically relate to. How would you feel about:

1. Wearing hand-me-downs to save money
2. Being asked to get an after-school job to help pay the rent
3. Sharing your apartment with another family to save rent
4. Doing cleaning work to help pay bills
5. Staying home from school to take care of a sick brother or sister so your parents don't lose a day's pay
6. Giving up your bedroom so it can be rented to a boarder
7. Buying shoes/sneakers you don't like because they're on sale
8. Moving to a smaller house or apartment to save money
9. Wearing the same clothes every day
10. Wearing old-fashioned clothes
11. Running out of school supplies and not having money for more
12. Your best friend's parent getting a better job and moving to a better neighborhood
13. Getting more change than you are entitled to at the store

14. Your parents being out of work and not able to buy you something you want
15. Your grandmother moving in with you to save money and sharing your room
16. Having to beg the grocer for credit
17. Your parents working and then going to school at night to learn English and get a better job, and you hardly ever seeing them

CLASSROOM ACTIVITY 8

MULTIPLE CHOICE EXERCISE—PROBLEMS OF IMMIGRANTS

The following exercise was prepared to show that there are many different answers to one question without one necessarily being more correct than another. However, it is interesting to discuss why we choose whichever answer we do. This is a nonthreatening way to express a point of view. The students may relate to some questions better than others. The teacher should use his or her discretion. The teacher may also add to the list.

1. If you moved to a new country, which would be hardest for you to get used to?
   (a) Eating strange new foods
   (b) Learning a new language
   (c) Making new friends

2. What would be the hardest thing for you to do in a strange new country where you don't speak the language?
   (a) Ask for directions to go somewhere
   (b) Ask for food in a restaurant
   (c) Ask for a job

3. If the kids in your new school made fun of the way you speak, would you:
   (a) Ignore it
   (b) Try to change the way you speak
   (c) Fight

4. If the teacher constantly corrected your speech in an embarrassing way, would you:
   (a) Try to improve
   (b) Complain to your parents
   (c) Tell the teacher to leave you alone

5. If your father and mother couldn't get jobs and were sick, would you:
  (a) Try not to spend money
  (b) Quit school to work
  (c) Ask friends and relatives to lend you money

6. If you saw many people at a fast food place eating something you'd never seen before, would you:
  (a) Buy one and try it
  (b) Not buy one
  (c) Ask a friend for a taste

7. If a group of kids at school made fun of the country you came from, would you:
  (a) Ignore it
  (b) Explain to them that what they are doing is wrong, and that they are prejudiced
  (c) Fight with them

8. If a new child came to this school from another country and all the kids laughed at his or her clothes and accent, would you:
  (a) Speak up for him or her
  (b) Mind your own business
  (c) Join in with the crowd

9. If you were an immigrant and your brother got sick here, would you want to:
  (a) Go back to the old country with him
  (b) Stay here with a relative or friend of the family while both parents take him home
  (c) Stay here with one parent while the other one takes him home

10. Which would be worse?
  (a) Getting cheated by a salesperson
  (b) Being made fun of by other people
  (c) Not understanding the language

11. Which would be the worst for you?
  (a) Living in one room with your whole family
  (b) Having to share a bathroom with three other families on your floor
  (c) Having to share your house with another family

12. What would you do if you couldn't get your favorite food because it is not available here?
  (a) Try to find a new favorite food
  (b) Forget about it
  (c) Go to different neighborhoods to try to get it

13. If all the children wore blue jeans to school and your parents didn't approve of that, would you:
    (a) Wear what they told you to wear
    (b) Buy blue jeans and secretly change when you got to school
    (c) Get some friends to help you convince your parents to change their minds

14. If your parents wanted you to go to after-school instruction to learn their native language and traditions (Greek, Japanese, etc.), would you:
    (a) Do it against your will
    (b) Refuse
    (c) Do it proudly

15. If your parents wanted to arrange a marriage for you, would you:
    (a) Run away from home
    (b) Marry the person
    (c) Refuse, and fight them on it

CLASSROOM ACTIVITY 9

A MULTICULTURAL CLASS

If the teacher is fortunate enough to have a multicultural class he or she may use any of the following strategies:

A. Interviews — students sit in pairs and interview each other about their backgrounds, traditions, impressions of the U.S., and so forth. They may share with the rest of the class or describe their experiences in journal writing.
B. If there is not enough variety in the class, the teacher can assign students to write questions as if they were reporters and then conduct interviews of students who are recent immigrants, with their consent of course.
C. Before any holiday discussions are held the teacher can list all the variations that come from combining more than one culture. This is especially effective when discussing Thanksgiving meals and what special foods students' families add to the traditional fare.
D. In a multicultural class the students can be asked to draw pictures of the flags of their country of origin (or family's country of origin). The teacher can create a bulletin board with these flags and photographs of the students. Students may enjoy creating the title for their bulletin board. For example, one group in our school chose the song title, "We Are the World."

CLASSROOM ACTIVITY 10

DEBATES DEALING WITH IMMIGRATION TODAY

The teacher should follow the procedure explained in the Debate chapter.

1. Should all illegal aliens be allowed to stay here and work?
2. Is someone who is an illegal alien really a criminal?
3. Should someone who is not yet a citizen of the United States be given:
   (a) Food stamps
   (b) Welfare
   (c) Medicaid
   (d) Unemployment insurance
4. Should immigrants who have become citizens and are then convicted of serious crimes be stripped of their citizenship and sent back to their countries of origin?
5. Should bilingual education be abolished?
6. Should we abolish all quotas for immigrants?
7. Should we stop immigration until all Americans have jobs?

CLASSROOM ACTIVITY 11

IMAGES OF IMMIGRATION

Many collections of photographs exist that illustrate the immigrant experience. The teacher may pass these pictures around the class or display them and have the students move about to view them. Students will write their impressions and feelings quickly as they look at each picture. At the end of the activity these short phrases and words can be turned into poetry.

CLASSROOM ACTIVITY 12

CULMINATING ACTIVITY–INTERNATIONAL FAIR

This is a wonderful culminating activity because:

- It allows for socialization and sharing among the students.
- It offers the family a chance to be part of a classroom activity.
- It enables the students to make use of everything they learned in the unit.

- It embodies the message that immigrants' contributions are a living part of the United States.

SUGGESTED ACTIVITIES

The teacher should plan for one block of time for the fair. It can be done in the classroom, school library, gym, or any other suitable area. It should have on display as many of the students' projects and reports as possible, and it may include any of the following:

- foods that are representative of immigrant groups (if the class does not have a variety of ethnic backgrounds, the teacher may assign different recipes to be worked on)
- costumes
- music and/or singing
- slide show
- handicraft exhibit
- artwork
- flag exhibit
- folk dancing
- language booth
- "Name the Immigrant" contest booth

CHAPTER TWELVE

The United States Becomes a World Power

INTRODUCTION

As the United States entered world affairs, it had to deal with many new problems and decisions. Starting as a country whose philosophical ties were to isolationism, it slowly became involved in foreign wars and colonialism. This chapter traces the steps toward becoming a world power from the Spanish-American War through World War I. Students will work on assignments and participate in activities that will help them understand the country's growing involvement and influence in world affairs. They will also deal with the responsibilities that this country assumed, whether welcome or not, in foreign lands and study the effect of our new role at home and abroad.

PROJECT LIST

1. Make a board game depicting different types of foreign policies.
2. Make a diorama of the sinking of the *Maine* or the *Lusitania*.
3. Make a three-dimensional map showing famous battles of the Spanish-American War and the new possessions gained by the United States after the war.
4. Write a short history of the Spanish-American War and its peace treaty as it might appear in either a Spanish, Cuban, or Filipino textbook.
5. Make a poster of heroes of the Panama Canal. Be sure to include William Gorgas, Theodore Roosevelt, George Goethals, and David Gaillard.

6. Make a working model of a ship passing through the Panama Canal or draw a detailed diagram.

7. Write an illustrated children's book about the building of the Panama Canal.

8. Write a research report using as many primary sources as possible on the foreign policy of one of the presidents below:
   - McKinley
   - Roosevelt (T.)
   - Wilson

9. Read poems about World War I. Analyze and possibly illustrate at least five.

10. Make a poster of weapons used in World War I.

11. Research any important battle of World War I and write a series of eyewitness accounts for a newspaper.

12. Write a diary or series of letters by a soldier in the trenches. Use actual primary sources for your research.

13. Read *All Quiet on the Western Front* by Erich Maria Remarque. After a short analysis of how the war affects the main characters, explain:
    (a) Why is this book considered one of the great antiwar, as well as war, novels of all time?
    (b) Did it matter to you that the protagonist was German?

14. Make a model of a plane used to fight in World War I (not store-bought).

15. Make a booklet of World War I fighter planes.

16. After doing research, write a short story about a World War I ace.

17. Write and tape a radio broadcast about one of the topics below:
    (a) Life in the trenches
    (b) Songs of World War I
    (c) Life on the home front

18. Write a series of letters from a wife, mother, sister, or girlfriend at home to a soldier. Have her describe her job, the hardships at home, and the efforts of civilians to help win the war. Be sure to use actual facts and specific examples.

19. Make a pamphlet that expresses the reasons for the antiwar movement and the opinions of its leaders during World War I. Be sure to use quotes wherever possible.

20. Write a report on the policy of segregation in the army during World War I.

21. During World War I, blacks held a demonstration protesting against the existing discrimination they faced at home. One of the signs asked the president to "make America safe for democracy." Using the quote as your title, compile a list of grievances with specific details and examples. Also include a list of demands.

22. Prepare a radio broadcast about Wilson's Fourteen Points. What was the outcome of his plan?

23. Write your own script for the meetings and writing of the Treaty of Versailles. Include all participants and the actual end result.

24. Do creative writing or artwork on any aspect of World War I.

25. Make a map showing all places in Europe where Americans fought during World War I.

26. Make an illustrated time line depicting the growth of the United States' participation in world affairs from the 1890s through World War I.

27. Write a series of radio scripts, including the music you would use for a program called *Good Morning, World War I*.

28. Prepare a public relations campaign to win World War I on the home front. Include slogans, radio commercials, posters, buttons, and fundraising activities.

HOMEWORK ASSIGNMENTS

THE SPANISH-AMERICAN WAR

1. Using the style of yellow journalism, write a headline and short article about your school.

2. Find coverage of the same event in two newspapers, one of which uses yellow journalism. Underline some of the major examples of how the articles are different.

3. Draw a cartoon or make a "Wanted—Dead or Alive" poster about "Butcher" Weyler.

4. Write a letter to President McKinley from any of the people below. Explain your position on whether the United States should or shouldn't get involved with the Cuban revolution against Spain.
   (a) An American businessperson who has invested in a Cuban sugar plantation
   (b) An American who feels that we should help Cuba's fight for freedom

(c) A Spanish diplomat who wants his country to avoid war

(d) A Cuban exile

These should be read aloud in class and discussed.

5. Write a list of unanswered questions about the sinking of the *Maine*.

6. Make up a slogan and poster to recruit men for the war against Spain.

7. Make a medal citation for Commodore Dewey after the American victory at Manila Bay.

8. Create a song or motto for the Rough Riders.

9. Draw a political cartoon showing America's position in the world before and after the Spanish-American War.

10. Write a diary entry for someone in Cuba, the Philippines, or Puerto Rico who has just learned that the United States will now be in charge.

PANAMA CANAL

1. How did winning the Spanish-American War lead to the United States' building of the Panama Canal?

2. Write a short explanation of how the United States obtained permission to build a canal in Panama from the following points of view:

   (a) Theodore Roosevelt

   (b) Colombia

   (c) Panama

3. Do you think the deal between the United States and Panama was fair? Explain your answer.

4. Write a letter from the French to the Americans warning of the problems found in building the canal.

5. Make up a hit parade of top ten song titles that will tell the story of how the canal was built.

6. Make a shopping list for the men who worked on the Panama Canal.

7. Write a page from a medical journal explaining how to reduce yellow fever and malaria in order to build the canal.

8. Pretend that you were on the first ship to pass through the Panama Canal. Describe how you felt and what you saw.

9. Make up a page for the Help Wanted section of a newspaper listing job openings for operating the Canal. (Example: Toll Collectors, must be good in math.)

10. It is the year 2000 and we are about to turn the Canal over to Panama. Make up a "How To Care For" list of things they should do to avoid trouble in the Canal.

11. It is the year 2000. Make up an acceptance speech by the leader of Panama when the Canal is turned over to them.

12. Make a new deed of ownership for the Panama Canal.

STEPS INTO WORLD INVOLVEMENT

1. Write the definition of the Open Door policy by an American, Chinese, Japanese, and European.

2. Draw a book jacket for a book called *The Open Door Policy*.

3. Make up questions for a press conference with Theodore Roosevelt in which he'll explain his position on the Monroe Doctrine. Include his answers.

4. Write an editorial in a Latin American magazine about the United States' intervention in Santo Domingo in 1905.

5. Describe the nineteen years of Marine "order" in Haiti from a Haitian's point of view.

6. Pretend you are a Marine in Haiti. Write a letter home describing your mission there.

7. Write a conversation that might have taken place if Pancho Villa of Mexico had talked to General John Pershing of the United States.

8. Make a poster urging United States' support for the court at The Hague.

9. Write a wish list for peace to the court at The Hague.

WORLD WAR I

1. Make up picture symbols to illustrate the causes of World War I.

2. If Archduke Francis Ferdinand of Austria had not been assassinated, do you think World War I would have started? Explain.

3. If you had been alive during World War I, which position would you have supported? Explain your answer.
   (a) Entering the war on behalf of England and the Allies
   (b) Staying neutral
   (c) Entering the war on behalf of Germany and the Central Powers

4. Write an editorial about Germany's policy of unrestricted submarine warfare.

5. Write a headline and short news article about the sinking of the *Lusitania*.

6. Make a poster urging the United States to aid England. Be sure to in-

clude what our ties were with that country. If you prefer, make a poster against entering the war.

7. Write a radio news bulletin announcing the United States' decision to enter the war. Include what you consider an important quote from President Wilson.

8. Make a recruitment poster for soldiers.

9. Write a jingle for a radio commercial urging civilians to support the war effort. It can be for Meatless Mondays, Wheatless Wednesdays, war bonds, or any other aspect of support.

10. Make a list of things that could have been given up for the rest of the days of the week besides Meatless Mondays and Wheatless Wednesdays.

11. Write a diary entry by a German-American about his or her reaction to words such as liberty cabbage, liberty measles, and other anti-German measures in America during the war.

12. Write a dialogue between two black people who have just read about some of the heroic deeds of the black soldiers in Europe.

13. Pretend that you are a woman who has just finished her first morning at her new factory job. Write her thoughts as she sits down for her first lunch break.

14. Write a letter home from the trenches.

15. Pretend you are a war correspondent. Send a telegram home describing any major battle studied in class.

16. Send a letter to President Wilson with your best wishes for his success at the peace treaty talks. Include your opinion of his Fourteen Points.

17. Write an editorial about the Treaty of Versailles from any point of view below:
    (a) German
    (b) American
    (c) French
    (d) English

18. Make up slogans for a rally to convince the Senate to vote for or against our participation in the League of Nations.

19. What would you bring for lunch on Wheatless Wednesdays?

20. Write a letter to a soldier in the trenches sending him encouragement from the folks back home.

21. Make a banner welcoming the soldiers back home after the war.

22. Write a petition urging the world to outlaw the use of poison gas.

23. Write a short essay on whether you believe the United States could ever truly stay in its own backyard again after World War I.

CLASSROOM ACTIVITY 1

FOREIGN POLICY HEARINGS

The following activity may be used throughout this unit as the teacher sees fit. Students will argue questions of foreign policy using the point of view of the characters listed below.

CAST OF CHARACTERS

- Isolationist Ida
- Expansionist Ethan
- Imperialist Ivan
- Neutralist Nellie
- Pacifist Pete
- Alliance Alice
- Jingoist Jill
- Freedom Freddy
- Businessman Bob
- Democracy Dave

FOREIGN POLICY QUESTIONS

1. Should the United States help Cuba fight against Spain?
2. Should the United States remain in Cuba after the war?
3. What should the United States do with the Philippines?
4. Should the United States build the Panama Canal?
5. Is it our business to insist on an Open Door policy in Asia?
6. Should we interfere in Mexico's revolution?
7. Should we join the League of Nations?
8. Who should we support, if anyone, in World War I?

CLASSROOM ACTIVITY 2

WHAT IS YOUR FOREIGN POLICY?

Using the same cast of characters as in Classroom Activity 1, the class will role-play reactions to the following situations:

1. An argument between your friends
2. A cry for help from the street

3. A young basketball team not playing well and taking up space and time in the gym
4. Mrs. Jones who does not plant very much in her garden which is right near your crowded one
5. The community center which needs donations for a new senior citizens' lounge

CLASSROOM ACTIVITY 3

FIND THE FACTS

This activity is designed to help students recognize facts and understand the difference between fact and inference. The teacher will reproduce the following passages. Students will read each passage and check off those sentences below it that are absolute facts as told in the paragraph.

After the students have completed each exercise, the teacher should go over each sentence and ask students to find the exact words in the paragraph to prove their answer. It will also be helpful and fun for the students to see how much we infer from material that is not specifically stated. The teacher should encourage the students to discuss what further information they would need to be sure that each sentence was a fact.

PARAGRAPH 1

Cuba wanted freedom from Spain. Many people in the United States sympathized with Cuba. The U.S. battleship *Maine* sailed into the harbor of Havana in order to protect Americans living in Cuba. It anchored there. On February 15, 1898, at 9:40 P.M. the *Maine* exploded. Over 260 men were killed. The United States blamed Spain.

Check Off Facts Below

1. The *Maine* was a U.S. battleship.
2. Spain blew up the battleship *Maine*.
3. This was a surprise attack.
4. Havana is a port city.
5. All the men who were killed were Americans.
6. It was nighttime when the ship sank.

7. It was very dark.
8. The explosion was due to an accident.
9. Spain treated Cuba cruelly.
10. Cuba asked for Americans to help them.

PARAGRAPH 2

In September 1899 U.S. Secretary of State John Hay asked Japan, France, Germany, Italy, Russia, and Great Britain to agree on an Open Door policy in China. He wanted all countries to have equal trading rights in China.

Check Off Facts Below

1. John Hay wanted China to be free.
2. The Open Door policy protected China.
3. China agreed to the Open Door policy.
4. The United States wanted to trade with China.
5. The Open Door policy originated in the United States.

CLASSROOM ACTIVITY 4

CIVILIANS AT WAR

Students will form committees to deal with different aspects of the civilian war effort. Each committee will make a list of all that they could do if World War I were being fought today.

1. *Scrap Drive Committee* will list all scrap material that could be collected for recycling.
2. *Food Committee* will list all the food made with sugar or wheat that could be given up on behalf of the war effort.
3. *Slogan Committee* will work on slogans to encourage people to support the war effort at home.
4. *Care Package Committee* will create care packages that they think would be appreciated by soldiers away from home.
5. *Hand Crafts Committee* will list all the things people could make that could be sent to soldiers away from home.

CLASSROOM ACTIVITY 5

IF WE HAD STAYED HOME

Divide the class into groups and ask them to project what the outcomes of each of the following would have been if we had not:

- built the Panama Canal
- had an Open Door Policy in China
- fought in the Spanish-American War
- entered World War I
- kept Puerto Rico after the Spanish-American War

After the groups have met they can share their ideas with the rest of the class. Students will then write a proposal for or against the action of the United States.

CHAPTER THIRTEEN

The Twenties

INTRODUCTION

A *time of* contrast, the twenties ran the gamut of experience from flappers to the Woman's Christian Temperance Union and from the gangsters of Chicago to the resurgence of fundamentalism in the Bible Belt. As great change such as women's suffrage began, we also had the Scopes Trial and the reappearance of the Ku Klux Klan. It was a decade in which Americans let their hair down, so to speak, and did their very best to forget the horrors of World War I and all the complications that come with world entanglements.

The twenties were especially vivid in terms of sight and sound – movies, jazz, sports. We filled this chapter with as many opportunities as possible for the students to recreate the sounds and life force of this decade.

PROJECT LIST

1. Make a scrapbook of fads of the twenties. You may include original drawings, magazine pictures, and selected photocopies from books. All illustrations must be explained.
2. Make a model of the *Spirit of St. Louis.*
3. Write a play about the Scopes trial or the trial of Sacco and Vanzetti.
4. Make up a radio script for a mystery involving the Palmer Raids.
5. Using jazz of the twenties as background music, write a radio show about life in this decade.
6. Make a map, globe, or mobile illustrating Lindbergh's flight from New York to Paris.
7. Make a poster of clothing fashions of the twenties.
8. Make samples of clothing of the twenties. This can be extended into a fashion show accompanied by jazz of the twenties.

143

9. Using poster board, draw or make samples of fashion accessories of the twenties, such as jewelry, hats, and handbags.

10. Use research to write an hourly log of Lindbergh's historic flight. Include what you think his feelings were.

11. Pretend you are a flapper. Make a calendar or diary of all your activities for a month.

12. Write a biography about a famous sports hero, movie star of the silent screen, or jazz artist.

13. Make up a department store catalogue of items for sale in any year of the twenties. You may include clothing, home furnishings, and appliances, along with prices and descriptions.

14. Make a model of the elaborate lobby of a movie theater of this decade.

15. Make a sales brochure for a Ford dealer in the twenties.

16. Write a research report on immigration laws that were passed in the twenties. Discuss what their major intent seems to have been and why they were passed.

17. Write a research report or radio script about the activities of the Ku Klux Klan during this era.

18. Do research on Al Capone and the Chicago gangs. Make up a movie script about their activities.

19. Make a booklet of newspaper front pages that covers a specific event or topic from start to finish. Any of the following would be suitable:
    (a) The Scopes Trial
    (b) Sacco and Vanzetti
    (c) Outstanding Sports Events
    (d) The Suffragette Movement
    (e) The Teapot Dome Scandal
    (f) The Presidency of Warren Harding
    (g) The Presidency of Calvin Coolidge

20. Draw a series of cartoons illustrating life under Prohibition.

21. Make up a short story or play using slang vocabulary of the twenties. Students may refer to Volume III of the Time-Life Series *This Fabulous Century*.

HOMEWORK ASSIGNMENTS

WHY THE TWENTIES ROARED

1. Pretend you are living during the twenties. Write a speech for or against women getting the right to vote.

2. Make up a dialogue between an angry mother and her rebellious flapper daughter. The mother is angry about her daughter's wild behavior.

3. Make up a rap song about fun in the "roaring twenties."

4. Make a list, diagram, or cartoon of tricks that stunt flyers could do.

5. Make an illustrated advertisement for a flying circus.

6. Make up a cheer or chant for Babe Ruth.

7. Imagine that you could go back to the twenties and see Babe Ruth play. Write a paragraph describing what would excite you the most.

8. Write a journal entry describing your first car ride.

9. Which activities of the twenties would have interested you the most? Why? Choose from: flagpole sitting, silent movies, jazz clubs, or any other activities discussed in class.

10. Make a shopping list of items that a flapper might buy.

11. Make up a sales pitch to convince a shopper to buy a Model T Ford on credit.

THE OTHER SIDE OF THE TWENTIES

1. Pretend you are either Clarence Darrow or William Jennings Bryan. Make up an opening speech for the trial of John Scopes.

2. Why was the Scopes trial nicknamed "The Monkey Trial"?

3. Do you think Sacco and Vanzetti were guilty? Explain. Do you think they would be found guilty if their trial were held today? Explain.

4. Write a newspaper editorial for or against the Palmer Raids.

5. Why was the Ku Klux Klan so afraid of black people after World War I?

6. Make up a newscast for a day in 1925. Include the following topics:
   (a) A Palmer Raid
   (b) Ku Klux Klan
   (c) Crash of an airmail plane
   (d) Beauty contest

7. Explain this statement: "Americans of the twenties both loved and fought against new ideas."

8. Pretend you are a senator. Explain to your constituency why you voted to limit immigration.

9. Why would a soldier returning from World War I want us to follow a foreign policy of isolationism?

PROHIBITION

1. Make up a secret password message that can be used during Prohibition to get someone into a speakeasy.

2. Make up a short story about a Chicago gang led by Al Capone that is planning to deliver some moonshine liquor.

3. Pretend you are a police officer in the twenties. Explain to your superior officer why you are having such a hard time arresting people who break the Prohibition law.

4. Make a cartoon illustrating one way that people broke the Prohibition law.

5. Compare the enforcement of Prohibition to the enforcement of marijuana laws today.

6. Make up a conversation between two people deciding whether they should or should not go to a speakeasy.

7. If you were an undercover agent during Prohibition, what would you have done to enforce the law? You may write your answer or do it in cartoon form.

8. (To be used with Classroom Activity 5) Prepare a list of questions for a roundtable discussion on the pros and cons of Prohibition.

9. Why did Izzie Einstein and Moe Smith stand out as law enforcement officers?

THE STOCK MARKET CRASH

1. If you could invest in the stock market today, which company would you invest in? Why?

2. Pretend you have just lost everything in the stock market crash. Describe your feelings.

3. Explain how buying on margin led to the stock market crash.

4. Make up a newspaper headline and article for October 29, 1929.

CLASSROOM ACTIVITY 1

HISTORY REPEATS ITSELF

Problems faced by people in the twenties were similar to many of those faced by people today.

The teacher may reproduce the following list or simply read it aloud and let the students raise their hands to indicate whether they feel the problem is or is not one that is faced by people today. If they feel the problem is not one faced by people today, they can go on to the next problem. If they feel the problem is similar to today's problems, then the teacher can pursue the discussion with such questions as:

1. Why do you think so?
2. Have you read about, or experienced, anything similar? What?
3. Do you feel this is a serious problem? Explain.

PROBLEMS

1. Parents feel their children are staying out too late.
2. Crime is on the rise.
3. Drunkenness is a serious problem these days.
4. Respected people are suddenly found to be taking bribes.
5. People are risking their savings by gambling on stocks.
6. People are spending money unnecessarily on things they don't need.
7. Young people spend too much time listening to the radio instead of doing their homework.
8. Women are spending less time at home being wives and mothers.
9. Young people are going out in cars and it is unsafe.
10. People are going to bars or speakeasies and breaking the law.
11. Today's new popular music is terrible, and it is ruining our young people.
12. Organized crime is a serious problem today.
13. "Nice" girls shouldn't smoke, wear tight skirts, or drink.

CLASSROOM ACTIVITY 2

SOUND EFFECTS

Radio was the new form of entertainment in the twenties. Everyone listened. There was no TV. Since there were no visual images, sound effects people were especially important.

Divide the class into groups of three or four and have them figure out ways to imitate sounds. For example: the sound of fire can be made by crumpling paper. Each group can decide what sounds they want to imitate. If they have difficulty coming up with ideas, the teacher may want to suggest the following:

1. Thunder
2. Rain
3. People running
4. Ambulance
5. Bird
6. Wind
7. Car starting

The class can then guess what each sound represents. As a follow-up activity, the students may enjoy writing a short radio script using sound effects and then presenting it to the rest of the class or to another class.

CLASSROOM ACTIVITY 3

TIME CAPSULE

The twenties was a decade of new things, of fun, of outrageous activities, and of new inventions and products. As a review, the students can name objects, for a time capsule, that are representative of life in the twenties. The teacher may begin with an example or go directly to volunteers in the class. The objects can be discussed in terms of how they changed or affected people's lives.

CLASSROOM ACTIVITY 4

SEEING THE OPPOSITE POINT OF VIEW

New things do not have the same value for everyone. Using the objects mentioned in Classroom Activity 3, the teacher will have the students take the point of view of someone who opposes them. They can be given a few minutes to write down their reasons for objecting to these new products. They can then come forward as if they were on a TV talk show and present their points of view. The teacher may even choose to have the other students argue back, as members of the audience.

CLASSROOM ACTIVITY 5

ROUNDTABLE DISCUSSION ABOUT PROHIBITION

This activity is to be used after the students understand the basics about Prohibition. The teacher will assign Homework 8 from the Prohibition section before starting this activity.

Student volunteers will participate in a roundtable discussion, but they must do it by choosing a role and representing the point of view of the character whose role they are taking on. They may choose from the following characters. The teacher may substitute or add others.

1. A member or leader of the Woman's Christian Temperance Union
2. A figure involved in organized crime
3. A Fundamentalist preacher
4. The owner of a speakeasy that was closed down
5. The chief of police
6. A flapper
7. A state senator who voted against Prohibition
8. A state senator who voted for Prohibition

The panelists will be seated in front of the room. Name cards should identify each one in terms of the character represented. The students may enjoy making up names for themselves and these should also be printed on the name cards.

The rest of the class can question the panelists by using the questions they prepared in Homework 8. If the class runs out of questions or is unprepared, the following questions may be used:

1. How do you feel about Prohibition? Are you in favor of it or against it? Why?
2. What do you think will happen if Prohibition ends?
3. What do you think will happen if Prohibition goes on?
4. How do you think Prohibition is affecting teenagers today?
5. As you know, many people break the Prohibition law. Why do you think they do that?

CLASSROOM ACTIVITY 6

YOU ARE THE JURY

The teacher will choose twelve volunteers to act as a jury. He or she will tell the story of the Scopes trial. The volunteers will be instructed to deliberate and reach a unanimous verdict.

The teacher may do the same thing with the Sacco and Vanzetti trial.

CLASSROOM ACTIVITY 7

INVESTING IN THE STOCK MARKET[1]

Investing in the stock market was very popular during the twenties because stocks kept going up and it seemed as if everyone was making money.

While this activity involves a little extra preparation on the part of the teacher, the student involvement and excitement that ensues make it well worth the effort.

The teacher will make a large wall chart listing the names of every student in the class. It will include vertical columns with headings that say: Student, Stock, Price, Date Bought. A number of blank columns should be included alongside these in order to fill in the prices of the stocks during the next few weeks.

Photocopies of the stock market page from a current newspaper should be distributed to the class. After the students understand how to read it, each one will choose a stock. They may discuss why they prefer one stock over another. It would be best for each one to choose a different stock. Each stock and the price will be listed next to the student's name on the large wall chart. The chart can be posted on a bulletin board that is easily accessible to the teacher and the students. One day each week can be established when either the teacher or the students (depending on the ability and responsibility of the class) will write down the prices of the stocks for that day.

This activity should culminate when the class is ready to study the stock market crash. Each student will calculate how much money he or she lost or gained. Students enjoy monitoring their own investments. The teacher will find that the students get very excited when they visually see their

---

[1]We thank Jerry Correll, a colleague at our school, for this idea.

stock going up in value and that they get upset when they see they are losing money.

An additional exercise can be to have the students keep a log of their feelings and reactions to the changes in the value of their stocks. Did they want to sell? Buy more? Did they panic? Did they wish they had bought something else?

The teacher can make use of current trends to have classroom discussions about the stock market.

CHAPTER FOURTEEN

The Great Depression

INTRODUCTION

The Great Depression was a time of poverty and misery for many people in this country. Most textbooks offer some insight into the causes and solutions to the depression but do not tell enough about the lives of the people.

Many of the problems faced by people during the depression are the same as those faced by large numbers of people today. We feel that students should be able to empathize with the problems faced by others in order to develop sensitivity and courage of their own. The assignments in this chapter attempt to open the students' hearts as well as their minds.

PROJECT LIST

1. Construct a Hooverville.
2. After doing research, write a short play, story, or series of poems dealing with how people lived and felt during the depression.
3. Read *The Grapes of Wrath* by John Steinbeck. Do one of the assignments below:
   (a) Write a report on the book. Include how the family's life was changed by the events of the depression, how they dealt with their problems, and your own feelings about the characters and events of the book.
   (b) Do a booklet of drawings to illustrate the main events of the book.
   (c) Write a play based on the book.
4. Using research from the thirties and magazines and newspapers of today, write a report comparing the problems of today's homeless people with those faced by people during the depression. You may also compare problems of farmers and problems of the unemployed.

5. If you have a relative or neighbor who lived during the depression, do an interview about their personal memories of that time. Prepare questions before the interview but also build on their answers to your questions. This interview may be taped.

6. Read about the Bonus Expeditionary Force's march on Washington D.C. in 1932. Write a newspaper that will feature the march as its headline. Include articles about speeches by Bonus Army leaders, response of the administration, General MacArthur's attack, Hoover's response. Also include an editorial, letters to the editor expressing more than one point of view, a few ads from this time, an agony column, and other relevant news items. This would be best as a group project.

7. Prepare a series of graphs showing wages and prices before, during, and shortly after the depression. Include costs of food items, appliances, luxuries, and basics such as clothing and rent.

8. Do research on the New Deal and its programs to end the depression. For each program write the following:
    (a) What problems existed during the depression that this program tried to solve?
    (b) How did this program attempt to solve this?
    (c) How successful was it?

9. Read about Herbert Hoover's philosophy and actions during the depression. Prepare a debate between him and Franklin Delano Roosevelt. Include questions by a moderator and both men's answers.

10. Make a collage showing activities of the depression. Include everything you can find that had an effect on people's lives, such as entertainment, leisure activities, breadlines, freight car hopping, and so forth.

11. Do a glossary of terms from the depression. Illustrate and explain such terms as breadline, Hooverville, dust bowl, Okie, soup kitchen, and so forth.

12. Write a paper dealing with ways in which the New Deal contradicted the spirit of laissez-faire. Include your opinion on the necessity and results of the New Deal.

13. Make a scrapbook of current newspaper and magazine articles that illustrate problems of today that existed during the Great Depression.

14. Do a photo-essay, with your comments, showing the effects that the recession of the nineties has had on the lives of people around you or the area where you live.

HOMEWORK ASSIGNMENTS

EFFECTS ON PEOPLE

1. Write a page in your diary describing a day of job hunting.
2. Draw or describe in writing a farm in the dust bowl. What problems did these farmers face?
3. Write a short story or poem using as many of the following terms as possible: breadline, dust bowl, freight car hopping, eviction, Okie, migrant, buying a job.
4. Why did emigration figures rise during the depression? Would you have left the country? Why? Why not?
5. This is a week's assignment:
   (a) Keep a budget journal of money you spend for a full week.
   (b) Pretend that amount must be cut in half. Write what you would be willing to give up.
   (c) Now cut it in half again. Record your feelings.
6. Make a list of inconveniences of living in a Hooverville or shanty town.
7. Why do you think farmers dumped their food and milk instead of just giving it away?
8. Pretend that you are jobless and homeless. Write a diary entry of your innermost thoughts about Hoover and the government.
9. You arrive at your bank and discover that it's closed for good. Write a letter to a friend describing how you feel.
10. Pretend there's a depression now. Make a list of things you would buy to feed your family using five dollars. Attempt the most nutritious meal possible.
11. Choose one of the following situations and describe how you would feel and all the actions you might take:
    (a) You lost your job because someone was willing to take it for less money.
    (b) The landlord just told you that unless you pay your back and current rent, you and your family will be evicted.
    (c) You are hungry and have no money.
12. Why do you think escapist entertainment was popular during the depression? What are some forms of escapism today?
13. Pretend you own a small store or factory. Write a letter to your employees explaining why you must lower their wages.

THE NEW DEAL

1. What do you think Franklin Delano Roosevelt meant by, "The only thing we have to fear is fear itself"? Do you agree? What were some of the things people feared during the depression?
2. Would you have voted for Franklin Delano Roosevelt? Explain.
3. Make a list of occupations that were helped by the W.P.A.
4. Pretend that you are part of the C.C.C. Write a letter home describing what you do.
5. Write a letter to the editor explaining your reasons for wanting the government to repeal Prohibition as a way to help end the depression.
6. Pretend that you are Franklin Delano Roosevelt. Write a fireside chat for broadcast on the radio.
7. If you were a bank manager, what would you tell your old depositors to convince them to trust your bank and begin saving there again?
8. Make a list of all the things you can think of in wartime that would create jobs.
9. How does preparation for war stimulate the economy? Illustrate this or diagram it beginning with one munitions factory.
10. Do you think the New Deal would have ended the depression even if World War II had not occurred? Explain.
11. Which program of the New Deal do you think was most helpful? Why?
12. Make a list of ideas to end the depression that were not used in the New Deal.

CLASSROOM ACTIVITY 1

CONTINUE THE STORY

This activity can work well in committee form or as a teacher-directed activity. The teacher begins the story (some examples are listed below). Then each student adds a sentence as they go around the room. If using committees, each committee will write its own story and then share with the class.

SAMPLE STARTERS

1. Mr. Jones lost his job in a hat factory and can't pay the rent.

2. The bank foreclosed on the Smith's farm. The family is suddenly homeless after generations of life in the same place.
3. Joyce saw her father selling apples on a street corner.

CLASSROOM ACTIVITY 2

HOW WOULD YOU FEEL IF . . . ?

The teacher may ask the questions below as part of a classroom discussion or may reproduce them and use the questions for a writing assignment. If students write their answers, time should be allowed for sharing their responses with the class. How Would You Feel If . . .

1. You are walking home from school and discover your mother in a breadline.
2. Your father leaves for work every day, but one day you see him in an employment line and realize he's been lying about having a job.
3. Your parents ask you to help the family by selling your prized stamp collection (or coin collection, bicycle, or anything else students care about).
4. Your aunt and uncle have lost their home and will be moving in with you. Your cousin will now share your room.

CLASSROOM ACTIVITY 3

MEETING WITH PRESIDENT HOOVER

President Hoover believed in rugged individualism and did not want any policies that might create dependence on the government. In this activity one student will portray Hoover. Other students may take the roles of advocates for aid needed by distressed farmers, the unemployed, the old, and the homeless. Students will act out the meeting.

If the class is advanced and understands Hoover's policies toward business, the teacher may add a fifth advocate to the meeting, someone trying to help businesses on the verge of failing.

CLASSROOM ACTIVITY 4

EXPERIENCING THE DEPRESSION

Students will understand more fully how people felt if they role-play certain depression experiences. Suggested situations are:

1. Three people standing in a breadline
2. Someone applying for a visa to leave the country
3. A worker offering to buy a job while a second worker stands by
4. A father (or older brother) telling his family why he's leaving home to try to find work
5. A group of people riding in a freight car
6. A family explaining to their child why she or he must leave college
7. A father or mother showing a child how to stuff cardboard in shoes to avoid resoling

CLASSROOM ACTIVITY 5

VIEWING PICTURES

Many collections of photographs have captured the sorrow, despair, and hopelessness plus the fight and spunk of the people who lived during the depression. The teacher may set up pictures around the room or use a book, such as *This Fabulous Century* 1930–1940, Time/Life Books, Volume IV.

Here are some suggested approaches.

1. Students and teacher may discuss the pictures one at a time. Some questions might include:
   (a) What is the mood of this picture?
   (b) Does anything disturb you?
   (c) Does anything remind you of today?
2. The teacher can show the pictures and have the students write down the first words that come to mind. The class will then read their reactions and discuss them. A follow-up to this would be to allow the students to develop their thoughts and reactions into poems or essays.

CLASSROOM ACTIVITY 6

TOWN MEETING

This activity would work well as the class reaches its study of the New Deal. It would be best to do it before actually teaching the solutions brought about by the Roosevelt administration.

Students will be told to imagine that they are all part of a town meeting. They might choose to be farmers, bankers, workers, storekeepers, married or unmarried, with or without children. They are at the meeting to discuss the problems brought about by the depression and to attempt to make suggestions for solving them. One or two students will act as secretaries. After the teacher has taught the New Deal, it would be very interesting to go back and reread the results of this town meeting.

CLASSROOM ACTIVITY 7

NEW DEAL HIT PARADE

This activity will help reinforce the concepts behind the various New Deal programs. The teacher will divide the class into groups and have each group come up with a list of New Deal Hit Parade song titles that reflect the goals of each of the following programs: TVA, CCC, AAA, NRA, FDIC, PWA, SSA, and REA.

As an alternative or additional activity students may enjoy writing a rap song or cheer with their group. When they are done they can perform their work.

CHAPTER FIFTEEN

World War II

INTRODUCTION

World War II involves more than just battles and battlefields. The concentration camps of Europe, the Japanese internment camps in the United States, and the decision to drop the atomic bomb are among the most devastating chapters in world history. Because the events of the era had such far-reaching effects, the students must be given ample time and opportunity to analyze and evaluate the material.

This chapter in U.S. history is very complex. Most Americans enthusiastically supported the war effort and our involvement. Once the war was over, Americans began to ask some critical questions about our wartime policies in terms of our treatment of Japanese-Americans and our decision to drop the atomic bomb. We want the students to understand both the patriotism of the time and the long-range effects created by the decisions made during the war.

PROJECT LIST

1. Pretend you are a Japanese commander. Write out the orders (including maps) that you will give to those airmen assigned to attack Pearl Harbor.
2. Make a poster showing the equipment issued to marines, soldiers, sailors, and air force men of the United States.
3. Make a map showing all the places where American troops fought.
4. Choose one year of the war. Make up a series of front pages of your local newspaper and cover some of the major events of the war that year.
5. Pretend you are a soldier in World War II. Write a diary telling about an invasion or battle that you participated in.

6. Pretend you are a soldier fighting on one of the following fronts:
   (a) The Pacific
   (b) North Africa
   (c) Europe
   Write a diary describing your surroundings and your activities.

7. Write a series of poems, short stories, or songs describing the life and feelings of a World War II soldier.

8. Make a map and accompanying description of one major American battle strategy of World War II.

9. Make a handbook called *This Is Army Life* outlining all the things that soldiers will encounter in their training period.

10. Make a poster of insignias representing the specializations of different members of the armed forces.

11. Make a program for a Christmas show with live entertainment for the soldiers overseas in World War II.

12. Pretend you were captured by the enemy, either in Europe or in the Pacific. Write a memoir of your experiences in a prisoner of war camp.

13. Make a model of a World War II airplane, ship, or aircraft carrier.

14. Write a report on segregation in the United States armed forces of World War II.

15. Make up a series of illustrated advertisements for commercial war films that served as propaganda and were made during World War II.

16. Write a book report on a novel dealing with World War II. In your report you can include:
    (a) A very brief summary of the plot
    (b) How the war affects the lives of the characters
    (c) Specific incidents or scenes that moved you, and why
    (d) What the author's point of view is

17. Make a poster or scrapbook illustrating all the ways civilians tried to help in the war effort.

18. Pretend you are living here during World War II. Write a series of letters to your brother who is fighting overseas. Describe how the war is affecting your life. You may include such things as air raids, rationing, scrap collections, and victory gardens.

19. Make an advertising supplement for your local newspaper with help wanted ads describing jobs that are available for women during the war.

20. Make up a week's menus based on ration coupons for a family of four or for your family.

21. Pretend you are a Japanese-American who was kept in an internment camp. Write a diary of your experiences and feelings.

22. Make a map of the United States showing the locations of all the Japanese internment camps.

23. Make a diorama of one specific Japanese internment camp.

24. Write a play about a family of Japanese-Americans which depicts what they went through as they got ready to go to an internment camp.

25. Research the attempts by Jewish leaders to help bring the Jewish victims of Nazism to the United States.

26. Pretend you are a war correspondent in World War II. Write a series of news releases describing the liberation of a concentration camp in Europe.

27. Write a report about either the development of the atomic bomb or the decision to drop it.

28. Make a poster showing medals that were given to war heroes. They should be hand-drawn.

29. Make up a calendar for the war years which highlights:
    (a) Holidays celebrating significant American battle victories
    (b) Memorial days in remembrance of battles in which many American lives were lost.

30. Write a research report on the Nuremberg Trials.

31. Some people say that Roosevelt gave in to Stalin on too many issues at Yalta in 1945. Do a research report and decide whether you agree or disagree.

32. Make a chart illustrating all the main parts of the United Nations and explain what their roles are.

33. Do a research report which discusses and weighs the strengths and weaknesses of the United Nations.

34. Write a short story describing the end of World War II and what would have happened to the United States and Japan if the atomic bomb had not been dropped.

35. Use newspapers and periodicals to research the role of the United Nations in world affairs today. Write your opinion on whether the United Nations is really fulfilling its role as a peacemaking organization.

HOMEWORK ASSIGNMENTS

EVENTS THAT GOT US INTO THE WAR

1. Make up a dialogue between an isolationist and someone who feels that we must get involved in the war.

2. Make up a balance sheet of reasons why we should or should not get involved in the war.

3. Make a political cartoon for or against getting involved in the war.

4. Pretend you are President Roosevelt. Make a radio speech for the American people explaining why you support the Lend-Lease Bill.

5. Make up a series of slogans in favor of the Lend-Lease policy.

6. Should the United States have declared war on the Nazis earlier? Explain.

7. Could the United States have done more to help the Jewish people in Europe? Explain.

8. Write a headline and newspaper article describing the surprise attack on Pearl Harbor.

9. How do you think the following Americans might have reacted to the attack on Pearl Harbor?
   (a) A small child
   (b) A nineteen-year-old man
   (c) His mother

10. Describe the attack on Pearl Harbor from Japan's point of view.

THE HOME FRONT

1. Imagine your family during an air raid drill. How do you think each member would feel and act?

2. Make a poster to get people to support the war effort and buy war bonds.

3. Make a list of all the scrap items today that you could save for recycling. What would they be used for?

4. Make a diagram for a victory garden. Label it.

5. Make up an advertisement calling for volunteers to work as air raid wardens. Describe the job and the qualifications needed for it.

6. Write a letter to your mayor explaining why you would make a good air raid warden.

7. Make up a dialogue between a boy and his girlfriend in which the boy explains why he is enlisting in the army.

8. Make up a rap song which tells the reasons why Americans support the war effort.

9. Make a greeting card to cheer up and encourage a friend in the army.

10. Write a letter to your senator explaining why you are for or against the 5 percent Victory tax on all income.

11. What problems did women face as they filled men's jobs during the war? How would you have handled these problems?

12. Make up an election poster to re-elect Roosevelt for a fourth term of office.

OVERSEAS

1. Pretend you are a bomber pilot. Make up a name and an illustration to put on your plane.

2. You are a soldier fighting on a Pacific island. Write a letter to your family or girlfriend describing your feelings.

3. Make a list of all the things you would miss most if you were sent overseas to fight. Try to put them into categories: people, things, sounds, smells, and experiences.

4. Imagine what it was like to be stationed on a ship in the Pacific. Make a list of all the things that you would find strange.

5. If you could interview a soldier who was fighting the Nazis or the Japanese, what questions would you ask him?

6. Make a list of all the non-combatant jobs that a WAC could do.

7. Prepare for a debate: During wartime it is often necessary to bomb cities.

JAPANESE INTERNMENT CAMPS

1. Pretend you are a Japanese-American. You have just been informed that you are being sent to an internment camp. Write a page in your diary describing your feelings.

2. You are a Japanese-American boy. Write a letter to President Roosevelt telling him why you want to be allowed to fight in the armed forces.

3. If you had to get rid of all the things you couldn't carry with you to an internment camp, which things would it be most painful for you to part with? Why?

4. If you were a Japanese-American living in California in 1942, what would have hurt you the most about being relocated?

5. Write a newspaper editorial explaining why your paper feels that the imprisonment of Japanese-Americans is just or unjust.

6. Make a list of rights that you believe were violated when Japanese-Americans were imprisoned.

THE END OF THE WAR

1. Make up an agenda for the Yalta Conference.
2. Why was it difficult for Stalin, Churchill, and Roosevelt to reach agreements when they met at Yalta?
3. Make a political cartoon showing Stalin, Churchill, and Roosevelt at Yalta.
4. Pretend you are a newspaper reporter. Make up a list of questions that you would ask Stalin, Churchill, and Roosevelt at the end of the Yalta Conference.
5. Make up an obituary for Franklin Delano Roosevelt.
6. Describe how you think Truman felt facing his first day of work as president after the death of Roosevelt.
7. Did we do the right thing in using the atomic bomb to end the war, or should we have continued fighting knowing that many thousands more American soldiers would have died? Explain.
8. If you had been on the crew of the *Enola Gay*, how do you think you would have felt?
9. Make up a statement to go on a memorial plaque for the victims of the atomic bombs dropped on Hiroshima and Nagasaki.
10. If you had been there to liberate the Nazi concentration camps, what do you think you would have said to and done for the first prisoners you met?
11. What was the significance of the Nuremberg Trials?
12. Pretend you are a prosecutor at the Nuremberg Trials. Make a statement explaining why you feel the Nazi leaders should be condemned as criminals.
13. The United Nations has been unsuccessful at stopping wars. Why do we continue to participate in it?

CLASSROOM ACTIVITY 1

GROUP DECISION MAKING

This activity is designed to help the students understand the impact of the Japanese relocation camps on the Japanese-Americans who were sent to internment camps. It is divided into several parts. The students will have to exchange ideas, compromise, and then express their feelings about the process. The age and level of maturity of the class will determine the end results.

The teacher will tell the students to imagine that they are Japanese-Americans living in California in 1942 and their family receives the order to report to an evacuation center for relocation at an internment camp. They are to bring along only the things they can carry. The teacher will divide the class into groups of four or five. Within each group, the students must assume the role of a different family member: mother, father, children, and possibly a grandparent. Every group must choose one "parent" to act as the group leader. They must make a list of all the things they have to do in order to get ready for their relocation. This list may include disposing of possessions, saying goodbye to friends, dealing with jobs, and deciding what they can and cannot take with them.

The teacher will walk around to each group and remind them that in their roles each one may have different things that are important to them. They should be reassured that there are no specific right or wrong items on the list and encouraged to include even seemingly unimportant details such as returning library books. It will be helpful for them to use their own lives as a frame of reference and consider some of the things they would have to resolve if they were personally involved in such an affair today.

When their lists are completed, they will share their results with the rest of the class. After they have heard all the lists, the teacher may want to hold a short discussion. This can be followed by an independent writing assignment to be started in class and completed at home, depending on the time available. The students can write a journal describing their feelings about the group activity they just participated in. They may want to include:

1. How they felt about working with their group
2. How they felt about preparing the lists
3. Whether or not they felt the other members of the group considered their needs and feelings

CLASSROOM ACTIVITY 2

REACTION REGISTER

We all react in a very personal way to different events depending upon who we are, how we live, and what our life experiences have been. The teacher will list the following feelings on the chalkboard so that the students can see them and weigh them throughout the course of this activity: happy, sad, angry, frustrated, afraid. He or she may want to add some others or delete some, depending upon the nature or maturity of the class.

As the following statements are read aloud, the students can register their feelings by raising their hands. As the teacher goes through the list, he or she can engage the class in discussion with the following questions:

1. Why does this make you feel this way?
2. Have you ever had a similar experience that gave you the same feeling?

STATEMENTS

1. Without warning, the Japanese attacked our naval base at Pearl Harbor.
2. The attack by the Japanese occurred early on a Sunday morning.
3. Franklin Delano Roosevelt was elected for a fourth term of office.
4. We don't want to get involved in the war between the Axis and the Allies, but we are lending the Allies war supplies.
5. Your class in school will begin planting a victory garden.
6. Your mother is going to work as a riveter in a factory.
7. We can only buy three gallons of gasoline for our cars each week.
8. All the letters sent home by soldiers are censored.
9. Your next-door neighbor's son was killed in the Philippines.
10. You can't have meat for dinner because your mother ran out of ration coupons.
11. Your best friend has enlisted in the marines.
12. Your sister has joined the WACS.
13. A Japanese-American student in your school is being sent to an internment camp.
14. You read that we are dropping bombs on the city of Dresden.
15. You read that we dropped the atomic bomb on Hiroshima.
16. You read that we dropped another atomic bomb on Nagasaki.
17. You read that Jews were being exterminated in concentration camps in Europe.
18. You read that American prisoners of war were being treated cruelly by the enemy.
19. You saw a picture of our men putting the American flag up at Iwo Jima.
20. You just read about Kamikazi pilots sinking an aircraft carrier.
21. Because of rationing, you couldn't have any butter on your bread.
22. You just found out your next-door neighbor is selling black market sugar.

CLASSROOM ACTIVITY 3

PANEL DISCUSSION ON ALTERNATIVES

This activity will enable students to evaluate the pros and cons of a controversial issue by discussion, pooling of ideas, and active presentation.

World War II seemed to be dragging out interminably, and the Japanese did not even seem to be near surrender. President Truman had to evaluate all the possible strategies for ending the war.

The following activity will be divided into two parts. The first part will involve group work, and the second part will consist of a panel discussion in which one member of each group will be chosen by the other members to express their ideas. The issue to be discussed is: what can be done to end the war with Japan? Divide the class into discussion groups. Each group will discuss the advantages and disadvantages of one of the following methods of ending the war with Japan.

1. Drop the atomic bomb on Japan.
2. Warn the Japanese of our plan to drop the bomb, and explain in detail what will happen to them if it is dropped.
3. Invite the Japanese leaders to a demonstration of an atomic bomb explosion on a deserted island.
4. Keep on fighting in the same way and invade Japan.
5. Make a deal with Japan. They can keep everything they've conquered, as long as they agree to stop fighting and stay out of American territory.

Each group can outline the pros and cons of their alternative. One person should record ideas in list form. When they are done, they can vote on one person to represent their committee in a panel discussion moderated by the teacher. After they have all had a chance to make their presentations, the rest of the class can comment or question members of the panel. The class can then vote on what they think is the best alternative.

For homework, or as a follow-up writing activity, the students can write their opinions as to what they think is the best way to end the war with Japan.

CLASSROOM ACTIVITY 4

PUBLIC SERVICE ADVERTISING CAMPAIGN

During World War II, there was strong public support for the war effort. Have the students work in groups to make either a radio advertisement or a poster for one of the following campaigns:

1. Buy war bonds.
2. Don't waste food or fuel.
3. Save scrap metal and rubber.
4. Join the armed forces.
5. Plant a victory garden.
6. Don't buy on the black market.

When they are done, the students can present their advertisements and posters to the class.

CLASSROOM ACTIVITY 5

DEAR MR. PRESIDENT

Have the students write letters to President Roosevelt in which they express their feelings, doubts, or questions from the point of view of one of the following:

1. A distraught mother whose only son has been drafted into the army
2. A conscientious objector who has received his draft notification
3. A black soldier who questions the policy of segregating the troops
4. A storekeeper requesting stricter law enforcement against black marketeers
5. A Japanese-American citizen who is being sent to an internment camp

After the students have finished writing their letters, they will be collected. The teacher will distribute the letters to the class at random. The students will write a response to their letters as if they were President Roosevelt. The next day it might be fun to read the letters and the responses aloud.

CLASSROOM ACTIVITY 6

ELECTION CAMPAIGN OF ROOSEVELT VERSUS DEWEY

When Roosevelt ran for his fourth term of office, there was a great deal of controversy over his candidacy. On the one hand, a continuity of leadership in wartime was of great importance, but on the other hand, the idea of one man retaining the office for four consecutive terms seemed incompatible with democratic principles.

The class can be divided in half to prepare campaigns for the two candidates, Roosevelt and Dewey. Once they are divided in half, the teacher can subdivide them into smaller more workable groups, and each group can be assigned a task:

1. Write a campaign speech.
2. Make a campaign poster.
3. Design a campaign button.
4. Make up a print advertisement.
5. Make up a campaign song.

When they are done, the students can present their material. When the presentations are over, the students can vote for the candidate of their choice.

CLASSROOM ACTIVITY 7

HIROSHIMA NO PIKA

The teacher will read aloud the book *Hiroshima No Pika* by Toshi Maruki, published by Lothrop, Lee & Shepard Books, New York. Although this is a book written for young children, it will move individuals of any age group. The teacher should be aware that this may lead to an emotional discussion with the students. However, we feel that this is a very important activity.

As an alternative to a class discussion, the students may write their reactions to the book. The teacher might prefer to give point of view writing to help the students focus. An example would be for students to pretend they are one of the crew on the plane that dropped the bomb. Write a letter to the family in the story either explaining why or apologizing for your act.

CHAPTER SIXTEEN

The Post-War Years: 1945–1959

INTRODUCTION

The post-war years of 1945 to 1959 have often been characterized as colorless, with people moving to the suburbs, fearing both communism and the House Un-American Activities Committee, focusing on buying material things, and conformity. Yet, it was also a time of commitment to other nations in the world, a time of civil rights and Martin Luther King, Jr., a time when Edward R. Murrow could speak out against Joseph McCarthy on television. It was a time of tentative beginnings amidst fear and apathy.

Many U.S. history teachers have difficulty teaching this period as they plow through a crowded curriculum. Yet the fifties form the bedrock for a future of civil rights, individualism, and radical changes in taste. They also hold the roots of the war in Vietnam and the problems of nuclear power.

Our assignments cover both the frivolous and serious aspects of the time.

PROJECT LIST

1. Write a short story or play describing the problems and experiences of a G.I. returning home from the war.
2. Write a manual to help the displaced persons arriving from Europe adjust to life in the United States.
3. Write a radio newscript describing one of the major strikes that occurred soon after World War II. Include concerns and points of view of both sides, interviews with bosses and workers, and opinions of concerned citizens who are affected by the strike.
4. Make a booklet of all the treaties the United States made after World War II from 1945–1950. Describe their intent.

5. Make a map of the world showing all the countries with which the United States made treaties immediately after World War II.

6. Make a collage showing fads of the fifties.

7. Make a poster showing fashions of the fifties.

8. Make a poster or booklet with original artwork for record jackets of hit songs of the fifties.

9. Write a short story or play describing teenage interests and activities during the fifties.

10. Choose any week during the fifties. After doing research, create a TV program guide with actual programs of that week. Write short descriptions of the programs.

11. Do a diorama or an architect's blueprint of a fallout shelter.

12. Write a report on the role of the United States in the Korean conflict. Include reasons for our heavy participation, military involvement, and the feelings of the people back home.

13. Make a special supplement for a newspaper covering the entire trial of Ethel and Julius Rosenberg. Include an editorial, letters to the editor, and all of the facts you have researched.

14. Read a book by an author from the Beat Generation, such as Jack Kerouac. What do you think *beat* means? How is this shown in the book you read?

15. Research any famous person from the fifties. Write a script for a TV show such as *This Is Your Life*. Include surprise guests from this person's past, friends and relatives, and people who will describe his or her accomplishments.

16. Make an illustrated dictionary of fifties' memorabilia.

17. Make up an autograph book signed by famous and infamous people of the fifties. Include what you think they would write.

18. Make a poster or booklet with original drawings of automobiles of the fifties.

19. Write your own script for a TV show about McCarthyism.

20. The boycott in Montgomery, Alabama, had many heroes and heroines. Write a paper about the roles of the little people as well as the more famous ones.

21. After researching the Montgomery bus boycott and the role of Martin Luther King, Jr., write a paper on whether events or people are most important in history. Use the situation in Montgomery for examples to back up your thesis.

22. Choose any event that was important in our foreign relations in the

fifties (for example, the Suez Crisis) and write a research paper describing who was involved, what events occurred, and what was the position of the United States.

23. Do research on the effect McCarthyism had on one individual's life and career. Put this into a TV documentary format.

24. Research and analyze the propaganda of the cold war in the fifties. Try to find examples of both American and Russian propaganda.

25. Make a board game showing how the United Nations works.

HOMEWORK ASSIGNMENTS

RETURN TO PEACETIME

1. Pretend that you are President Truman. Write a speech outlining your plans for returning the country to peacetime life. Include plans for the returning soldiers, the end of rations, and the return of business to a peacetime economy.

2. Make a shopping list of items you would want to buy once you are off rationing.

3. Pretend you are a G.I. returning from World War II. Write an entry in your diary describing your reactions to your first day at home.

4. Imagine that your father has just returned home from the war. Describe your feelings.

5. Write a conversation between a refugee or displaced person arriving in the United States and his or her American cousin.

6. Make a strike poster with a slogan and reasons for striking for any of the following post-war industries:
   (a) Automobile
   (b) Coal
   (c) Steel

7. Pretend you are a woman who worked in a factory during World War II. Describe how you feel when your job is given back to a returning G.I.

8. Why was inflation such a major problem after World War II?

9. Compare the attitudes of people after World War II with the attitudes of people after World War I. Give specific examples of similarities and differences.

10. Pretend you are a German during the Berlin Airlift. How might you change your attitude about the Americans?

11. Prepare for a debate for/against entering the North Atlantic Treaty Organization. This will be used for Classroom Activity 2.

12. Make up a political cartoon commenting on the new statehood of Alaska or Hawaii.

13. Make a campaign button for either Eisenhower or Stevenson.

14. Make up a newspaper headline and short article announcing that Jackie Robinson has just been signed by the Brooklyn Dodgers in 1947.

15. Pretend you attended Jackie Robinson's first game as a Dodger. Write a letter to a friend describing what you saw and what you felt.

CULTURE DURING THE FIFTIES

1. Make up a page from a teenage manual of the fifties on how to behave on a date.

2. Use the following words in a little song, limerick, or story:
   (a) Poodle cut
   (b) Ducktail
   (c) Hula hoop
   (d) Pop beads
   (e) Crinoline
   (f) Poodle skirt

3. Make a list of slang words from the fifties. Translate them into today's slang.

4. Pretend you are a teenager during the fifties and you are planning a party. Make a list of some hit songs you need, the food you will serve, and what you intend to wear.

5. Make a poster advertising a 3-D movie. You may use any movie.

6. Write a list of all the new products, jobs, vocabulary, and customs that have entered American life because of television.

7. Do you think television has done more good or harm in American life? Explain your answer.

8. Prepare a commercial for TV dinners.

9. Pretend that you are a bobby soxer. Plan out your clothes for school tomorrow. You may draw or describe your answer.

CIVIL RIGHTS DURING THE FIFTIES

1. Pretend that you are a lawyer for either Mr. Brown or the Topeka Board of Education. Write your final argument for the Supreme Court.

2. Write a headline and article, or an editorial, or make a political cartoon reacting to the Supreme Court decision of *Brown v. Board of Education* in 1954.

3. Pretend that you are one of the first black students attempting to attend Little Rock High School and had to be escorted by federal troops. Describe how you would feel.

4. Make up interview questions for Rosa Parks after her arrest. You may include how you think she would have answered them.

5. Make a notice encouraging people to support the bus boycott in Montgomery, Alabama.

6. Write a sentence or two expressing how you think each of the following might have felt about the bus boycott in Montgomery:
   (a) Bus driver
   (b) Boycotter
   (c) Owner of the bus company
   (d) White resident of Montgomery

FEAR OF COMMUNISM

1. Pretend you are a speech writer for Joseph McCarthy. Write a speech for Congress warning of the danger to our country from communism.

2. Write a rap song about the "reds" among us.

3. Make up a list of questions that McCarthy might have asked someone who was testifying before the House Un-American Activities Committee.

4. Write an editorial explaining why so many people feared communism in the fifties.

5. Make up a list of questions that you would ask Senator Joseph McCarthy about his beliefs.

6. Write an editorial against McCarthyism.

7. Interview people today and ask: "Are you afraid of communism?" Ask why or why not and record all the answers.

8. Make up a list of accusations against Joseph McCarthy enumerating all the injustices he committed.

9. Would you have signed an oath swearing you were not a Communist? Why? Why not?

10. Pretend you are a young child in the fifties. Your class has just had its first air raid drill in which you took cover by hiding under your desk. Write an entry in your diary describing how you felt.

11. Make a list of things you would personally take into a fallout shelter if you were going to be there for three months.

12. If you could take any nine people into your fallout shelter, who would you choose? Why?

FOREIGN AFFAIRS

1. Interview your parents or grandparents about their memories of:
   (a) The Suez Crisis
   (b) Sputnik
   (c) Nikita Khrushchev's visit to the United States
2. Compare American civilian involvement during the Korean War with involvement during World War II.
3. Write a speech explaining the policy of containment.
4. Make a symbol to illustrate the policy of containment.
5. The following events and issues spanned more than one decade. Show their roots in the 1950s:
   (a) The Nuclear Arms Race
   (b) The Vietnam War
6. What does "cold war" mean? Describe an episode of a "cold war" in your personal life.
7. Write your own version of a United Nations Charter to be signed by every country in the world.

CLASSROOM ACTIVITY 1

CONGRESSIONAL COMMITTEES

After World War II, Congress had to deal with many issues in order to return the United States to a peacetime economy. It was difficult for Congress to prioritize and act on such a variety of concerns. This activity will demonstrate this difficulty.

The teacher will write the list of post-war concerns on the board. Students will be grouped in committees. Each committee will be assigned one issue. They will then prepare a list of arguments for Congress enumerating the reasons why their issue should be dealt with immediately. The students will present their arguments to the class, and everyone can vote and rank the issues in order of importance.

ISSUES

1. Aid to education
2. Low-income housing

3. Equal rights for all Americans
4. Repeal of the Taft-Hartley Law
5. Federally funded health insurance
6. Aid to the elderly
7. Expansion of social security benefits
8. An end to price controls
9. Raising the minimum wage
10. Ways to forestall inflation

CLASSROOM ACTIVITY 2

NATO DEBATE

Joining the North Atlantic Treaty Organization (NATO) was an important and controversial issue after World War II. There was a lot of discussion over the degree of involvement that the United States should take in foreign affairs. Opinions ranged from isolationism to an active role in the post-war world.

Students will prepare for this debate by doing Homework 11 in the Return to Peacetime section. After the debate, the class may enjoy voting.

CLASSROOM ACTIVITY 3

MEDIATION

The end of World War II generated new social problems for Americans. The divorce rate went up, the role of women was in a state of flux, and returning G.I.s had to reenter the job market and readjust to civilian life.

Students often feel overwhelmed by problems in interpersonal relationships and would benefit from using the following experiences as a starting point for exploring problem-solving techniques. Students will volunteer to participate in the socio-dramas below. A mediator should be included in each situation to help facilitate clarification of the problem. The role of the mediator is to:

- ask each party to explain his or her point of view
- encourage both parties to listen to each other and to respond to each other
- rephrase or mirror what each party says when necessary

The class can also ask questions and give suggestions of alternative possibilities for solving the problem.

SITUATION 1: CAN THIS FAMILY BE SAVED?

Husband: My wife is more independent than I remember. She ran the house without me when I was away at war. She doesn't seem to need me anymore.

Wife: My husband is a stranger. He seems cold and withdrawn.

Child: I don't know my father. I wonder if I'm to blame for his seeming so unhappy to be home.

SITUATION 2: CAN THIS MARRIAGE CONTINUE?

Husband: I just got home and I want to start a family immediately. We've wasted so much time.

Wife: I'm still angry at being replaced at my job by a returning soldier. I don't know if I want to stop working.

SITUATION 3: IS LIFE FAIR?

Soldier: I put my life on the line for this country. The least they can do is give me back my old job.

Boss: I found a worker who is superb and I want to keep him.

Current Worker: I am handicapped and couldn't fight in the war. Before then, it was hard to even get a job. I knew that once hired I'd give my all and convince the boss that I'm good, and I have. Why should I leave now?

SITUATION 4: CAN THE ROOMMATES REMAIN?

Soldier: I need time to study. I'm twenty-six and in a rush to get on with my life now that I've returned from the war.

Roommate: I'm eighteen and want to enjoy college. He's too serious.

SITUATION 5: CAN WE BE FRIENDS AGAIN?

G.I.: I have nightmares and can't talk to anyone anymore.

Friend: He's so silent! I don't know what he's been through, and he won't let me help.

SITUATION 6: CAN WE LIVE TOGETHER?

Parents: He left a boy and returned a man. Now it's hard to live with him, but we'd hate to lose him again.

G.I.: They don't give me any space. They're always around and they ask too many questions. I feel like a kid again and I resent it.

CLASSROOM ACTIVITY 4

FALLOUT SHELTER DECISIONS

During the fifties, the fear of a Communist attack led many Americans to plan and build fallout shelters. Their elaborate plans for what to include helped switch the focus from fear of death to how to survive, unlike most of today's youngsters who believe that nuclear war will be the end of the world. This activity will help students understand and empathize with the outlook of the fifties.

Students will be asked to make lists of what they would include if they were to spend three months in a fallout shelter of limited space. They should keep in mind their personal feelings as well as the belief that what they bring will be used to start a new life after an atomic war. Students may divide their lists into two sections—what they need for survival and what they want to bring for personal reasons.

The teacher may either lead a discussion about the students' lists or put the students into committees where they will share their lists with each other. If the teacher wants to add drama to this activity, he or she may direct the committees to vote on what they would accept into their shelter. If committees are used, the students should write a follow-up log on how they felt working together.

Some discussion questions follow to help the teacher culminate this activity.

1. How did you feel as you wrote the list?
2. Did you eliminate any items you really wanted? Why?
3. What was hard/easy about working with the group?
4. Did they question any of your choices? Did you question any of theirs?
5. Were there many arguments? How were they resolved?
6. What did the committee choose as their final items for the shelter?

CLASSROOM ACTIVITY 5

CONFORMING

The fifties was called a time of conformity. Teenagers, especially, went to any length not to appear different. Today's teenagers will probably identify with some of the adolescent concerns of the fifties. This activity will help them clarify just how much conforming means to them. Comparisons may be made to the fifties when appropriate.

The teacher will read the questions and choices to the class. Students may substitute their own answers if they wish.

1. If your friends belonged to a local youth group and you preferred another activity, would you
   (a) Join anyway just to be like them
   (b) See your friends less often
   (c) Try to convince them to join your group

2. Which would bother you the most?
   (a) Wearing a shirt that is out of style
   (b) Getting a haircut that isn't like your friends'
   (c) Having to wear shoes when everyone else wears sneakers

3. Girls: If your parents would not let you wear makeup and your friends already did, would you
   (a) Obey them but feel embarrassed and different
   (b) Obey them and not care what anyone else thinks
   (c) Put on makeup when you get to school

4. What would upset you the most?
   (a) To be shorter than your friends
   (b) To be fatter than your friends
   (c) To be taller than your friends

5. If you really didn't like the music that all your friends listen to, would you
   (a) Tell them about what you do like
   (b) Pretend to like it
   (c) Complain or walk out when they play theirs

6. If you went to a party and all your friends began to smoke (or drink, misbehave, or make out) and you didn't want to, would you
   (a) Leave
   (b) Refuse to do what they are doing
   (c) Do it anyway

7. If you belonged to the Boy/Girl Scouts and your friends made fun of it, would you
   (a) Quit
   (b) Tell them you enjoy belonging
   (c) Change friends

8. Your family still enjoys doing things together and feels that you should join them. They plan on all attending a movie on a date night (Saturday night). Would you

(a) Go and have a good time
(b) Pretend you are sick and stay home
(c) Go and hope you don't run into any of your classmates

9. You are visiting a friend whose parent makes a racist remark with which you disagree. Would you
   (a) Keep quiet because it's polite and you don't want to make trouble
   (b) State your point of view
   (c) Keep quiet but later discuss this with your friend

10. Your teacher makes a derogatory comment about a politician that you and your family admire. You
    (a) Wait to see if anyone else in class challenges the teacher
    (b) Ask why the teacher feels this way
    (c) State your own point of view

CLASSROOM ACTIVITY 6

DEBATES

The following debate topics are outgrowths of concerns of the 1950s.

1. Should TV watching time be limited for children?
2. Does TV encourage violence?
3. Should public servants (such as teachers) be forced to sign oaths swearing that they are not Communists?
4. Was Robin Hood a Communist? This is based on a real event when a member of the Indiana State Textbook Commission wanted to prohibit the use of a textbook in which Robin Hood was mentioned as robbing from the rich to give to the poor.
5. Did McCarthyism stifle independent thinking?
6. Did the growth of suburbs ruin American individualism?
7. Should we contribute to the United Nations when we have so many problems at home?

CLASSROOM ACTIVITY 7

THE FIFTIES JUKE BOX

Humor is very important in a classroom. This game can be used after the students have learned enough about the fifties to participate fully.

The teacher or a student will draw a large juke box on the chalkboard or on a large sheet of poster paper. Students may work alone or in committees to make up names of "hit songs" that express some aspect of life during the fifties. They must include an original title plus the singer or group. As the students brainstorm to think of titles, there should be noise and laughter. The final results should be written into slots on the juke box.

Examples: "The Color Red" by Joe McCarthy
"Feet of Fury" by The Bus Boycotters

CLASSROOM ACTIVITY 8

TO CONFESS OR NOT TO CONFESS

Joseph McCarthy's search for Communists in the U.S. was a "witch hunt." He accused many citizens of being involved in Communist activities. If they refused to answer questions or refused to cooperate fully with his investigation they often found that they lost their jobs and that their friends abandoned them. Their lives were often ruined. Therefore, those people who were questioned felt tremendous pressure to cooperate.

This activity is designed to parallel the situation and the types of questions used by the members of the House Un-American Activities Committee. It will help the students to explore their reactions and feelings in a similar type situation, and to better understand the events of the McCarthy era and the effect that fear can have on people.

The teacher will present the following situation to the class. If the topic of condoms is not relevant to the class the teacher can substitute any other volatile issue that the students will relate to (banned books, controversial art or music, etc.).

The teacher will say:

"An investigation by the school administration has shown that there are students in this school who are distributing free condoms. Unless the problem is resolved by getting rid of those students who are doing this, funds will be stopped and this school will be closed down. Therefore, in order to save this school we must investigate and question all of you. You have to answer our questions. If you refuse to answer it will go down on your record and you will be placed in a special school for troublemakers until you graduate. You will not be able to get into a good high school, nor will you be accepted into any college. Your future will be ruined."

Students will be asked to answer the following questions (under oath):

1. Have you ever distributed free condoms or attended any meetings where distribution was discussed?

2. Have you ever been offered a free condom here?

3. Have your friends or schoolmates ever been offered, or accepted, free condoms?

4. Tell us the names of those students you know who have distributed or accepted free condoms.

As each question is asked discuss the following:

1. How did you feel about answering the question?

2. Did you feel you had to answer? To confess?

3. What pressures are affecting your answer?

As a wrap-up, the students can write their reactions to this activity using a journal type format.

CLASSROOM ACTIVITY 9

THE DINNER PARTY (A CULMINATING ACTIVITY)

Often, dinner parties throw together very diverse people with a variety of opinions and outlooks on life. This activity is designed to allow students to interact in a role-playing situation while reviewing material learned during this unit. It might even be fun to have the students eat lunch during this activity to make it more lifelike and pleasurable.

The teacher may choose from suggestions below but hopefully won't feel limited by them. The characters can be real people in history or personalities that might reflect outlooks of the fifties. Students will choose or be assigned their roles and then have a few minutes to prepare. The "party" should be limited to six members in order to give everyone a chance to participate. We suggest a ten- to fifteen-minute time limit in order to have more than one dinner party per class period and time for a discussion afterward.

Suggested personalities include the following:

1. A member of the House Un-American Activities Committee

2. A former Communist

3. The real estate agent for a new development of split-level houses in the suburbs

4. A bus boycotter from Montgomery

5. A TV salesman

6. Someone who testified during the HUAC hearings

7. Someone who didn't testify during the HUAC hearings
8. Someone who believes in segregated schools
9. Someone who believes in integrated schools
10. A white collar commuter
11. A strong fan of Douglas MacArthur

POSSIBLE FIGURES FROM THE FIFTIES FOR THE DINNER PARTY

Martin Luther King, Jr.
Joseph McCarthy
Edward R. Murrow
Marilyn Monroe
James Dean
Elvis Presley
Adlai Stevenson

CHAPTER SEVENTEEN

The Sixties

INTRODUCTION

The sixties were a time of upheaval and radical change. To many who lived through it, the memories are alive today—memories of commitment, social revolution, music, protests. To others, it remains a puzzling and threatening time. Hanging over everything were assassinations, a war that split the nation in two, and a willingness by many to break laws and traditions that had never before been challenged with such vehemence.

In order to capture the spirit of this decade, many of our activities directly involve the students in the process of choosing and evaluating their levels of comfort in activities that are reflective of the sixties.

The units on the sixties, seventies, and eighties also offer the students an opportunity to do many projects and homework assignments based on interviews. Oral history is a dynamic and exciting method of learning. Students are given the chance to explore on their own and to develop the skills of questioning, organizing, and listening. As they gain practice, they will also learn to build new questions based on the answers they hear and to use follow-up questions to uncover more specific details.

If students are uncomfortable with this form of learning, the teacher might find it beneficial to run practice interviews in class. The students or the teacher may act as subjects. Students will build on each other's questions and analyze what they learned, left out, and still need to ask.

Although the purpose of this book is not to list sources of audio-visual material, we feel that no unit on the sixties can be complete without making use of the wealth of tapes and filmed material available. For example, music, famous speeches such as Martin Luther King, Jr.'s "I Have a Dream," footage from newscasts of protests, music festivals, love-ins, Vietnam, or the deaths and funerals of the Kennedy brothers and Martin Luther King, Jr. can all be included in an attempt to make this decade more vivid and alive to the students.

187

PROJECT LIST

1. Make an illustrated catalogue for a store that sells memorabilia from the sixties.

2. Make a series of ten front covers and accompanying articles for a news magazine using the topic "Person of the Year" or "Event of the Year."

3. Make a guidebook for someone taking a trip back in time to the sixties. Include what clothes, etiquette, slang, mores, and famous names of the decade to be prepared for.

4. Write the script of a documentary entitled *The Primaries of 1960*.

5. Richard M. Nixon began the 1960s as vice-president to Eisenhower and as the loser of the presidential election to John F. Kennedy. By 1969, he was president of the United States. Research his career for the years in between and write a report in the style of either:
   (a) A date book or diary
   (b) A photo album with titles
   (c) A series of articles and headlines about his activities

6. Write a report tracing the accomplishments of the U.S. space program during the sixties.

7. Make a model of a spaceship.

8. Make a poster of diagrams of spaceships developed during the sixties.

9. Research the life of any of the astronauts of the sixties (for example, Alan Shepard, John Glenn, Scott Carpenter, Neil Armstrong, David Scott, Virgil Grissom, Roger Chaffee, Edward White, Edwin Aldrin, or Michael Collins). Write a paper portraying this astronaut as explorer, hero, scientist, dreamer, or any other characteristic that you feel describes him.

10. Make a poster or booklet of the people in President Kennedy's cabinet. Include their backgrounds.

11. Using primary sources of information, write a report on the death of President Kennedy. Include all the events from the assassination to the funeral, the effect on the people of this nation, and your analysis of the coverage from that time.

12. Prepare a script for a TV documentary about the Kennedy presidency. Include excerpts from his speeches.

13. Make a fashion magazine for the sixties.

14. Make a dictionary of new words, phrases, activities, and slang of the sixties.

15. Write a paper entitled *The "Ins" of the Sixties* (for example, sit-in, love-in) about either the civil rights movement or the activities of the "hippies."

16. Do creative writing on the assassinations of the sixties.

17. Prepare questions for interviews with people who remember the life and death of Martin Luther King, Jr., John F. Kennedy, and Robert F. Kennedy. Tape-record or write up the interviews.

18. Do an illustrated time line showing major events in the civil rights movement during the sixties.

19. Write a report on Ralph Nader's efforts to secure automobile safety. Include material from his book, *Unsafe at Any Speed*.

20. Compare the beliefs of Martin Luther King, Jr. with any of the men below. Use speeches and other primary material.
    (a) H. Rap Brown
    (b) LeRoi Jones
    (c) Malcolm X
    (d) Eldridge Cleaver
    (e) Stokely Carmichael

21. Collect material from the antiwar movement in the sixties. Make a collage, videotape, or scrapbook.

22. Prepare oral history interviews with one of the people below. This may be done on tape or in writing.
    (a) Somebody who was involved in the antiwar protests of the sixties. Include questions on why they participated, what they did, what they accomplished, and how they feel about it today.
    (b) A veteran of the war in Vietnam. You may ask questions about his experiences and also about his feelings about the protests at home.

23. Prepare a tape or cassette for a radio show on music of the sixties. Include the disc jockey's patter and a few commercials.

24. Write an essay with detailed specific examples showing how the music of the sixties reflected ideas, beliefs, and life in that time. You may also tape the music to accompany your report.

25. Using the format of press conferences, recreate the public life and philosophies of one of the following men:
    (a) Robert F. Kennedy
    (b) Eugene McCarthy
    (c) Hubert H. Humphrey

26. Make a board game about the space program in the sixties.

27. Research and report on any of the student movements of the sixties. Be sure to include goals and accomplishments of the group.

28. Make a collage of famous faces from the sixties.

29. Design wallpaper with themes from the sixties.

30. Choose any five people who were important in the sixties and write short essays on what happened to them, what they have done, and where they are now.

31. After doing research, make a series of watercolors or charcoals giving your impressions of the sixties.

32. Write a pamphlet explaining to parents and children why the polio vaccine is so important. Include a history of the disease and how destructive it was before the vaccine.

HOMEWORK ASSIGNMENTS

MOVING INTO THE SIXTIES

1. Make a list of questions about the sixties that you would like to have answered.

2. Why were people so surprised when the students at Berkeley protested so violently?

3. Write an entry from a journal about the U-2 incident using the point of view of any of the following:
   (a) Francis Gary Powers
   (b) President Eisenhower
   (c) Nikita Krushchev
   (d) De Gaulle of France or Macmillan of England as they prepare for the Big Four Summit

4. Why did the U-2 incident end the Big Four Summit?

5. Write a speech for the defense or prosecution of Francis Gary Powers to be given in Moscow at his trial for spying in the summer of 1960.

6. In President Eisenhower's farewell speech he warned against letting the military-industrial complex get too powerful. What do you think he meant by that? Looking at the speech from the perspective of today, do you think he was right or wrong? Explain.

7. Why do you think John F. Kennedy had to deal with the "Catholic problem" during the 1960 primaries? What does this tell you about our country at that time?

8. Make up campaign buttons or posters that state the philosophies of Richard M. Nixon, Henry Cabot Lodge, John F. Kennedy, and Lyndon B. Johnson.

9. Make a political cartoon illustrating how television hurt Richard Nixon during his first debate with John F. Kennedy.

10. Write a letter of advice to any of the candidates of 1960 stating what you think the problems of this country are and what you hope he'll do about them.

11. Interview someone who voted in the 1960 election. Ask about his or her memories of the campaign and, if the person is willing, who he or she voted for and why.

THE KENNEDY YEARS

1. Make a chart with two columns. In one column write what you expect from your country. In the second column write what you can do for your country.

2. Write a letter describing the failure of the United States in the Bay of Pigs from the point of view of one of the people below:
   (a) President Kennedy
   (b) Fidel Castro
   (c) An anti-Castro Cuban living in the United States

3. Interview any adults who remember the following events and ask about their feelings at the time:
   (a) Bay of Pigs
   (b) Berlin Wall
   (c) Soviet Missile Crisis and President Kennedy's address on television

4. Pretend you were alive during the Soviet Missile Crisis and watched President Kennedy's speech on television. Write a diary entry expressing your fears and hopes about the next few days.

5. Make a recruitment poster for the Peace Corps.

6. Write a page from an instruction manual for new members of the Peace Corps.

7. The Peace Corps still exists today. Would you consider enlisting? Why? Why not?

8. How does the Supreme Court decision of 1962 about compulsory prayer in public schools affect you today? How do you feel about this?

9. What do the following show about President Kennedy's beliefs?
   (a) Choice of cabinet
   (b) Encouragement of Green Berets' training program
   (c) Test ban treaty

10. Make up questions for a press conference with President Kennedy on the topic of our involvement in Vietnam.

11. Write two letters on the right of James Meredith to attend the University of Mississippi. One letter is from President Kennedy to Governor Ross Barnett of Mississippi; the other is from Governor Barnett to President Kennedy.

12. Interview adult members of your family and neighbors who are old enough to remember the death of President Kennedy. Ask where they were when they heard the news, how they felt, and what they did.

13. Make a list of questions for the Warren Commission to answer in their report on President Kennedy's assassination.

14. Write a poem or do original artwork about the death of President Kennedy.

15. Pretend you were alive when John F. Kennedy was assassinated. Write a letter of condolence to his family.

16. Make a chart about the Kennedy administration. Include columns for accomplishments, failures, and unfinished business.

THE JOHNSON YEARS: DOMESTIC ACCOMPLISHMENTS

1. What were some of the ways President Johnson tried to reassure the people of the United States and the world that he was capable of being president in those first weeks after he took office.

2. Write a speech for President Johnson outlining the main points of the "Great Society."

3. Make up a slogan for either Lyndon Johnson or Barry Goldwater to be used in the campaign of 1964.

4. List the differences between Johnson and Goldwater in how they would deal with the following issues:
(a) Use of military strength
(b) Domestic problems

5. Pretend that you are a black person living in the South on July 2, 1964, when the Civil Rights Act becomes law. How would your life be different now? Give specific examples from the new law.

6. Using President Johnson's words "War on Poverty," write a letter to the editor listing what that war should accomplish.

7. Interview your grandparents or any senior citizen about what benefits they get from medicare.

8. Pretend you are a black person voting for the first time. Write a letter to a grandchild explaining what this occasion means to you. Include how you hope his or her life will be different.

9. Make a political cartoon from any point of view on President Johnson's "War on Poverty."

10. Write a letter from a child of 1965 thanking President Johnson for his Aid to Education Law.

CIVIL RIGHTS IN THE SIXTIES

1. How was the sit-in at Woolworth's in Greensboro in 1960 different from the bus boycott in Montgomery in the 1950s?

2. Write a speech that you might have given in school in the sixties if you had wanted to awaken student awareness of what they could accomplish for civil rights.

3. Write a letter to a friend describing James Meredith's arrival at the University of Mississippi from the point of view of a:
   (a) State trooper
   (b) Student at the university
   (c) Black high school senior

4. Could you have been a freedom rider? Why? Why not?

5. Pretend you were present at Martin Luther King, Jr.'s "I Have a Dream" speech during the march on Washington in 1963. Write your reactions.

6. Do you think Martin Luther King, Jr.'s dream has come true? Give reasons for your answer.

7. Write short diary entries about the riots of Harlem, Watts, Cleveland, Chicago, Newark, or Detroit from the point of view of all of the following people:
   (a) A looter
   (b) A white store owner
   (c) A person who lives in the neighborhood

8. Write a eulogy for Martin Luther King, Jr.

9. Would you have followed Martin Luther King, Jr. or one of the more militant leaders (such as Malcolm X, Stokely Carmichael, and so forth)? Explain your answer.

10. Jesse Jackson had an important role in the 1988 primaries and in the National Democratic Convention. Reflect on his role in our country and in the civil rights movement from the point of view of a black person who first registered to vote at the age of fifty in 1968.

11. Why is the work of Cesar Chavez an important step in the civil rights movement in the United States?

VIETNAM: A WAR AT HOME AND ABROAD

1. Write a newspaper article about the role of the United States in Vietnam during the sixties. Include the following terms:
   (a) Civil War
   (b) Viet Cong
   (c) Escalation
   (d) North Vietnam
   (e) Tet offensive
   (f) Domino theory

2. Explain the term *credibility gap* and give an example from either Vietnam or recent news.

3. If you had been against our participation in Vietnam, which of the following ways would you have chosen to protest? Explain.
   (a) Teach-in
   (b) Moratorium
   (c) Letter-writing campaign
   (d) Bombing a military recruitment center
   (e) Protest march
   (f) Burning your draft card
   (g) Leaving the United States

4. Draw a political cartoon about the difference between "hawks" and "doves."

5. Write a dialogue between a "hawk" and a "dove."

6. Write a song or poem entitled "The Whole World Is Watching" about the protests at the 1968 Democratic Convention in Chicago.

7. How did the war in Vietnam affect the election of 1968?

8. Do you agree with the opinion that the war in Vietnam was an immoral war? Explain your answer and give specific examples to back up your feelings.

9. Make a report card for President Johnson.

THE SPACE PROGRAM

1. Make up a series of movie or song titles to depict the progress of the space program in the sixties.

2. Make up a time line showing the progress and problems of the space program in the sixties.

3. If you could have accompanied the astronauts who went to the moon in 1969, would you have gone? Explain.

4. If you could have given Neil Armstrong one thing (besides the flag)

to take to the moon that symbolizes the United States, what would it have been? Explain.

5. Compare the astronauts of the sixties with the explorers who came to the New World hundreds of years ago. How are they alike? How are they different?

HOW LIFE CHANGED

1. Pretend you were alive in the sixties and had just read Betty Friedan's *The Feminine Mystique*. Write a letter to the author asking any questions you might have and expressing your opinion on her ideas.

2. Make a bumper sticker for or against the Equal Rights Amendment.

3. How is life different today because of the early work of the women's liberation movement?

4. Use as many of the following terms as possible in a poem, short story, or song about life in the sixties:

Woodstock	Groovy	Commune
Trip	Hippies	Love beads
Love-in	Acid rock music	Flower child
Bell bottoms	Psychedelic	

5. What would have to happen to make you angry enough to form a protest group to take over the administration office in your school? Explain.

6. If you could go back to the sixties, what would you most enjoy doing? What would you be least likely to enjoy? Explain.

7. Is there anything in your culture now that had its roots in the sixties?

8. Write a dialogue between a drug user of the sixties and an addict of today. What warning might the addict give?

9. Take a poll of sixties memories by asking at least five adults about the first three things they remember about that time.

10. Make up the table of contents for a magazine whose cover says, "Goodbye Sixties, Hello Seventies."

CLASSROOM ACTIVITY 1

MOVING INTO THE SIXTIES

Vivid images of this decade abound, and it would be very productive for the students to use their own knowledge, impressions, and even misinformation to introduce the sixties.

The teacher will begin the class by asking the students to take a few minutes to write down everything that comes to mind when they hear the term *sixties*. The teacher will tell the class that nothing is too trivial to include and that the students should not edit the list.

When the writing is over, the students will read their lists. The teacher will write their contributions on the chalkboard. The class will discuss:

1. Why some of the impressions were shared by so many
2. Where they got their ideas—from the media, parents, books, movies, other sources?

The teacher will point out how much the class already knows and also allow the students to see the areas of misinformation and stereotypes that exist. This activity may be followed by Homework 1 from the section on Moving into the Sixties.

CLASSROOM ACTIVITY 2

INTERVIEWS

The teacher may choose to be interviewed alone[2] or bring in invited guests. Students will use their questions from Homework 1 of the Moving into the Sixties section.

This activity works beautifully if two or three parents, interested neighbors, or other teachers come into the class for the interviews. The teacher may also invite people from a senior citizens' center, which makes for a lively learning experience for adults and children alike.

The students will read from their questions but will be instructed to listen carefully to answers and ask new questions based on them. The best results occur in an informal setting. When the activity is over, it would be productive for students to discuss the success of the interview and their questions—what more they could have asked; what they would have changed, if possible; and what else they want to learn. They might also discuss the limitations, opinions, and possible prejudices in the answers of the interviewees. They might then make suggestions for future interviews.

CLASSROOM ACTIVITY 3

"ASK NOT . . ."

This activity is designed to help students internalize and explore the

---

[2]The teacher must of course be old enough to have lived through the sixties.

meaning of President Kennedy's words, "Ask not what your country can do for you; ask what you can do for your country."

Four different approaches follow. The teacher may choose to do one or all of them depending on the age and interest of the class. It is hoped that students will recognize how often they can truly make a difference.

PART 1: MULTIPLE CHOICE

Although the following questions seem to have right as well as wrong answers, the teacher should stress that these are for clarification and not judgment. Students should be allowed to discuss their answers and might even complain about the multiple choice format. This is fine and allows for honesty and analysis. Students should be allowed alternative answers if they choose. The teacher should lead the discussion with as little opinion and judgment as possible but focus on the students' feelings and reasons.

1. You are walking down the street and have some trash in your hands that you wish to discard. You would
   (a) Carry it around until you find a trash can
   (b) Only throw it in a trash can if one were conveniently available
   (c) Throw it in the street
2. If you see a blind person preparing to cross the street, you would
   (a) Offer to help
   (b) Help if you're asked
   (c) Keep your distance
3. An old person gets on the bus. You would
   (a) Offer your seat
   (b) Get up if you are asked
   (c) Look out the window and not make eye contact
4. The school desperately needs people to work on the student play. You would
   (a) Volunteer
   (b) Feel that you wouldn't be of any help because you can't act
   (c) Feel that you are too busy with work for school to get involved
5. Your homeroom teacher asks your class to clean out the desks every morning, even though other classes use the room as much as you do.
   (a) You resent it since you didn't leave any papers in the desk
   (b) You help
   (c) You volunteer to be the monitor and carry the garbage can around the room
6. The community center has a sign asking for volunteers to help shop for home-bound neighbors. You feel

    (a) The sign does not apply to you

    (b) It would be nice to help someone

    (c) You should apply but you're too busy doing school work and help-
ing out at home

7. The Parent/Teacher Association is having a meeting about curriculum. The teacher gives you a notice to bring home. You

    (a) Bring it home

    (b) Stuff it in the desk because you know your parents are too busy to
come

    (c) Decide to attend the meeting yourself since curriculum affects you

8. Your school needs new equipment or supplies. You

    (a) Suggest that the student council try to raise money with a cake
sale or dance

    (b) Start a petition to the mayor or school board asking for more
funds

    (c) Complain that nobody cares about kids

9. You learn about an anti-fly campaign in a town in China in which all
the citizens actually carried fly swatters and killed off the flies.

    (a) You think it's great for China but could never work here

    (b) You think it's funny

    (c) You think it only worked in China because the people are afraid
of their government

10. Your community is having a white elephant sale to raise money for the
homeless. You

    (a) Volunteer to help at the sale

    (b) Plan to go to the sale and buy something

    (c) Ask your parents to find things to contribute

PART 2: WHAT I LIKE ABOUT MYSELF

Studies show that altruism is most often the result of self-confidence and
a feeling that what you do makes a difference. Often, students have a weak
sense of self-esteem and underrate their own talents and abilities. This activity will help them clarify their own qualities and worth and make them
realize how these qualities might be used for service to others.

Students will be instructed to make a list of everything they like about
themselves. They should include personality traits, character, accomplishments, talent, and ability. They should also list what makes them feel
proud about themselves.

When the students are finished, the teacher will tell them to skip a line
and now write a list of things they can do but tend to take for granted and

thus never thought to include in the above list. Examples may be given, such as sew on a button, cook, speak a second language.

As a culmination to this activity, the teacher may ask the class to write either:

- what they learned from doing this exercise
- a list of things they discovered about themselves

The students will then meet in committees. They will share their lists and help each other find ways to contribute their unique traits and talents to others. They will answer the following questions:

- What can I do for my family?
- What can I do for my school?
- What can I do for my community?
- What can I do for my country?

PART 3: CAPABLE AND WILLING

This variation of the exercise would help students explore for themselves what they are able and willing to do for others. They will answer the following questions either as a writing assignment or during a class discussion.

1. I am capable of doing the following for my family, school, community, and country.
2. I am willing to do the following for my family, school, community, and country.

PART 4: YOU DO MAKE A DIFFERENCE

Students sometimes overlook how much they do (or can do) to help others. The teacher will use the questions below to lead the class in a discussion. He or she may wish to point out how much one really does to help others and how much it matters. The discussion can also include the various degrees and levels of service that people give.

1. Do you ever hold the door for someone?
2. Have you ever donated money or things to charity?
3. Have you ever given food or money to a homeless person?
4. Do you help other students with their homework?
5. Do you ever wash dishes, take out the garbage, sweep or vacuum, dust the furniture, or do the marketing for your family?

6. Have you ever written a letter to your senator, representative, or to the president?
7. Have you ever called the police or the fire department?
8. How many of you are monitors for teachers or work on squads or belong to the student council?
9. How many of you feel that if we went to war you would enlist in the armed forces?
10. Has anyone ever rescued a stray dog or cat?

CLASSROOM ACTIVITY 4

A GREAT SOCIETY

The teacher will break the class into groups. Each group will try to answer the following questions:

1. What is a great society?
2. Do we have one? Explain.
3. If not, what would we have to do to have one?

Committees will report back to the class, and the teacher will tie together their findings and opinions.

CLASSROOM ACTIVITY 5

CHECKLIST FOR A GREAT SOCIETY

The teacher will reproduce the list below, and students will check off those items that they feel make a great society. If the teacher or the class wishes, the students may number each item according to what they think is the order of importance for a great society.

1. Employment for all
2. Enough food for everyone
3. Strong armed forces
4. Up-to-date weapons
5. Enough affordable housing for everyone
6. A space program
7. Public education

8. A good welfare system
9. Federal medical insurance
10. Clean air and water
11. Care for the aged
12. Federally funded child care for working parents
13. Animal rights
14. Women's liberation
15. Strong religious influence
16. Tough laws for drug dealers
17. Death penalty
18. Civil rights for everyone
19. Strong prisons to punish criminals
20. Effective rehabilitation programs

CLASSROOM ACTIVITY 6

STUCK IN AN ELEVATOR

The students may act out meetings between people listed below who happen to be in the same elevator when it gets stuck.

ELEVATOR 1

1. A black rioter/looter from Watts, Los Angeles
2. A white police officer
3. A black police officer

ELEVATOR 2

1. A follower of Martin Luther King, Jr.
2. A Black Panther
3. A freedom rider

ELEVATOR 3

1. An owner of a newly integrated restaurant
2. A black student enrolled in a white school
3. A southern sheriff who believes in segregation

ELEVATOR 4

1. A draft card burner
2. A G.I. who just returned from Vietnam
3. A hawk (who is not in the army)
4. A dove (who has not really participated in any war protests)

ELEVATOR 5

1. A hard-working parent
2. A young person who lives in a commune
3. A radical feminist
4. A male chauvinist

CLASSROOM ACTIVITY 7

HOW FAR WOULD YOU GO?

  Because the sixties offered so many forms of protest, people discovered how far they were willing to go for what they believed. In this activity students will examine their own activism. Students can check off the answers that apply to them from the questions below. If there is more than one answer, they should number them in order of preference, with number 1 denoting first choice.

1. I would be comfortable
   (a) In a sit-in
   (b) Boycotting a product
   (c) Storming an office and taking it over
   (d) Marching in protest
   (e) Giving a speech
   (f) Signing a petition
2. If I truly believed in something (or was very much against something), I would be willing to
   (a) Go to jail for my beliefs
   (b) Leave the country
   (c) Commit violence
   (d) Write protest letters
   (e) Participate in civil disobedience
3. Injustice and inequality to others would

    (a) Make me furious
    (b) Have me out there marching and protesting
    (c) Spur me on to give time to the organization that would help them
    (d) Get me to stand on street corners to get petitions signed
    (e) Not really bother me

4. If I had lived during the sixties, I would have been most likely to get involved in
    (a) Antiwar movement
    (b) Nader's raiders
    (c) Women's liberation movement
    (d) Civil rights
    (e) Student organizations to reorganize my school

5. To me, someone who burned his draft card was
    (a) A coward
    (b) A hero
    (c) A criminal

6. I believe that someone who avoided the draft was
    (a) An idealist
    (b) Not a good American
    (c) A coward

7. If I had been drafted, I would have
    (a) Gone to Canada
    (b) Gone into the army
    (c) Done non-combatant service

8. If friends of mine had wanted to burn their bras, I would have
    (a) Joined in
    (b) Been ashamed of them
    (c) Wished them well
    (d) Tried to convince them to change their minds

9. If I believe a law is immoral and wrong, I would be willing to
    (a) Disobey it and be arrested in order to challenge it in court
    (b) Write letters of protest and petitions against it
    (c) Organize others to join me in disobeying it

10. The worst thing for me to do would be to
    (a) Spit on the flag
    (b) Disobey police officers
    (c) Use drugs
    (d) Make fun of a president of my country
    (e) Hurt my parents

After the students have completed this activity, they might benefit from writing or discussing in class what they learned about themselves and their classmates.

CLASSROOM ACTIVITY 8

"SIXTIES-IN"

As a culmination to this unit, the class might enjoy creating the kind of "in" so popular during the sixties. The classroom, school library, or gymnasium can be decorated with posters, artwork, projects, portraits of famous people of the sixties, and displays of record album covers. Booths and tables can display memorabilia from the sixties, scrapbooks, old magazines and newspapers, buttons, and so forth. Music of the sixties should be played. Skits can be presented, as well as readings from speeches of that time. Neighborhood adults and other teachers should be invited to participate—it might even be fun to make a tape of their memories.

Students and adults who wish to can wear clothes in the style of the sixties.

The planning, preparation, and production of this activity will be both educational and enjoyable for all.

CHAPTER EIGHTEEN

The Seventies

INTRODUCTION

The seventies brought America its 200th birthday. It gave Americans the opportunity to celebrate the achievements and relearn the principles of this country. It was a time of fireworks and big boats and flag waving.

It was also a decade in which Americans watched almost helplessly as the country lost power and influence. Our escape from Vietnam erased any joy at finally ending our participation in the war. We were impotent in the face of the Ayatollah and his followers when our embassy was attacked and Americans were taken hostage in Iran. Three Mile Island and Love Canal, along with the energy crisis, renewed doubts about the infallibility of technology. The resignation and pardon of a disgraced president further eroded trust in the government.

By the end of the seventies we begin to see more of a multicultural awareness in American society. The Voting Rights Act of 1975 created bilingual elections to serve the needs of our growing Hispanic population, which had reached over fourteen million by the end of the seventies. After 1975 "boat people" from Vietnam and Cambodia began to resettle here. In general there was a larger influx of immigrants from Latin America and Asia than there was from Europe.

Further attention was drawn to the plight of Native Americans when in 1973 AIM occupied Wounded Knee, South Dakota for several weeks as a reminder of our government's failure to keep its treaties.

The women's rights movement continued to press forward with the 1972 congressional proposal for an equal rights amendment to our Constitution.

We have tried to open up this decade for the students—warts and all. History hasn't yet brought enough distance and perspective, but students will have access to a wealth of eyewitness accounts. They will also see the continuity of history as they trace social issues and movements from the past through this decade and into the present.

PROJECT LIST

1. Do research and make a poster of slogans, signs, buttons, and bumper stickers that expressed the opinions of both antiwar protesters and war supporters in the seventies.

2. Make a time line of United States' participation in Vietnam, stretching back to the Eisenhower administration.

3. Using your own questions, interview people who remember the end of the war in Vietnam.

4. Prepare questions for an interview with any woman who has been or is still active in the women's movement. Send her the questions (keep a copy for yourself and the teacher in case she doesn't reply) and ask her to answer your questions in order to help you understand the movement more clearly from an eyewitness point of view.

5. Read and compare copies of women's magazines from the 1920s through the 1970s. Write a report on the similarities and differences, including the changes in approach, outlook, and choice of topics. Also include what has stayed the same. Analyze how the magazines reflect the changes in women's lives and the impact of the women's movement.

6. Study pollution in your area and write a report on its sources and possible solution.

7. Pretend you are an anthropologist. Watch reruns of the TV show *All in the Family* for at least two weeks. Observe and write a report on as many of the following as possible:
   Family customs
   Relationships
   Use of language
   Clothing and artifacts
   Interests
   Prejudices
   Values
   Describe the basic points of view and analyze how this show reflects the seventies.

8. Research any prison reform program. Describe it, evaluate it, and add your own suggestions for improving it.

9. Research magazine and newspaper accounts of Watergate. Make a booklet of original political cartoons illustrating this scandal.

10. Make up a series of indictments against all the people and organizations who were accused of criminal acts in the Watergate scandal.

11. Make a newspaper supplement on the Senate hearings about Watergate.

12. Make a time line from the Watergate break-in to President Nixon's resignation.

13. Research the present activities and whereabouts of all the participants in the Watergate story and make a chart entitled "Where Are They Now?"

14. Using newspapers and magazines as your sources of information, write a report on terrorism in the seventies. (Since we are all affected by the horror of this, the report does not have to include only instances in which Americans were victims.)

15. Prepare a celebration for the 200th birthday of the United States in 1976. Include a giant birthday card, a collage or poster of what America is and has accomplished, a menu for the feast, and a wish list for the future.

16. Draw a mural or make a model of a bicentennial fair. Label all the booths and activities that you would include.

17. Write a short story about the seventies called "The Me Decade." Use magazines and newspapers for your research.

18. Make up questions and interview people who remember the following events of the seventies.
    (a) Three Mile Island
    (b) Takeover of the U.S. embassy in Teheran and capture of American hostages

19. Write an investigative report for a newspaper about Love Canal. Include interviews with residents and business people.

20. Make a poster showing progress of the space program in the seventies.

21. Write a report on solar energy and how it can be used. Include diagrams.

22. Make a ledger for the United States in the seventies. Include pages on assets and liabilities (positive and negative events in U.S. history during those years). Also include people whom you would consider assets or liabilities.

23. Research the "boat people" who fled Vietnam and Cambodia in the seventies. Write a first person account from the time of departure to resettlement in the United States.

24. Using research, interviews, and photographs write a magazine article about Asian and Latin American immigrants who have settled in your area since the 1970s.

25. Write a report on the demands and progress of several minority groups in the United States during the seventies. At the end you can evaluate their success.

HOMEWORK ASSIGNMENTS

VIETNAM CONTINUED: A WAR AT HOME AND ABROAD

1. Write a letter to President Nixon expressing your opinion about his plans for Vietnamization. Use the point of view of either:
(a) An American soldier stationed in Vietnam
(b) Someone who believes the war should end immediately
(c) Someone who feels we should stay in Vietnam until the war is won

2. Write a memorial service for the students who were killed during the demonstration at Kent State University.

3. Write a political cartoon defining the silent majority.

4. Prepare a case for or against Lt. William Calley for his participation in the My Lai Massacre of 1968. (This will be used in Classroom Activity 1.)

5. Was Daniel Ellsberg a hero or traitor for leaking the Pentagon Papers? Explain your answer.

6. Write a newspaper article or editorial using the following quote from Henry Kissinger as your headline: "Peace is at hand."

7. Pretend you are living during the seventies. Which would bother you the most about the war in Vietnam? Explain your answer.
(a) Soldiers who are missing in action
(b) Use of napalm
(c) Antiwar protests at home

8. Why weren't there parades and celebrations when the American participation in the Vietnam War ended?

9. Write the questions for a press conference for G.I.'s returning from Vietnam after the fall of Saigon.

10. In Vietnam and the U.S. the war affected civilians as well as soldiers. Write how and give specific examples.

11. Many people considered antiwar protesters "tools of the Communists." Do you think this was true? Do you think they had a right to protest? Explain.

12. Write a short play describing a confrontation between antiwar protesters, hardhats, and the police.

13. Write a last will and testament from the war in Vietnam. What is its legacy to the U.S.?

SOCIAL ISSUES AND MOVEMENTS

1. Interview your parents on their opinions about legalized abortion. Include questions on how they felt when it was first legalized in 1973.

2. As the seventies progressed, the women's movement ran into problems with "backlash." Write a dialogue between two women—one who believes in women's liberation and the ERA and one who doesn't.

3. Write your own definition of liberated women.

4. Before there was a women's liberation movement, there were liberated women. Write about anyone you know, or have read about, who you feel fits the description of liberated.

5. Ask your parents to tell you all the jobs they remember that were once restricted by gender and are now open to both.

6. Write a rallying chant for Cesar Chavez's lettuce boycott.

7. Draw a poster promoting Earth Day or any other environmental concern.

8. Pretend you are a reporter for a news magazine. Write the questions you would have prepared for an interview with the leader of one of the cult religions that existed in the seventies.

9. Make a list of drug-related problems that existed in the seventies. Check off the ones that still exist today.

10. Write a proposal to prevent a repeat of the Attica uprising.

11. As doctors have found better ways to help more people live longer, what new problems and questions are created for society? Which do you think is the most difficult to solve? Why?

12. Write an answer to a TV editorial regarding affirmative action.

13. How would an affirmative action policy affect your admission to college? How do you feel about it?

14. Do you think prisons or prisoners are to blame for the high rate of recidivism? Explain.

15. Make a list of topics for a women's consciousness raising group.

16. Write something a family member has told you about your ethnic background that makes you proud.

17. How is ethnic pride different from assimilation?

18. Write a dialogue in which two eighteen-year-olds discuss their new right to vote and what new responsibilities come with it.

19. Write a series of questions you would want to have answered about the Karen Ann Quinlan case in which the New Jersey court ruled that she had the right to die. Your questions might be addressed to her family, the doctors, or the judges.

20. Write a list of interview questions for the Native Americans who occupied Wounded Knee, South Dakota in 1973.

21. Do you think election materials should be bilingual? Explain.

22. Make a list of all the places where you see and hear languages other than English (signs, conversations, TV).

23. Do you think we should provide bilingual education for students? Explain.

NIXON'S PRESIDENCY AND WATERGATE

1. Make up a toast for Richard Nixon to give at his meeting with Premier Chou-En-Lai during his historic visit to China.

2. Make up a peace prize citation for President Nixon after his visits to China and Russia in 1972. Explain what his visits accomplished toward peace.

3. Why do you think people didn't pay a lot of attention when the Watergate break-in was first reported?

4. Write an account of the Watergate story using as many of the following terms as possible:

Break-in	Tapes
Plumbers	Impeachment
Bugging	Stonewalling
Dirty tricks	Smoking pistol
Leak	Senate hearing
Kickback	Resignation
"Saturday Night Massacre"	Pardon
Sanitized money	"Political base"
Cover up	Obstruction of justice

5. In what ways did the Watergate scandal disgrace this country? In what way did the country find honor?

6. How did the Watergate Senate hearings and investigation prove that even a president is equal before the law?

7. Write a telegram to Nixon urging him to resign.

8. Write a letter to President Ford reacting to his pardon of Nixon.

9. Because Watergate led to much distrust among Americans toward politicians, it would be interesting to poll the level of trust today. This homework should take a few days to do. Students will make up questions for a poll on trust in government and ask as many people as possible to answer them. They will then tally the results and report back to class. If the teacher prefers, he or she may use the questions below for this poll.

(a) Is there any politician that you trust today? Who?

(b) How often do you believe campaign promises?
  1. All the time
  2. Most of the time
  3. Very seldom
  4. Never

(c) Do you consider politicians to be more honest or dishonest?

(d) Do you believe elected officials really care about the people they work for?

(e) Do you think all politicians are rich?

(f) Do you think politicians are more interested in public service or wealth and power?

(g) How often do you feel that you're happy voting for someone?

(h) Do you vote in every election?

THE CARTER PRESIDENCY

1. Write a news bulletin about the results of the Camp David meetings between President Carter, Menachem Begin, and Anwar Sadat.

2. Write questions for a press conference with President Carter on his return from six days of negotiations in Cairo and Jerusalem for the peace agreement between Israel and Egypt.

3. Describe the opening of full diplomatic relations between the United States and China from the following points of view:
  (a) United States
  (b) China
  (c) Taiwan

4. Write a letter to your senator giving reasons why he or she should ratify (or not ratify) the Panama Canal treaties.

5. Pretend you were a member of the family of one of the Americans held hostage in Iran. Write a diary entry or a letter to a friend expressing your feelings and fears.

6. If you had been an Iranian student studying in America when the embassy in Teheran was taken over, what would have been your reaction? Explain.

7. Write a letter to the hostages to let them know Americans are thinking of them and wish them well.

8. Write a letter to President Carter urging him to do more on behalf of the hostages. Write his answer in which he explains his reasons for his policy.

9. Make a political cartoon for or against President Carter's policy with Iran.

10. If you could have sent a care package to the hostages for Thanksgiving, what would you have sent? Draw or describe.

11. Make a public service commercial for television urging Americans to hang out yellow ribbons on behalf of the hostages in Iran.

12. Make a poster explaining how even/odd days for gasoline worked in the seventies.

13. Make a cartoon about waiting in a gas line.

14. Write slogans to convince Americans to conserve energy.

15. Why do you think President Carter was not reelected for a second term of office?

CLASSROOM ACTIVITY 1

TRIAL OF LT. WILLIAM CALLEY

Students will have studied the massacre at My Lai and prepared Homework 4 from the Vietnam homework section before doing this activity.

The teacher will ask for volunteers to read their arguments for and against Lt. Calley. The class will then split into juries of six to twelve students and discuss the case until each reaches a decision. All juries will report back to the class.

In the follow-up discussion the teacher may want to focus on when following orders is not an excuse, possible alternative behavior and options during the massacre, and whether Lt. Calley would still be convicted today.

CLASSROOM ACTIVITY 2

SEXUAL STEREOTYPES

The following short exercises are designed to help students recognize sexual stereotypes and prejudices. The teacher may do one or all of these exercises to open up a discussion or as writing assignments.

EXERCISE 1

Students will write male, female, or both after the characteristics below.

Sensitive	Loud
Strong	Cries easily
Tough	Persevering
Good at math	Cooks well
Loves children	Tender
Helpful	Gentle
Worries a lot	Kind
Athletic	Artistic

EXERCISE 2

Students will follow the instructions in Exercise 1. The following words should make them think of male, female, or both.

Flower	Butterfly
Rock	Stone
Bird	Hawk
Tiger	Blue
Pink	Lily

EXERCISE 3

Students will list the first five words that come to mind when they hear the term masculine and when they hear the word feminine.

EXERCISE 4

Students will read the list below and write female, male, or both next to the jobs.

Automobile mechanic	Photographer
Ballet dancer	Model
Secretary	Police officer
Nurse	Salesperson
Construction worker	Lawyer
Doctor	Veterinarian
President of company	Bus driver
Librarian	Teacher

EXERCISE 5

Students will list any jobs that they feel are not appropriate for either men or women. A discussion should follow either in committees or as an entire class.

CLASSROOM ACTIVITY 3

DEBATES ON ISSUES OF THE SEVENTIES

1. Should abortion be legalized (1973)?
2. Should tne ERA be passed?
3. Will bussing really help integration?
4. Should gay rights be protected by law?
5. Should eighteen-year-olds be allowed to vote (Supreme Court decision 1971)?

CLASSROOM ACTIVITY 4

REVERSE DISCRIMINATION?

The Supreme Court Bakke decision was very controversial and led to heated arguments for and against affirmative action. This activity will help students grapple with the complex issues involved, as well as with their emotional impact.

The format for this activity is a TV discussion show in which both guests and audience participate. The program takes place right after the Supreme Court decided that Bakke, a white male, had indeed been the victim of reverse discrimination. However, the discussion should not be limited to the decision but should also deal with its concept.

Volunteers will choose from the suggested list of guests below. They should have enough time to get into character and prepare statements or anecdotes expressing their opinions and experiences. The rest of the class will act as a TV studio audience and question the guests. They will also be allowed to argue with the guests and express their own opinions. The teacher, or a strong student, will act as a moderator. The activity may begin with the moderator reviewing the Bakke decision and asking the guests for their opinions. The teacher should warn the students that this can become a heated discussion and that there are no easy answers or even fair ones for everyone.

GUESTS

1. A white man who was not hired for a job because of affirmative action
2. A black woman who got the job the white man wanted
3. A woman who had been denied a promotion because of her sex
4. A woman who states that a male colleague is making more money than she is for doing the same job
5. An older black man who has lived through years of discrimination
6. A civil rights activist
7. Two high school seniors—one black and one white
8. A black college student who was admitted because of affirmative action

At the end of this activity, students may vote on whether affirmative action leads to reverse discrimination and/or whether affirmative action is necessary to solve problems caused by years of discrimination.

CLASSROOM ACTIVITY 5

IDENTIFYING FEELINGS

Feelings are not always rational, and many Americans faced a variety of emotions when they learned about the capture of the American hostages in Iran. The teacher will allow the students to choose from the emotions described below. They will then act out a town meeting held at a local school in which people gather to share their concerns and feelings. Other students might choose to react to what is said. While all feelings are valid, it might be helpful for the teacher to point out instances of overreactions.

FEELINGS

1. Anger at the Iranians in the United States
2. Shame that the United States was so weak
3. Fear that the followers of the Ayatollah Khomeini would kill the hostages
4. Frustration with your powerlessness as a country or as an individual
5. Hopes that the United States would bomb Iran off the face of the earth
6. Sympathy for the hostages' families
7. Hatred of the Ayatollah

CLASSROOM ACTIVITY 6

MULTICULTURAL MULTIMEDIA CELEBRATION

To celebrate the growing awareness of the multicultural nature of our society, students can work in groups and prepare a display or production to illustrate this concept. Students can elect to work in the area in which they feel most comfortable and competent.

- art for a bulletin board display or mural
- photo essay
- poetry
- play
- music (tape mix)
- rap songs
- videotape
- dance
- performance art

This could be an ideal opportunity for the teacher to use the talents of other staff members to make this a schoolwide celebration.

CHAPTER NINETEEN

The Eighties—Moving into the Nineties

INTRODUCTION

This chapter will deal with some of the issues that have been prominent during the eighties. Many of the themes reflect ongoing or recurrent problems with which the students are familiar on some level, either personally or by exposure through the news media. These include social problems and concerns about health, ethics, and the environment. Because of the immediacy of many of the topics, the students will be given ample opportunity to go out into their communities to gather information by carefully observing, taking notes, and interviewing. There are also numerous opportunities for research using newspapers, magazines, and interview techniques.

The students will explore and seek solutions for many of the unresolved problems since the eighties, both in class activities and in homework assignments.

PROJECT LIST

1. Do a photographic essay on the senior citizens in your community.
2. Visit a community center that services senior citizens. By interviewing employees and members, make a brochure that shows how the senior citizens are serviced.
3. Make a blueprint with explanations for a senior citizen center for your area. Include:
   (a) Housing and other basic needs
   (b) Entertainment
   (c) Provisions for health and emergency care
4. Make a booklet describing the programs in your community, city, or state that deal with the problem of drug or substance abuse.

5. Do a research report on the effects of illegal drugs on individuals and society.

6. Using newspapers, magazines, and interviews, make a special Sunday supplement for a newspaper about the problem of the homeless.

7. Do a research report on both the short-term and long-term solutions that different cities are using to resolve the problem of the homeless.

8. Make an original plan for an ideal city. Include a labelled diagram with all the services that would be provided.

9. Do a photographic essay showing all the ways in which your city serves its children.

10. Pretend you are a disc jockey. Make up songs and titles for an hour of "Issues That Concern Kids of Today." This can be taped.

11. Visit one or more day-care centers in your area. Observe and interview employees for a report on whom they service and how they serve the needs of the community. At the end you may write your own evaluation.

12. Do a poster illustrating new roles that both men and women have taken on in recent years, along with new family arrangements that have become more common.

13. Make up an *Entertainment Guide of the Eighties or Nineties* highlighting some of the newer forms of entertainment such as video games.

14. Make up a public service advertising campaign to inform people about how AIDS is spread. Make up both TV and print ads and indicate where and when they would be shown, and why.

15. Make a series of graphs which illustrate how AIDS has spread in recent years within different segments of society, including drug users, homosexuals, heterosexuals, babies, and hemophiliacs.

16. Do a newspaper exposé on the latest scientific information regarding the causes of cancer. Include the destruction of the ozone layer, asbestos in buildings, radiation leaks, acid rain, cigarettes, and sun exposure.

17. Using community and government resources, investigate what programs exist for pollution prevention and control, toxic waste disposal, and recycling. Write your report in the form of a public service information bulletin.

18. Make a poster with examples of today's causes of air pollution.

19. Using local newspapers, research and write a report on race relations in your community or city during recent times.

20. Make a sales catalogue of items that promote health and fitness.

21. Make a directory of institutions and places in your city or town where

the services of volunteers could be used. Write a brief description of each.

22. Make up an original video game about life in the eighties or nineties.

23. Make up a TV program schedule for a week with original titles that illustrate the interests and concerns of people today. Include politics, race relations, technology, and social issues.

24. Do a survey of integration in your community in terms of schools, places of employment, and housing. You may use interview techniques for gathering information.

25. Make a series of graphs which compare income levels and education levels of white and black people. Analyze the information and then try to work out a program to even out the gaps.

26. Make up a police blotter of some of the top business people of the eighties and nineties who were accused and convicted of insider trading, embezzlement, or tax evasion. Include brief descriptions of their jobs, their salaries, and their crimes.

27. Based on research about the Iran-Contra affair, make up a *True Confessions Magazine* highlighting the explanations given by all the major figures involved.

28. Make a special newspaper supplement giving a full account of the *Challenger* explosion.

29. Make a calendar for the coming year with holidays honoring outstanding citizens of the eighties and nineties. Include their contributions.

30. Make a scrapbook of memorabilia from the Reagan years.

31. Do an in-depth report on President Reagan's economic policies.

32. Make a labelled diagram or model of a computer with a descriptive list of all the discs covering the major events during President Reagan's terms of office.

33. Write a day-by-day account, in diary form, of one specific hostage situation involving Americans.

34. Make a magazine special on outstanding women of the eighties, including Sally Ride, Sandra Day O'Connor, Geraldine Ferraro, Christa McAuliffe, and Jane Fonda. You may add names of women in the news today.

35. Make a map showing the places where the United States had critical foreign involvements during the eighties and nineties.

36. Make a scrapbook of disasters of the eighties. Include the *Challenger* explosion, the *Achille Lauro* tragedy, the murder of John Lennon, the shooting of an Iranian passenger plane by the United States, and racial violence that reached the front pages of newspapers.

37. Write an illustrated guide to keeping healthy for people of the next decade. Include the things that people should and should not do.

38. Gather information from Alcoholics Anonymous and other sources and write a report entitled "Alcoholism as a Disease."

39. Make a memorial service or poster about famous people who have died from AIDS.

40. Make a map showing all the political changes that have taken place in Europe. Write a short analysis of how this affects U.S. foreign policy.

41. Using periodicals and newspapers do one of the following:
    (a) Make a time line of the important events in the Persian Gulf war.
    (b) Write an analysis of the results of the Persian Gulf war.
    (c) Describe the roles of George Bush, Norman Schwarzkopf, Colin Powell, and Peter Arnett.

42. Write a paper about the Persian Gulf war entitled, "The TV War."

43. If students are old enough to remember the Persian Gulf war they might write a paper describing their memories and feelings as they watched the war progress.

44. Write a report on the role of women in the Persian Gulf war.

45. Make a poster showing all the legislation vetoed by President Bush during his term.

46. Using research and current events do a poster comparing the Great Depression and the economy of the early nineties.

47. Interview any neighbors or family members who fought in the Persian Gulf. Write your questions. The interview may be done on tape.

48. Make a time line entitled; "From Desert Shield to Desert Storm."

49. Using primary sources for research, write a series of editorials, rap songs, or a script for a TV documentary following the events from the arrest of Rodney King to the riots in Los Angeles in 1992.

50. Do a videotaped interview or photo essay describing the range of problems facing urban communities today.

HOMEWORK ASSIGNMENTS

HEALTH, ENVIRONMENT, AND TECHNOLOGY

1. (To be assigned before Classroom Activity 1) Make a list of people (by job) in your community who have contact with drug abusers.

2. (This homework will be assigned in conjunction with Classroom Activity 1, after the students know who will be speaking to the class.) Make up a list of questions for the people who are invited to speak about drugs.

3. Interview five people and ask them how they think the drug problem can be stopped.

4. Make up an original public service advertisement against drugs or alcohol.

5. Choose a print or TV advertisement against drugs. Analyze who it is aimed at and why you think it is or is not effective.

6. How do you think the law should handle drug pushers? Why?

7. Write a letter to your mayor explaining why you feel clean needles should or should not be given to drug addicts.

8. What would you do if you discovered that your sister, brother, or parent is using drugs?

9. Make up an editorial either for or against on-the-job mandatory drug tests.

10. Make a list of the things in your life that would be ruined if you started using drugs.

11. Write a scene from a TV drama in which a school counselor or friend explains the risks of being the child of an alcoholic.

12. Make up an advertisement warning about the connection between cigarettes and cancer.

13. Do you think the manufacture and sale of cigarettes should be prohibited? Explain.

14. Write a letter to your senator explaining why you are for or against raising the drinking age.

15. Walk around your neighborhood or community and make a list of every example that you see of litter or pollution.

16. What things do you notice in your community that point out people's concerns about fitness and health? Why is this so?

17. Look at yourself, a member of your family, or a friend and list all the things you would change in order to live a healthier life.

18. Make a list of all the places where you see computers used in a day.

19. Make a list of all the technological advances that have taken place since you were born. Do they make life better or worse?

20. Write a page for an addition to a dictionary defining all the new words related to computers.

SOCIAL ISSUES

1. Describe one memorable experience you have had with an elderly person. How did you feel about it?

2. (To be assigned before Classroom Activity 2) Make a list of the needs or problems that are unique to the elderly.

3. Interview a senior citizen in your family or neighborhood. Find out:
   (a) How he or she spends the day
   (b) What he or she enjoys doing
   (c) What other things he or she wishes were available to do

4. Walk around your community and write down your observations regarding the homeless. These could include places where the homeless are given food or shelter or simply instances of people living in the streets.

5. Write a poem expressing your feelings about the problems of homeless people.

6. Who, if anyone, do you think should be responsible for resolving the problem of the homeless? How could this person resolve it?

7. Make a list or a diagram of all the other services that must be provided when housing is built for large numbers of people.

8. What other problems are created for people as a result of homelessness? Which do you feel is the worst one? Why?

9. Write a speech as if you were running for president and explain the programs you propose for improving race relations in this country.

10. Make a button with a slogan that encourages improved race relations.

11. What do you think can be done in your community or school to improve race relations?

12. Why was the candidacy of Jesse Jackson in the 1988 Democratic primary so important? Explain.

13. Make a list of all the minority groups in your community or school. Do they get along well? Explain.

14. List the names of all the organizations of today that are working to get more rights for those they represent.

15. Do you think the role of women will change in the next decade? Explain.

16. Make up a song about the rights of children.

17. Write a letter to a factory or large business in your area urging them to set up a day-care center for the children of their employees.

18. Make a list of all the ways you think children could be better served by our society.

19. Why don't abused children tell on their parents?

20. Make a poster to alert adults to signs of child abuse.

21. Using the telephone directory, make a list of all the help lines that offer crisis intervention in your city.

22. Make an original poster urging teenagers to stay in school.

23. What advice would you give to a teenager who wants to drop out of school?

24. Do you think surrogate parenting should be allowed? Explain.

25. Make a cartoon about Yuppies.

26. Make a calendar of activities for a week in the life of a Yuppie.

27. Make up a Yuppie shopping list.

28. Why do you think TV evangelists have such a large audience?

29. Interview three adults and ask them how they were affected by Reaganomics.

30. Make up titles for a TV series about terrorism.

31. Make up an instruction sheet for government officials who deal with terrorists, including what they should and should not do.

32. If you could nominate an outstanding American of the decade, who would it be and why?

33. Do you think welfare should be abolished? Why? Why not?

34. Make a list of things you would include in a time capsule that are representative of the eighties and nineties so that future generations could know about us.

35. Interview five people of different ages and ask them what they think are the three biggest problems the United States has to face in the future. (This is to be assigned before Classroom Activity 7.)

ETHICS IN GOVERNMENT AND BUSINESS

1. Have you ever disobeyed orders from an adult because you felt they were wrong? Explain.

2. You are the president of a large brokerage house and are about to fire one of your top executives for insider trading. What will you say to him or her?

3. Write a dialogue between a stock broker and his or her child in which the stock broker explains what insider trading is and that he or she was just fired for it.

4. You are a bank executive who has just been convicted of embezzling bank funds. Write what you will say to the judge before your sentencing.

5. Should people convicted of white collar crimes be sent to low security prisons with better conditions than those found in regular prisons?

6. Why was the Iran-Contra affair nicknamed Iran-Gate?

7. Make up some original names for the title of a movie about the Iran-Contra affair.

8. Name one way in which you think the Iran-Contra affair could have been stopped, and by whom, before it went so far.

9. Interview someone in your family and ask him or her what they remember as most shocking about the Iran-Contra affair.

10. Oliver North claimed that he was just following orders in everything he did and that he considered himself a good soldier. Do you agree? Explain.

11. Conduct an interview among your family and neighbors on the following questions:
    (a) Do you think government leaders have the right to withhold information from the American people in the name of defense? If so, when?
    (b) Do you hold the president responsible for everything our government does? Why? Why not?

12. Interview family members or neighbors about their opinions on paying taxes.

THE PERSIAN GULF WAR

1. What did the yellow ribbons during the Persian Gulf conflict signify?

2. Write a diary entry of one of the following people in the reserves who have just received notice to appear for duty in the Persian Gulf:
    (a) Mother of two children
    (b) Someone who has just received a promotion at work

3. Write a list of all the adjustments children of war participants had to make in their daily lives.

4. Why wasn't there a larger anti-war movement during the Persian Gulf war?

5. Write a letter from an American stationed in an Arab country describing all the differences and restrictions he or she faces because of culture and religion.

6. Do you agree with the U.S. policy forbidding religious identification by U.S. personnel stationed in the Middle East? Explain.

7. Why do you think people supporting the war often compared Saddam Hussein to Adolph Hitler? Do you agree? Explain.

8. What domestic problems were forgotten (or shelved) during the Persian Gulf conflict?

9. What new terms entered the U.S. vocabulary because of the Persian Gulf war?

10. Write an argument for or against the statement: If Kuwait was not rich in oil we would not have gone to war with Iraq.

11. Did the United States achieve its goals in the Persian Gulf war? Explain.

12. Write a poem or rap song about the victims of the war on both sides.

CLASSROOM ACTIVITY 1

INTERVIEWING THE EXPERTS

This activity is divided into three components, and each one is to be handled on a separate day.

DAY ONE

Using the information the students gathered in Homework 1 in the Health, Environment, and Technology section, the teacher will make a list on the chalkboard of all the people and organizations in the community that have contact with drug abusers. The students can then decide whom they would like to interview during a class session. The teacher or student volunteers can arrange the appointments.

DAY TWO

Prior to the visit, the students must complete Homework 2 in the Health, Environment, and Technology section. It is very important that the teacher go over the questions and help the students formulate additional ones. The better their questions are, the more information they will get from their guest. Good questions from the students will also serve to put the speaker at ease and enable him or her to provide them with information that is interesting to them. It is a sure way to prevent a boring lecture.

DAY THREE

Once the visit is over, the class can evaluate the experience. The teacher may ask:

1. Did you learn anything new? Surprising?
2. Is there anything else you wish you had asked? What?
3. Is there anything else you would like to learn about the problem of drugs? (The teacher must try to be sensitive to the needs and problems of the students. If, in fact, there appear to be individual cases of drug abuse in the class, the teacher may be able to pursue the situation with the guidance department in the school or with one of the drug agencies in the community.)

CLASSROOM ACTIVITY 2

INTERACTION WITH SENIOR CITIZENS

This activity will be more productive if it is done after the students have completed Homeworks 1, 2, and 3 in the Social Issues section. Using their homeworks as a point of reference, the teacher will make a list on the chalkboard of problems senior citizens of the community have to face.

The teacher will divide the class into committees and assign each committee a different problem. Each committee can discuss possible ways of solving the problem. They can then report back to the class, and when everyone is done, the teacher may ask:

1. Are there any ways in which our class or school can interact more with the elderly to help solve their problems?
2. Could our senior citizens possibly be of any help to us here in the school?

Depending upon the class and the nature of the community, this may be an ideal opportunity to launch an outreach program between the students and the senior citizens. Ideally it should come from the students, but the teacher can be instrumental in channeling the discussion to help the students recognize what they would like to do and what is possible to do, considering the limitations of age and time. This activity could generate a program to help the elderly or one in which the elderly could be brought into the school or class to tutor or interact with the students.

CLASSROOM ACTIVITY 3

WHO GETS THE HEART TRANSPLANT?

Advancements in science and medicine have created a new set of problems for society. The teacher will present the following problem to the class.

You are all in charge of the most advanced hospital for heart transplants. There are six patients waiting for a donor heart, and they will die shortly if they don't receive one. You have just heard that a donor heart has been found and will be flown in immediately. You must decide who gets the heart transplant. In other words, you will decide who gets to live. The teacher will list the patients on the chalkboard. In order to make this activity as meaningful as possible, the teacher may substitute or add to the list of patients.

1. A high school honors student
2. A young mother with two small children
3. The senator from your state
4. A homeless twenty-four-year-old high school dropout
5. A brilliant thirty-eight-year-old doctor who works in your hospital
6. A sixty-three-year-old grandmother

Before there is any discussion, the teacher will ask the students, by a show of hands, to indicate who they think should get the transplant. The discussion can follow with these questions:

1. Why did you vote the way you did?
2. What factors should be weighed in deciding who gets the transplant?
3. Does one person deserve to live more than another?
4. Why is this such a complicated problem?
5. How do you think problems such as this one will get resolved in the future?

CLASSROOM ACTIVITY 4

A QUESTION OF ETHICS

Because of the Iran-Contra affair and the insider trading scandal, the issue of ethics in government and business has gained renewed interest. In this activity the students will have an opportunity to explore their ideas about a variety of questions regarding ethics.

The teacher will read each of the following statements aloud and ask the students, by a show of hands, if they agree, disagree, or are unsure. Whenever there appears to be interest or disagreement, the teacher can encourage discussion of the issue by asking the students why they feel the way they do.

1. It's alright to keep the change when a cashier makes a mistake in your favor.

2. You are still telling the truth even if you leave out a few of the details.

3. Doing a good job means doing everything you are told to do.

4. It isn't stealing when you take money from your parent's wallet.

5. It isn't stealing when a hungry person takes a loaf of bread without paying for it.

6. It's alright to drive just a little above the speed limit since everyone else does it.

7. While it may be illegal to carry a weapon, it's alright if you need it for protection.

8. Using recreational drugs once in a while is okay, so long as you don't make a habit of it.

9. When someone does the homework most of the time, there's nothing wrong with copying someone else's once in a while.

10. Since everyone cheats a little on income tax, there's nothing really wrong with it.

11. If the teacher leaves a test on the desk before giving it, it's perfectly understandable that the students will take advantage of the situation and use it.

12. If a student finds the test, makes copies of it, and sells it, that's good business.

13. Anyone who saw a carton of brand-new calculators lying on the street would take one.

14. It's perfectly okay for the boss to ask an employee to lend him or her money.

15. If the bus driver doesn't ask for the fare, then there's no reason to pay it.

16. When you know that a classmate is going to call for the answers to the science homework, it's alright to have your brother say you're not home.

17. If you are babysitting and you have a big test the next day, it's alright to let the kids watch TV even though the parents said that they shouldn't watch it for more than an hour.

18. You broke your neighbor's window, but there's no problem because no one saw you do it.

19. It's no big deal if you take money from the cash register where you work, so long as you return it.

20. When two companies are bidding for a contract, it's logical to give it to the one who will return some of the profits after the job is done.

21. It makes good sense to do a job "off the books" so that you don't have to pay taxes on the money you earn.
22. When you see someone shoplifting in a grocery store, it's none of your business to do anything about it.
23. When you see someone shoplifting in your uncle's grocery store, it's none of your business to do anything about it.
24. There is a toll-free number to call if you suspect that someone you work with is committing fraud or is involved in something unethical. It's easy to make that phone call and report it.

CLASSROOM ACTIVITY 5

INDEPENDENT DECISION MAKING

Many people involved in the Iran-Contra affair claimed that they felt they had the authority to do the things they did. People make many decisions every day, both on and off their jobs, for which they take responsibility even though there are no specific rules guiding them and no one watching them every minute.

The teacher will have the students make a list of every independent decision they personally made in the last week regarding their family life, friends, school work, behavior, and after-school activities. Have them put a star next to those items which could have gotten them into trouble.

When they are done, they can share their lists. Discussion can be motivated with all or some of the following questions where appropriate:

1. Do you feel that was the only thing/best thing you could have done in that situation? Why?
2. What kind of trouble could you/he/she have gotten into? How would you handle that kind of trouble?
3. What else could you/he/she have done?

CLASSROOM ACTIVITY 6

WHAT'S WRONG HERE?

When the United States government needs fighter planes or MX missiles or any other defense equipment, it turns to privately owned corporations. They bid for the job and one of the bidders is selected. In recent years it has been found that many unethical things have been done. Divide the class into groups to discuss the reasons why each of the following is wrong.

1. Falsifying product test reports
2. Inflating labor costs
3. Paying off a government employee (an insider) to find out how much the competing companies are bidding
4. Bribing a poor foreign government official in order to get him or her to place an order
5. Treating a key American government worker to expensive meals and gifts so as to get him or her to award the contract to you

When the groups are done, they can report back to the class. The activity can be concluded with a discussion of how these abuses can be avoided or brought under control.

CLASSROOM ACTIVITY 7

ADVICE FOR FUTURE GENERATIONS

The teacher can motivate this activity by going over Homework 35 in the Social Issues section. As the students name the problems they elicited during their interviews, they should be listed on the chalkboard.

The teacher will tell the class that they are going to try to work out words of advice for future generations to help assure an improvement in the quality of their lives. The class will be divided into groups, and each group will work on a specific category or problem from the list on the chalkboard. The advice may be written in rhyme form, chant form, or as a rap song. The students might also enjoy writing it as a fortune teller or palm reader would say it.

If the assortment of topics is not large enough to work with, some of the following can be added to the list:

- nuclear war
- terrorism
- drugs
- crime
- racism
- AIDS

- cancer
- child Abuse
- air pollution
- water pollution
- acid rain
- extinction of animals

When they are done, each group can assign a member to read their completed work aloud, or the entire group can read it aloud as a chorus.

CLASSROOM ACTIVITY 8

WHERE SHOULD THE MONEY GO?

The United States' government has a multi-million dollar budget, and each year Congress decides what to spend it on.

The teacher will list the following areas of government expenses on the chalkboard. Although there are other high expense budget items, these were chosen because they will stimulate the interests of the students. The teacher should feel free to substitute or eliminate any of the categories listed:

1. Defense
2. Welfare
3. Education
4. Aid to farmers
5. Health care
6. Environment
7. Foreign aid

The students will be asked to think about why each of these budget items requires a large amount of money. They will then be divided into committees. Each committee will choose or be assigned to work on one of the above budget areas. They will have to tell Congress why they need more money than any other group. Once they have worked out their arguments, one committee member will report to the class. After all the committees have reported, the class can vote on what they feel the government should spend the most money on, in order of importance.

CLASSROOM ACTIVITY 9

DIFFICULT TO RESOLVE

Advancements in science and technology have created difficult moral and ethical problems for society. The teacher may divide the class into groups of two or three to go out and interview people about one of the following issues:

1. Genetic engineering
2. Surrogate parenting
3. The danger of nuclear power

4. Socialized medicine

5. The right to die

6. Stress and push-button warfare

The students can break up into groups to work out the questions for their interviews. The interviews can be arranged with other classes, school personnel, and individual students from other classes. The students will find it more enjoyable and comfortable to share their interview assignments rather than go out alone.

When they return, they can report their findings to the class, and the entire class can discuss their feelings about each issue and why each one presents problems that are so difficult to resolve.

CLASSROOM ACTIVITY 10

SOCIAL ACTION GROUPS

"Balancing the budget" has become a much-heard phrase in federal as well as local government. Most students have had personal experience with budget cuts in education and social services.

In this activity students would begin by listing all the lost services due to these budget cuts. They would then form small groups of three or four and star the items that appear on most of their lists. Each small group will report back to the class and the teacher will list the results on the chalkboard. Students will then vote on which losses affect them most seriously. The teacher will then form new committees called social action groups. These groups will work on a campaign or plan on how to either get the services returned or find alternative ways of funding them.

It is hoped that the groups will take action based on their plans.

CLASSROOM ACTIVITY 11

RETURN OF THE HOSTAGES

As American hostages returned to their families in 1991 students witnessed emotional reunions and press conferences. This activity would encourage students to express their own curiosity and reactions.

Working in groups the students would choose one format:

1. Interview questions for the hostage or family

2. Interview questions for government officials on what they did to try to get the hostages home

3. Letters of welcome
4. Poem of welcome
5. Journal from point of view of returned hostage
6. Questions the hostage might have about what has been happening in the United States
7. Guide for the hostage about all that has changed since his captivity

After the students write their assignments there should be a discussion in class as well as sharing of their work.

CLASSROOM ACTIVITY 12

WISH LIST FOR THE TWENTY-FIRST CENTURY

As they live through the 1990s students will see many of today's problems solved and many new problems created. This activity will depend on the conditions that exist at the time it is used.

Students will make collages, original art, or poetry for display in which they illustrate their vision of a better world. This activity is suitable for the end of any year, decade or century.

CHAPTER TWENTY

Current Events—The Nineties and Beyond

INTRODUCTION

The reading, writing, and discussion of events in the news is a basic component of any social studies course, and particularly the study of U.S. history. It enables students to see the connections between events of the past and the present. Current news events become more meaningful when they are understood within the larger context of history. In this sense, current events lessons often become extensions and reinforcements of curriculum content lessons. Students are in a better position to share ideas, evaluate events, and often debate their points of view regarding these events. These discussions produce a greater awareness of the larger issues that affect our country politically, socially, and economically. It is another way to prepare the students for active participation, as adult voters, in a democratic society. Of course, the historic importance of any event can only be determined with the passage of time.

Because the events of the nineties are so current, the perspective that is needed to objectively evaluate their historic importance is simply not there. The impact that the Persian Gulf crisis or the Clarence Thomas appointment to the U.S. Supreme Court have on U.S. history and policy will only become clear with the passage of time. However, by critically evaluating the events, the students begin to see the impact that they have on society, and frequently on their own lives. For this reason we treat current events as history in the making.

The traditional method of having the students summarize articles in the "who, what, why, where, when, and how" mode can be augmented, varied, or replaced with the following approaches.

EXPRESSING OPINIONS

If students prepare their current events at home they should write their opinions in addition to their summaries. This takes the students beyond the basic facts and the rote process of repeating information. It is a way of encouraging them to formulate their value system. During the class discussion the teacher will encourage the expression and sharing of diverse opinions.

COOPERATIVE LEARNING

Students are placed in groups of four or five where they can share their news items. This is a non-threatening way for them to express themselves. After they have worked cooperatively, each group can present some of the more stimulating news items to the rest of the class. In this way the students teach each other. This type of activity lends itself to journal writing at the end, where the students can express their feelings about working with the group.

NEWS BROADCAST

Some classes enjoy forming groups of four or five to plan and present news broadcasts, modeled after those they see on TV. They use their summaries for the actual presentation. They enjoy preparing original commercials, a weather forecast, and any other broadcast features that appeal to them. Because our students are so widely exposed to TV news formats we have had some unexpected surprises in the presentation of weather forecasts. They insist on using large maps such as the meteorologists on TV do, and then point out weather trends throughout the country. This gives the entire class an additional experience in learning map skills and provides a wonderful opportunity for the teacher to "sneak in" a little geography lesson here and there. This format also allows for a lot of humor which is a welcome addition to any class.

CLASSROOM WRITING

The teacher can present an important current event to the class. Students will then choose from the following writing assignments:

1. Make up interview questions for the major person or persons involved.
2. Write an editorial about the event.
3. Write a letter to the editor about the event.

4. Write a letter to one of the people involved in the event offering advice, condolences, congratulations, or any other relevant opinion or feelings.

5. Write a list of things you don't understand about this event.

6. Rewrite the event the way you wish it had happened.

POLITICAL CARTOONS

The teacher can reproduce political cartoons for class analysis, or students can work independently or in groups to make up original political cartoons based on a given event.

SKILL HONING

Students prepare written summaries and opinions of news articles for homework. In class they pair up and exchange their papers. Each student is required to proofread his or her partner's paper looking for missing information. Students also respond to each others' opinions in writing and may add questions. This helps students to focus. It lends itself to a culminating discussion about what the students learned from each other and whether they agreed with each other's views.

DEBATE

The teacher can suggest that students seek articles on a specific topic or issue that is currently in the news: homelessness, rise in crime, disarmament conference, illegal aliens, drugs. Students will be asked to prepare for a debate on that issue. Students will use the information in their articles to strengthen their positions.

NEWS AS RESEARCH

As events occur, one way for students to keep up with history as it is being made is to use the newspaper as a textbook.

News can be assigned topically, geographically, or with any other focus that stimulates the interests of the students and broadens their knowledge. During election time they may be encouraged to seek articles relating to the candidates, campaigns, and issues. Students can be encouraged to go beyond the newspaper in their research. They can collect material from campaign headquarters if they are researching an election. They may want to gather information by interviewing people, taking surveys, or collecting and analyzing printed opinion polls. For other topics students can do background research. For example, an event in the Middle East would be better understood after researching its history.

KNOW YOUR NEWSPAPER

Younger and middle grade students often have little knowledge about the content of a newspaper. The teacher may devote special lessons to these sections of a newspaper:

- Entertainment—students can examine the weekly TV guide and look for programs that are relevant to their current unit of study. This can be extended to theater, movies, museum exhibits, and so forth.
- Obituaries—insight into the character, personality, and accomplishments of local and national figures can be obtained by reading and discussing their obituaries.
- Editorials—by reading editorials the students are exposed to clearly formulated opinions. This gives them guidelines for expressing themselves more clearly. Editorials can be used for class discussion and followed up by having the students write their own editorials or letters to the editor.

Depending on the age and ability level of the class, other sections of the newspaper can be used to integrate a specific topic with current news. For example, the Business Section lends itself to the study of the Stock Market Crash of 1929. The Sports Section contains in-depth articles about sports figures and sports events. They are often especially meaningful and inspiring to the students.

The pleasure and value of reading a newspaper goes beyond its front page and it is the teacher's responsibility to familiarize students with this.

Current events is a total learning experience in that students gain practice in gathering information, reading comprehension, writing, presenting ideas verbally, working independently and cooperatively, and developing and expressing opinions. They also develop skill in critical thinking, organization of ideas, and active listening. It is up to us, as teachers of U.S. history, to make the time for this invaluable aspect of the curriculum. We must not forget that history is an ongoing subject.

CHAPTER TWENTY-ONE

Term Papers

INTRODUCTION

Writing a term paper or research report need not be an overwhelming or forbidding task for students, whatever their age or ability level. We have found that students feel more self-confident when we break the process down into short-term assignments with due dates. This is a building process in which the students will ultimately produce a finished research paper. By guiding them through this process, the teacher simplifies each task into basic skills, without forgetting the overall goal.

As in sports where the coach provides training exercises to help the team reach its potential, we as instructors must do the same in our area.

We teach the following steps:

- choosing an appropriate topic
- locating information
- writing a preliminary outline
- note-taking
- revising the outline
- writing a rough draft
- rewriting the final draft

CHOOSING AN APPROPRIATE TOPIC

An appropriate topic is narrow enough to be done in depth, manageable for the age and ability level of the student, and one that has enough material available for research.

Students tend to choose topics that are too broad. The teacher can illustrate how to limit a subject. For example, The Roaring Twenties is too broad a topic. The teacher can guide the students into narrowing the topic down into any of the following:

- Scopes Trial

- Suffragette Movement
- Teapot Dome Scandal
- Organized Crime as an Outgrowth of Prohibition
- Jazz in the Twenties
- Ku Klux Klan in the Twenties
- Trial of Sacco and Vanzetti

and many more.

Of course the teacher will work within the needs of his or her students, the curriculum, and the time frame.

LOCATING INFORMATION

It is very helpful to work with the school or local librarian at this early stage. If possible, the librarian can give a book talk. This is also the perfect time to teach research skills and familiarize students with the use of the following: the card catalogue, reference books such as encyclopedias, atlases, dictionaries, and almanacs, Reader's Guide to Periodical Literature, and Computer Index.

If the students are not already familiar with the uses of primary and secondary sources, this is the time to teach them.

It is helpful at this point for the students to prepare a preliminary bibliography in order to be sure that enough material is accessible on their topics. We teach standard bibliography form and expect the students to use it throughout the assignment.

WRITING AN OUTLINE

A preliminary outline will serve as a guide so that the students can see what the scope of their research will be. The following is an example of a preliminary outline for a paper on Manzanar, the Japanese Internment Camp:

I.   Location
II. Physical Set-Up
     A. Housing
     B. Security
III. Inhabitants
     A. How selected
     B. Age breakdown
     C. Professions
IV. Services Provided
     A. Schools
        1. Attendance

    2. Quality
    3. Curriculum
  B. Health care
  C. Entertainment
  D. Sanitation
V. Effect on Lives of Prisoners
  A. Physical
  B. Psychological

It must be made clear to the students that the preliminary outline will serve as a guide and can continually be revised, based on where their research takes them.

NOTE-TAKING

Our students use three by five index cards for their note-taking. A special bibliography card is made for each source used. Each note card contains only one idea or fact. The following are examples of how they would look:

BIBLIOGRAPHY CARD

Cordero, Wilma and Kintisch, Shelly

Breaking Away From the Textbook

Lancaster, Pennsylvania: Technomic
    Publishing Co., Inc., 1990.

NOTE CARD

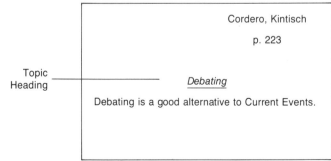

                                    Cordero, Kintisch
                                          p. 223

Topic
Heading ———————————— *Debating*
        Debating is a good alternative to Current Events.

Choosing a topic heading for each card is vital to note-taking because the cards will be organized according to the headings. Students may be given class practice in note-taking using a textbook. Once the students feel comfortable using this method, note-taking flows, and they pick up speed. By putting only one fact on each card the students are less likely to copy long passages word for word. They learn to focus more clearly, and are better able to integrate many sources of information. The author and page number on the note card is necessary for footnotes. The bibliography cards will be used for compiling the bibliography at the end of the paper.

REVISING THE OUTLINE

Once all research is completed and the note cards have been arranged according to topic, the students can revise their outlines. This is the time for them to omit or add topics.

WRITING A ROUGH DRAFT

Using their revised outlines and their note cards the students can write their rough drafts. Before they begin writing we give a few lessons on writing style and footnoting. We require that footnotes be done in the new simple form, citing the author and page in parentheses directly after the fact, quotation, or cross reference.

We encourage the students to include their own ideas and interpretations, as well as facts and quotes, throughout the paper. After they have submitted their rough drafts, we conference with each student.

REWRITING THE FINAL DRAFT

They are now ready to prepare the final typed draft. Those students who have no access to a typewriter or word processor may print their papers by hand.

Although this may seem like a very long process, it is one that produces a great deal of satisfaction and pride in the students. We often spend a few days having the students present their papers orally to the class. This is an opportunity for the students to teach each other and to share their work and their knowledge.

CHAPTER TWENTY-TWO

A Special Classroom Library – Beyond Reference

INTRODUCTION

During twenty plus years of teaching we have each collected many books for our classroom reference libraries. Students have access to a variety of primary sources, high-interest texts, and atlases. There are good dictionaries, sets of pictures and documents, newspapers and magazines, as well as a budding collection of videotapes of relevant films and quality TV programs that expand on topics discussed in class. Everything comes in handy for classroom use and, as most teachers probably do, we haunt bookstores and comb the city for anything that will help increase our students' interest in learning. History is an ongoing subject and we try to make use of any sources or techniques that help create a living and stimulating classroom.

It has been said that good teachers are never off duty. Most U.S. history educators are continuously building their own libraries and resources. Maps, globes, photographs, music, and a multitude of supplies for group and individual projects are essential for the social studies classroom. Teachers need essentials but essentials are not enough.

For years we had dreamed about creating a classroom library that would offer students the opportunity to read fiction as a vehicle for studying history. We each had our own memories of favorite scenes and characters from books read during childhood and adolescence. These memories remain alive and vivid today. More to the point, reading fiction opened up our interest in history and led to further reading and study.

Such experiences are priceless and we hoped to entice our students away from video games and TV sets into the solitary and highly satisfying world of reading a book. We felt that having novels, poetry, folktales, and biographies visible and available in the classroom would encourage students who might hesitate to use a regular library. We wanted our students to be comfortable holding a book, reading for fun as well as for an assignment, losing their hearts to a character, and getting totally engaged in someone else's story. Passion, idealism, making difficult choices, might be better understood and internalized through reading a novel or a biography. Students of all ages are capable of seeing the relationship between history, life, and literature. They often need to relate to an event or character on an emotional level before beginning the process of critical thinking. Reading an enjoyable book could motivate students to do further reading and study on their own. Offering non-threatening material might break down the walls of fear many children have of reading history. The benefits abound but first we needed the books.

Therefore we applied for and received grants to create this library. We shopped for books on many reading levels in order to meet the needs of our heterogeneous classes. We received advice from bookstore clerks, librarians, and English teachers.

We placed the books in glass cases and on open shelves—to be looked at, touched, opened, borrowed—an integral part of the classroom. We included them in lessons, classroom activities, and project lists. This library truly added a new dimension to our U.S. history classes. We have included our booklists and guidelines for writing reports at the end of this chapter. The booklist continues to grow as we get more suggestions and more money.

The following are some suggested techniques for using fiction and biographies in a U.S. history classroom.

INTRODUCING A UNIT

Each new unit of study may be introduced by displaying relevant books and reading selections aloud. The teacher may also describe the plot of a book, stopping at a point that leaves the students wondering what will happen next. For example, *The Crossing* by Gary Paulsen is an excellent way to introduce current problems relating to immigration. Students empathize with the youth of the main character and are horrified by the poverty and misery of his life in Mexico. Such a book sensitizes students to why immigrants will often go to any lengths to get to the United States.

Students may choose a novel or biography for their projects. However, they often opt to do one of the other projects from our list and borrow a book to read just for fun. This often leads to added insights and participation during class discussions.

ENHANCING LESSONS

Throughout any lesson, interesting, humorous, and exciting passages may be read aloud to illustrate material being taught or to stimulate discussions and questions. A short poem, song, personal description or letter help students relate to events that might seem distant at first glance. Our students tend to be more interested in stories with characters of their own age group and reading from such books helps bring history to life for them.

The teacher may also reproduce and distribute relevant reading selections to the students. This can be followed by journal writing or a homework question based on the reading.

Journal writing would focus on the students' reactions and feelings. The teacher may also choose to give a direct question based on the reading. For example, after any selection dealing with the problems involved in making a difficult decision, the teacher could have the students write answers to the following:

1. Have you ever had to make a decision like this?
2. What advice would you give to the character in the story?
3. What problems would you personally have facing the same dilemma?
4. What decision would you make in this situation and why?

Often reticent students will write their hearts out in this type of assignment. Sharing of answers in small groups or during a class discussion is another option for a culminating activity.

USING CHILDREN'S PICTURE BOOKS

While elementary school teachers are well acquainted with many techniques for using children's picture books, the secondary school teacher might hesitate to use such books with older students. Our students react with sensitivity and feeling to such books as *Hiroshima No Pika* and *Faithful Elephants*, two books dealing with World War II. Children's books may be read in their entirety during one class session. Written assignments for class time or homework would be perfect follow-ups to the reading and class discussions. Students might also enjoy using these books in small groups. They could take turns reading aloud and discussing the story.

Our older students use children's books as inspiration for:

1. Creating their own picture stories
2. Continuing the story
3. Giving the story a new ending
4. Introducing a new character

Many picture books today deal with serious issues that touch students of all ages.

INDEPENDENT SILENT READING

Providing a quiet calm environment is often the first step toward hooking students into reading a book. We distribute books from our libraries and set aside time for a simple reading period. If the teacher is interested in a more structured activity he or she may write a question on the chalkboard for directed reading. For example, a question asking the students to describe one character or conflict covers most books. Students would then focus and also have a written activity to augment their reading.

This is also a way of introducing students to a book that they will continue at home. Teachers might choose to begin an individualized reading program as part of their curriculum. Students can keep literature journals as they read the book or write a report based on our guidelines at the end of this chapter.

PRESENTATIONS

Fiction readers and students who have done research for their projects can be grouped together by topic; for example, slave life on a plantation. The students would pool their information and choose a method of presentation. This could be done as a play, TV or radio script, quiz show, or art show. The finished product could be presented to the class or at a school assembly.

This is a wonderful opportunity for teachers to share their expertise with colleagues. Art, music, literature, and drama teachers could work with the U.S. history teacher for a cooperative effort. For example, students could create costumes and sets for the scripts. They could work on such projects as murals, collages, and quilts. If there is a home economics teacher, students could prepare regional meals or dishes that are representative of different ethnic groups across the country. Often students will come up with their own creative ideas for presentations.

Great care must be taken by the teacher to organize the groups and tasks according to the age and ability levels of the students so that they end up with a sense of accomplishment.

HISTORICAL MAGAZINE

Many schools today have desktop publishing. Magazines may be created as culminating activities at the end of a term or unit. Any or all of the following may be included:

- book reviews

- trivia gathered from reading
- creative writing based on the books read by the students
- art work
- point of view articles "written by" characters from the books read
- drawings of characters, scenes, and settings from the books
- poetry
- editorials
- a theme magazine based on the era of novels read

LENDING SYSTEM

It is important to set up a well organized lending system to keep track of books. Students must learn to take responsibility for the books they borrow. Parent cooperation in the care and use of the books should be encouraged and would allow parents to share the students' experiences with the books. Parents might even help raise funds to add to the library once they see how exciting fiction is to their children. Since nothing we teach or study is done in isolation, it is important to include family support in our efforts at school whenever possible. This special classroom library can become a wonderful joint project of teacher, parents, and students.

GUIDELINES FOR BOOK REPORTS BASED ON HISTORICAL FICTION

1. Read the book for pleasure in a quiet place. Give yourself enough time to read at least one chapter at a sitting.

2. If necessary, take notes as you go along. Do not ruin the pleasure by taking too many notes.

3. When finished, write a report using the questions below as guidelines:
   (a) Write the title and author of the book.
   (b) Write a short summary of the plot. What part does history play in the plot? Give examples.
   (c) Write about the characters in relation to the times in which they live. What problems do they face? What choices do they have? How does the time and place affect and shape their lives?
   (d) Would you have wanted to live at this time? Why? Why not?
   (e) Write your own reactions to, and feelings about, the book. Did reading this book add to your knowledge about the history of the time? Be specific.

GUIDELINES FOR BOOK REPORTS BASED ON BIOGRAPHIES

1. Write the title, author, and a short summary of the person's life.
2. How did events affect the person's life? Include problems, choices, and conflicts the person faced.
3. What did this person do that affected the lives of other people?
4. Is the world a better or worse place because this person lived? Why?
5. Would you have been willing to work with this person? Why? Why not?
6. Write a short eulogy for this person (optional).

BOOK LIST FOR U.S. HISTORY

EARLY COLONIAL LIFE

Blos, Joan W. – *A Gathering of Days: A New England Girl's Journal*
Fritz, Jean – *The Double Life of Pocahontas*
Speare, Elizabeth George – *Calico Captive*
Speare, Elizabeth George – *The Witch of Blackbird Pond*

AMERICAN REVOLUTION

Caudell, Rebecca – *Tree of Freedom*
Collier and Lincoln – *My Brother Sam Is Dead*
Fast, Howard – *Citizen Tom Paine*
Forbes, Esther – *Johnny Tremain*
Lawson, Robert – *Ben and Me*
Lawson, Robert – *Mr. Revere and I*
Rinaldi, Ann – *Time Enough for Drums*
Brady – *Tolliver's Secret*
Fritz, Jean – *Traitor (Benedict Arnold)*
Haynes, Betsy – *Spies on the Devil's Belt*

PIONEERS AND WESTWARD EXPANSION

Brink, Carol Ryrie – *Caddie Woodlawn*
Conrad, Pam – *Prairie Songs*
Holland, Isabelle – *The Journey Home*
Keats, Ezra Jack – *John Henry, An American Legend*
Lane, Rose Wilder – *Let the Hurricane Roar*

McNear, May — *The California Gold Rush*
Moore, Robin — *The Bread Sister of Sinking Creek*
Speare, Elizabeth George — *The Sign of the Beaver*
Van Steenwyk, Elizabeth — *Levi Strauss the Blue Jeans Man*
Wisler, G. Clifton — *Piper's Ferry*

SLAVERY AND THE CIVIL WAR

Claflin, Edward Beecher — *Sojourner Truth and the Struggle for Freedom*
Crane, Stephen — *The Red Badge of Courage*
Fox, Paula — *The Slave Dancer*
Freedman — *Two Tickets to Freedom*
Fritz, Jean — *Stonewall*
Hamilton, Virginia — *Anthony Burns: The Defeat and Triumph of a Fugitive Slave*
Hamilton, Virginia — *The House of Dies Drear*
Hamilton, Virginia — *The People Could Fly — American Black Folktales*
Hansen, Joyce — *Which Way Freedom*
Hunt, Irene — *Across Five Aprils*
Keith, Harold — *Rifles for Watie*
Lester, Julius — *Long Journey Home*
Lester, Julius — *To Be a Slave*
Steele, William O. — *The Perilous Road*
Sterling, Dorothy — *Freedom Train — The Story of Harriet Tubman*
Sterne, Emma Gelders — *The Slave Ship*
Taylor, Mildred D. — *Roll of Thunder, Hear My Cry*
Yates, Elizabeth — *Amos Fortune, Free Man*

WOMEN IN THE 19TH CENTURY

Lauber, Patricia — *Lost Star — Story of Amelia Earhart*
Meltzer, Milton — *Mary McLeod Bethune*
Oneal, Zibby — *A Long Way to Go*

IMMIGRATION

Angell, Judie — *One-Way to Ansonia*
Levinson, Nancy S. — *I Lift My Lamp — Emma Lazarus and the Statue of Liberty*
Lord, Bette Bao — *In the Year of the Boar and Jackie Robinson*
Mayerson, Evelyn W. — *The Cat Who Escaped From Steerage*
Paulsen, Gary — *The Crossing*
Smith, Betty — *A Tree Grows in Brooklyn*

INDUSTRIAL REVOLUTION, EARLY URBAN LIFE, AND LABOR

Finney, Jack—*Time and Again*
Rappaport, Doreen—*Trouble at the Mines*
Sinclair, Upton—*The Jungle*

WORLD WAR I

Remarque, Erich Maria—*All Quiet on the Western Front*

THE DEPRESSION

Cannon, Bettie—*A Bellsong for Sarah Raines*
Lyon, George Ella—*Borrowed Children*
Mazer, Harry—*Cave under the City*
Olsen, Violet—*View from the Pighouse Roof*
Steinbeck, John—*The Grapes of Wrath*
Taylor, Mildred—*Let the Circle Be Unbroken*

WORLD WAR II

Adler, David A.—*We Remember the Holocaust*
DeJong, Meindert—*The House of Sixty Fathers*
Greene, Betty—*Summer of My German Soldier*
Houston and Houston—*Farewell to Manzanar*
Kerr, Judith—*When Hitler Stole Pink Rabbit*
Levi, Primo—*Survival in Auschwitz*
Roth-Hano, Renee—*Touch Wood*
Serraillier, Ian—*Escape from Warsaw*
Strasser, Todd—*The Wave*
Tsuchiya, Yukio—*Faithful Elephants—A True Story of Animals, People and War*
Yolin, Jane—*The Devil's Arithmetic*

CIVIL AND CONSTITUTIONAL RIGHTS

Armstrong, William—*Sounder*
Bradbury, Ray—*Fahrenheit 451*
Brown, Claude—*Manchild in the Promised Land*
Haley, Alex—*Malcolm X*
Hansberry, Lorraine—*To Be Young, Gifted and Black*
Hentoff, Nat—*The Day They Came to Arrest the Book*

Lawrence and Lee—*Inherit the Wind*
Parks, Gordon—*The Learning Tree*
Quayle, Louise—*Martin Luther King, Jr.—Dreams for a Nation*
Thomas, Piri—*Down These Mean Streets*
The Words of Martin Luther King, Jr.

VIETNAM

Paterson, Katherine—*Park's Quest*

Debates

Debating offers students of all ages the opportunity to do individual and team research, formulate opinions, express and defend them, and possibly even change these opinions. The students also develop self-discipline, which allows for a more structured presentation of ideas than in simple classroom discussions or arguments.

We have used debating as an alternative to current events. It can also be used to enhance and give immediacy to a controversial topic in any unit in the U.S. history curriculum.

Preparation for a debate takes time. It teaches that opinions need facts to back them up. We introduce the topic a week before the debate. The entire class is encouraged to discuss the topic with parents, other teachers, friends, and classmates, and to do research in newspapers and books on their own. Each student prepares a written argument. This will be handed in at the end of the debate. On the day of the debate, students volunteer and sides are chosen. An alternative method could have students choose sides and teams when the topic is announced so that they may prepare together. Both ways are effective.

Since this is not a team competition, the main goal of our debating is to open up as much participation as possible. Two or three students make up each side. They debate in front of the class using the following format: for, against, rebuttal, final statement. Then, the topic goes to the class, and they may question points made by the debaters or bring up their own arguments and ideas. At this stage, the teacher may allow for more informal use of argument and expression of emotions, even anecdotes or examples, to prove a point.

Before debating, teachers might enjoy asking their classes for lists of topics that they would like to discuss. In our debates we used student-suggested topics as well as our own. We also discussed many problems and controversies of the time. Any local issue that is of interest to your particular student body can be incorporated into debate time, i.e., should taxpayer money be spent on a town swimming pool?

We feel that debate is part of U.S. history and democracy. Below is a list of some successful and still arguable topics. (Specific debate topics for individual units are listed in those unit chapters.)

TOPICS FOR DEBATE

1. Should children with AIDS be allowed to attend school?
2. Should teachers be tested for AIDS?
3. Should teachers be tested for drugs?
4. Should parents be held responsible for crimes committed by minors?
5. Should the drinking age be lowered?
6. Should the drinking age be raised?
7. Should children be consulted during a divorce about which parent they want to stay with?
8. Should abortion be illegal?
9. Should condoms and birth control advice be made available to students in high school clinics?
10. Is capital punishment right?
11. Does an individual have the right to decide if a law is "bad" and then to break a "bad" law?
12. Should prayer be allowed in public schools?
13. Should animals be used for medical experimentation?
14. Should a citizen have the right to carry and use arms for self-defense?
15. Does our jury system work?
16. Should welfare be abolished?
17. Should welfare be strengthened?
18. Should we have the right to decide when we die?
19. Should marijuana be legalized?
20. Should music albums be given ratings?
21. Should minors be given adult punishment for adult crimes?
22. Do you think minors should be tried by a jury of peers—other minors?
23. Should the draft registration be abolished?
24. Should school boards (or librarians, teachers, government, parents) have the right to decide what children should read?
25. Should the peace draft be reinstituted?
26. Should we continue to make nuclear weapons?

27. Should the United States continue spending money on weapons?
28. Should the voting age be lowered?
29. Should the voting age be raised?
30. Should citizens have to pass a test to vote?
31. Should citizens have to pass a test to be on a jury?
32. Is affirmative action fair?
33. Are women really liberated?
34. Should bathrooms be unisex?
35. Should the ERA be adopted?
36. Should women be drafted?
37. Should students be allowed to choose their own courses or teachers?
38. Should all students have to do some sort of volunteer work as part of their school credit?
39. Should newspapers, TV, or radio be prevented by the government from giving news to the public that might be deemed dangerous to national security?
40. Is it the government's responsibility to provide housing (or work or education) for everyone?
41. Is freedom of speech possible?
42. Should teenagers or their parents make the decision about what to do if a girl gets pregnant?
43. Is it ever alright to cheat?
44. Should a gay rights amendment be passed?
45. Should towns and cities have curfews?
46. Should AIDS testing be part of everyone's physical checkup?
47. Is affirmative action necessary?
48. Should a doctor be allowed to decide when to withhold life support systems?
49. Should we have socialized medicine?
50. Should the United States send money to foreign nations in need?
51. Should the United States send military aid to our allies?
52. Should men be given time off for child care?
53. Should guns be outlawed completely for anyone but the police?
54. Should all health care workers be tested for AIDS?
55. Should homeless people be forced into shelters "for their own good"?
56. Should all adults be obligated to serve on jury duty?
57. Should we have mandatory military service for all eighteen year olds?

58. Should all people who receive welfare be obligated to perform some work or public service in return?

59. Should doctors be allowed to help dying patients commit suicide?

60. Should school officials have the right to censor student publications?

61. Should violence on TV be censored?

62. Is it a violation of first amendment rights to rate movies?

About the Authors

Shelly Kintisch and Wilma Cordero have worked together for over twenty-five years. They are firmly committed to public education and through the years have developed multicultural curriculum for heterogeneous classes, team taught, supervised student teachers, mentored new teachers, and coached the debate team. They are still involved in these activities as classroom teachers of social studies in New York City.

Shelly Kintisch has her Bachelor of Arts and Master's degrees from New York University. She developed, wrote, and teaches a special primary source curriculum in anthropology. She is faculty advisor of the student government, and coordinates the community service activities for the program she developed at her school.

Wilma Cordero is a graduate of Brooklyn College and holds a Master's degree in political science from the New School for Social Research. Ms. Cordero has developed a law course which she teaches to middle school students. She has also worked on writing an experimental social learning curriculum at Yeshiva University.

Shelly Kintisch and Wilma Cordero are recipients of several grants that have helped them expand their activities. They have also given numerous workshops for teachers, and are presently at work on a new book.